NORTHWEST COAST INDIAN PAINTING

Gwayasdums village on Gilford Island photographed during the first decade of the 20th century. The painted facade house front at the right decorated the Sea Monster House and belonged to the Scow family. The painting depicts the face of a powerful sea being, a crest of the Scow family. Photograph courtesy Royal British Columbia Museum, PN 235.

NORTHWEST COAST INDIAN PAINTING
House Fronts and Interior Screens

EDWARD MALIN

Timber Press
Portland, Oregon

Published in 1999 by
Timber Press, Inc.
The Haseltine Building
133 S.W. Second Avenue, Suite 450
Portland, OR 97204, U.S.A.

Printed in Hong Kong

Library of Congress Cataloging-in-Publication Information

Malin, Edward.
      Northwest coast Indian painting: house fronts and interior
screens/Edward Malin.
            p.   cm.
      Includes bibliographical references and index.
      ISBN 0-88192-471-7
      1. Indian painting—Northwest Coast of North America. w. Indian
painting—British Columbia. 3. Indian painting—Alaska. I. Title.
E78.N78M33 1999
759.195'089'97—dc21   98-39230
                                                                              CIP

To Benigna, the woman of my dreams, 1952–1996

mina mihal kita, baba i

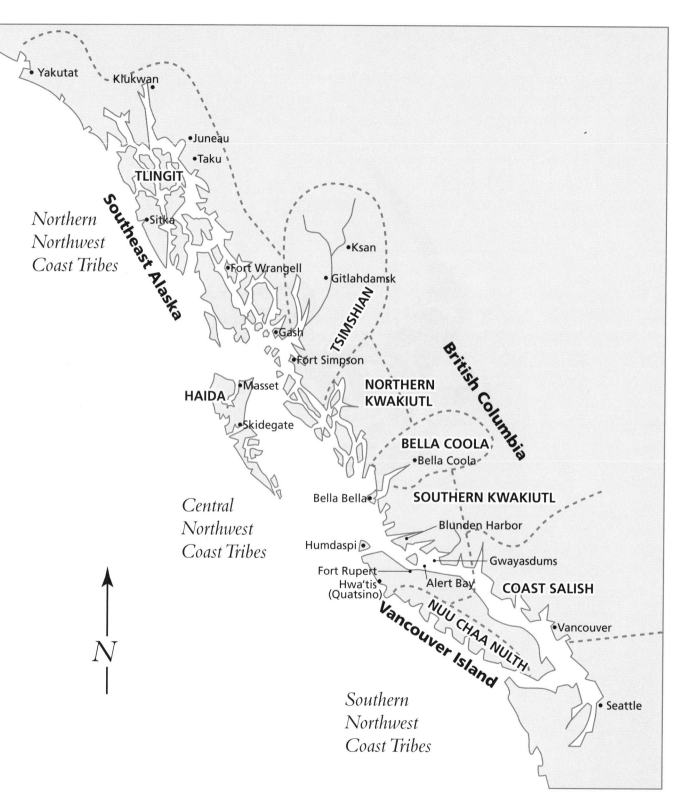

Map of Tribes and Major Villages

Yakutat

Klukwan

Northern Northwest Coast Tribes

Southeast Alaska

Juneau

Taku

TLINGIT

Sitka

Ksan

Fort Wrangell

Gitlahdamsk

TSIMSHIAN

Gash

British Columbia

Fort Simpson

Masset

NORTHERN KWAKIUTL

HAIDA

Skidegate

BELLA COOLA

Bella Coola

Central Northwest Coast Tribes

Bella Bella

SOUTHERN KWAKIUTL

Blunden Harbor

Humdaspi

Gwayasdums

Fort Rupert

Hwa'tis (Quatsino)

Alert Bay

COAST SALISH

NUU CHAA NULTH

Vancouver

Vancouver Island

Seattle

Southern Northwest Coast Tribes

N

CONTENTS

ACKNOWLEDGMENTS

MY EARLIER book *Totem Poles of the Pacific Northwest Coast* (1986) was strictly a labor of love. This book, a more ambitious effort, I view in a somewhat different light. It represents my swansong. It was a six-year effort, the culmination of 55 years of interest in and pursuit of an understanding of Pacific Northwest Coast Indian art and culture.

This volume had a tender inception. I was introduced to the paintings in Tlingit clan houses during an ethnographic research expedition to Alaska in 1949. The thought of writing about them never crossed my mind. But ideas have a way of incubating over time; ultimately they coalesced into an agreement with Timber Press to write about monumental flat paintings of the Pacific Northwest Coast Indian people.

I began the Introduction in early 1990 and worked on the largest portion of the illustrations from 1991 through 1993. However, a flood of interruptions impinged upon these pursuits. At one point I discontinued writing altogether for almost a year. Picking up the threads once again seemed agonizingly difficult. But perseverance with the project, along with further encouragement from my publisher and numerous associates and friends, eventually paid off. It is with immense satisfaction and relief that my initial objective has been realized.

I owe an enormous debt to many people who assisted me along the way. To my teacher, colleague, and friend, Frederica de Laguna, emeritus professor of anthropology at Bryn Mawr University, I express special appreciation for the watershed experience serving as her research assistant. To the Clark Foundation and Maybelle Clark MacDonald Fund I wish to express my heartfelt thanks for the financial assistance provided through travel grants. Special gratitude I give to Fred Koch, M.D., for his interest in my research and for the generous financial assistance he provided over the years in order for this book to come to fruition.

There are others who helped along the way: Dan Savard of the anthropological collection section of the Royal British Columbia Museum in Victoria, British Columbia; Peter Corey of the Sheldon Jackson Museum in Sitka, Alaska; Steven Brown of the Seattle Art Museum; Steve Henrikson of the Alaska State Museum; Lucy Williamson of the Museum of Archaeology and Anthropology, University of Pennsylvania; Lynn Maranda of the Vancouver Museum; and last but by no means least to Johanna Scherer of the Handbook of American Indians Project of the National Museum of Natural History in Washington, D.C. To each and all my deepest expression of gratitude. My thanks go to other institutions that helped with photographs, including the Vancouver Public Library, the British Columbia Archives and Records Service, the American Museum of Natural History, the Chicago Museum of Natural History, the Canadian Museum of Civilization, the Denver Art Museum, the National Archives of Canada, the Vancouver City Archives, and the Alaska State Library.

Special memories of my friend, the late Norman Feder of Sidney, British Columbia, involve our years of association while he was curator of native arts for the Denver Art Museum. And I offer gratitude to Bill Holm, whose prolific writings have stimulated and inspired all writers interested in the cultures of the Pacific Northwest Coast.

There are a number of contributors who for various reasons prefer to remain anonymous, but I wish to acknowledge my debt to each and every one of them for their perceptive insights and suggestions. I also thank Dempsey Bob, the Tlingit artist from Prince Rupert, British Columbia, for permission to quote from his reminiscences of his beloved late grandmother, Eva Carlick of the Stikine Tlingit tribe.

Most profoundly of all, I wish to express my deepest appreciation to Mr. Richard Abel, my editor and the former publisher of Timber Press. He provided unstinting support for this effort as well as a thousand vital comments, criticisms, and suggestions, all of which suffuse every chapter in this book as well as each page. Without his initial interest in the project and his wholehearted support thereafter, this volume probably would not have come into being.

INTRODUCTION

"Perhaps the supreme virtuoso performance of the Northwest Coast artists was in flat painting. But only a few achieved that level of excellence. When it happens I don't really know how—it's almost like a miracle. They could produce absolute perfection of line and form on a rough wood surface."

Bill Reid
Form and Freedom:
A Dialogue on Northwest Coast Art

I DISCOVERED Pacific Northwest Coast Indian flat painting during a single moment of astonishment in July 1949 while at Klukwan (Old Honored Town), a Tlingit village located along the Chilkat River some 20 miles (32.2 km) north of Haines, Alaska. It was to change my life in a hundred different ways. I was a member of an archaeological-ethnographic reconnaissance team led by the eminent anthropologist Frederica de Laguna, an outstanding authority on Pacific Northwest Coast Indian and arctic cultures. The team had earlier in the summer spent six weeks in Yakutat, the northernmost of all Tlingit settlements. We had planned to stay several weeks in Klukwan before moving southward to a third village, Angoon on Admiralty Island. One day while in Klukwan Professor de Laguna, or Freddie as we came to affectionately call her, announced she had arranged with the matriarch of the Kit Hit or Killer Whale House to enter the lodge to view its cultural treasures. The rules were no photographs, note taking, or questions.

The fragile structure was not built in the traditional Tlingit architectural style, rather it was a two-story, frame building typical of the Western frontier style. The old long house had vanished but its name and its treasures were retained for this new location. This collection once belonged to the powerful leader with the eminent name Kudenaha and had been kept intact with great pride following his death many years earlier. What an experience that visit turned out to be! The treasures of the clan, viewed in that hour-long visit, remain vividly imbedded in my memory.

Some weeks earlier I had received permission to make drawings of the painted wall partitions—clan heirlooms called screens, or *nahen* in the language of the Tlingit people—of two important Yakutat families (Figures 6 and 7). I recall the pleasure of drawing these partitions, but the practice had done little to prepare me for the impact of the screens that stood in Kudenaha's old Klukwan clan house. We were met by an astonishing array of superbly wrought treasures: chiefly staffs, dancing batons, feast dishes and bowls, clan hats, and dramatic animal masks were all collected from ages past and held in great esteem. They reflected the power of the clan. The sight, however, that took my breath away was the house screens—not one but two large flat paintings with black figures shown in profile representing killer whales. Each panel was about 14 feet (4.3 m) long, and they were positioned on opposite walls of the main room of the house (Figure 1.1; Plate 1).

That single experience drove my interest to the point of bewitchment with the paintings of the Northwest Coast Indians.

That fascination has remained undiminished through the years despite my extended immersion into other aspects of the Northwest Coast Indian tradition, including extensive study of first the masks and then the totem poles of these remarkable people. Finally I turned my attention back to that stunning experience in Kudenaha's clan house, and in 1990 I began to prepare some drawings that might be useful for a book on Northwest Coast Indian painting. The deeper I probed the more numerous and illuminating were further discoveries about the tradition, which, of course, only further stimulated my interest. My study led me to conclude that there is no Native American or First Nations art form in the Western Hemisphere that equals the flat paintings on the house fronts and interior screens of the Pacific Northwest Coast Indians, with the exception of the paintings from Toltec civilization and the brilliant polychrome murals done by the ancient Mayan peoples in Mexico and Guatemala from the 7th through the 9th centuries, A.D. This book then is an outcome of that growing understanding and appreciation and my interest in sharing these discoveries from the Northwest Indian tradition.

Before I proceed further, let me define the focus of this book. House front paintings are plank wood exterior facades considerably larger than the front wall of the large cedar dwellings of the Northwest Coast Indians. Designs representing animal, bird, sea creature, or a combination of these and other-than-worldly beings are painted on the wood planks in bold configurations and are emblazoned with primary colors (Figure 22; Plate 2). House front paintings vary in size from 10 to as much as 50 feet (3.0 to 15.2 m) in length and often reach considerable heights, some exceeding 20 and more feet (6.1 m). Some paintings cover the entire surface of the house front itself, a scale that may strain our imagination as well as our willingness to believe.

Interior screens, on the other hand, are partitions made of wood planks on a single plane or in some cases dual planes. The screens function to separate the living quarters of the ranking member of the house and his wife or wives from the space occupied by the rest of the kin group; the leader's living space is always located at the rear of the long house. The wood surfaces facing the forward part of the house serve as a gigantic canvas for painting symbols of a complex nature laden with especially potent meaning for the occupants of the household (Figure 2; Plate 3).

Other types of paintings also will be examined in the following study, including painted canvas and muslin screens as well as mortuary figures that were commonly placed near the graves of deceased members. Both these forms arose from the same flat painting art as house fronts and interior screens and represent later phases in the ongoing painting tradition of the Northwest Coast peoples.

The region in which screen and house front paintings were made extends from the northernmost panhandle of southeastern Alaska southward almost to the Juan de Fuca Strait, which separates the westernmost portion of the Province of British Columbia from that of the State of Washington (See map p. 6). Though the Northwest Coast culture extended across the strait into the Olympic Peninsula and southward, the monumental paintings that are the principal concern of this book were not produced by the many tribes located in what is now Washington State. Little is known about this artistic tradition prior to the mid- to late 18th-

century Age of Discovery by Western powers, but we are certain that monumental painting evolved and spread throughout much of the Northwest Coast in the early 19th century.

The monumental paintings from the past survive in the dim and fading memories of a handful of tribal elders, in rare and often unexhibited holdings of a few museums, or in the photographs made by European and North American explorers, anthropologists, and tourists, photographs that have fortunately been preserved through the years ultimately to find their way into museum archives and libraries in Canada and the United States. These scant materials have been vigorously and ingeniously employed by a number of single-minded North American historians and cultural anthropologists determined to learn about and document the distinctive culture of the region, which was in the latter 19th century being consciously and summarily discarded by some of the natives in favor of ways being introduced by the expanding migration of Western culture.

The meager photographic records have become invaluable resources in the pursuit of information about the past. The ability to comprehend and assess what once transpired on these shores would be seriously limited without this thin vein of visual records. They provide vivid testimony relative to the achievements, interests, and activities of the native people.

While pursuing the research for this book I examined the greatest proportion of the extant photographs contained in the libraries and archives of both western Canada and the United States. Some were dated and their geographic locations recorded, which proved immensely helpful, but most lacked any information as to the village photographed or the lineage or clan residing in it. Critical information regarding the owners of the houses was largely absent, as was the presumed meaning of the symbols. Information bearing on such matters was gleaned by painstakingly tracking through whatever other sources were available. Most of these photographs fall within the period of the 1870s to early 1900s. Unhappily, few exist from before 1870. Had photography developed into a more readily usable technology earlier, the foundations of this painting tradition and all its richness at the zenith of its practice would undoubtedly have been more thoroughly traceable. As it is, many of the extant photographs are washed out, dark, fuzzy, and often hard to read. I was able in a limited way to penetrate some of the obscure secrets hidden within these early, dim photographs by using a magnifying glass, a constant companion.

I have located 188 examples of house front or house partition paintings. A few have managed to survive intact despite their highly refined and complicated execution on and with quite perishable materials. I firmly believe my findings to be but the tip of the iceberg, as it were. Though paintings of this genre do not seem to have been commonplace within the culture during the 18th and 19th centuries, many more than are now evident were made but discarded, as was a common practice with totemic objects. Furthermore, every tribal group of this region is represented in the examples, suggesting a well-established, indeed entrenched, tradition, one that evolved over a few hundred years into increasing complexity.

The paintings vary in quality from true masterpieces to those less than mediocre, but most are legitimate examples of a mature and sophisticated art form. The photographs reproduced in this book and my drawings accompanying them, though widely representative, are not the end of the story. In the years ahead, I believe, additional screens now hidden will surface. Additional photographic evidence of now lost or hoarded clan treasures will ultimately come to light, adding to our wonder and admiration as well as our sense of loss.

The drawings in this book were prepared over a two-year period. Each was selected to assist the reader in discovering and recognizing the details of as well as the subtleties in composition, line, and form. Photographs can provide an overview of a painting but the details are commonly elusive and not readily visible. Therefore, I spent much time searching out and recreating not only the intricacies of the design but also the formal characteristics of the composition, its details, and the color scheme integral to the artistic organization of each screen illustration.

I had several objectives in mind when I began working on this volume. One was to document in a single volume the details of as many examples of house front and house screen paintings as I could discover. It became a formidable task. Several important examples are sequestered in museum collections and are not accessible for study. Others have simply vanished, destroyed by decay, floods, or fires that occasionally swept away entire villages. Some others were destroyed as an outcome of over-zealous missionary and government policies. A few superb specimens remain hidden in old clan houses, such as those I was so fortunate to observe years ago in Klukwan. I have been unable to track down others that were recorded by travelers, scholars, and interested observers during the late 19th century. Some of them undoubtedly remain hidden in the conservative villages throughout the Northwest Coast region, continuing to play a covert role in the lives of the people. In all these cases I have had to depend upon the often hard-to-decipher photographic records.

Three other objectives presented themselves through my investigation. One was to describe the different forms of this painting tradition. Some paintings are representational in contrast to others that employ conventional themes; some are action-oriented rather than static; early types contrast with later types; stylistic features separate those used by one group from those used by another. Secondly, I set out to provide an account of the historical and social context in which the paintings were produced and used. How were the screens judged? What constituted a masterpiece separating the work of a master from a mere technician? And how did the artists achieve their objectives? What compelled the leaders of important houses to commission artists to create such works? Thirdly, I wanted to highlight those gifted artists who wielded the brushes and created the myriad symbols. Very little is known of them. My search for information bearing upon these issues led down numerous blind alleys, like searching for (but usually not finding) the proverbial needle in the haystack. People do not remember names or they choose not to do so for various reasons. In pursuits such as mine the investigation is always confronted by the suspicion-induced reticence arising in response to inquiries made by outsiders or strangers.

A number of hypotheses began to take form in my mind as I became increasingly conversant with the growing volume of data I was gathering related to the flat-painting tradition. The first was that house front paintings and screen partitions have not been given the attention in the literature that they so richly deserve. I was forced to this conclusion by the limited and even rare number of articles published on the subject.

Secondly, flat painting appears to be an early art expression that was quite widespread geographically though never common, but the making and use of flat-painted screens and partitions gradually gave way to an increasing vogue of totem pole carving. This impression grew in part out of the brief statements made by early observers writing on the region. For example, William Beynon, a Tsimshian Indian and scholar, wrote in the early 1920s: "In the old days house front paintings were more numerous than totem poles. They were also more important. These paintings were the real crest boards whereas the totem poles were only commemorative" (Barbeau 1950:777). John Swanton, a scholar associated with the Bureau of American Ethnology in Washington, D.C., wrote early in the 20th century: "It seems very certain there were once far more examples of house front paintings among the Tsimshian than we suspect. Most have disappeared through many misfortunes." The late Viola Garfield, professor of anthropology at the University of Washington in Seattle, commented: "The most spectacular products were paintings which covered the facades of houses and timbers carved with symbolic figures generally known as totem poles. Facade paintings seem to have been more popular with Coast Tsimshian who carved few columns compared to the numbers in Gitksan and Nishka villages" (1966:46).

Philip Drucker, another Northwest Coast Indian scholar, added to these conclusions: "House front paintings and screens were not as commonly found as totem poles but they clearly represent the heyday of monumental art prior to the introduction of metal tools on a wide scale. They became the driving force in the springboard to an explosion of totem pole carving in the mid-19th century" (1950:251). His hypothesis was supported by the house front and screen evidence that I was able to discover—I uncovered much more than anticipated in light of the paucity of published literature.

My investigation brought to light a third hypothesis: it seemed increasingly apparent that some clans and tribes distinctly preferred to utilize painted house fronts to proclaim the important status of their families rather than employing totem poles to do so.

Lastly, I concluded that house front paintings and interior screens represent a continuing commitment to an earlier tradition of monumental art developed along the Northwest Coast. The beginnings of this tradition of symbolic art go well back in the records of the prehistory of the Northwest Coast Indians. But by the later 19th century the monumental form of house front and screen painting was utilized almost exclusively by the most highly esteemed and wealthiest of families, despite the fact that the older 18th-century tradition of flat painting was largely displaced by the increasingly popular vogue for totem pole carving. By the late 19th century only a few clans retained their traditional regard for monumental flat-painted screens and partitions.

A scattered few house screens have not only survived to the present but remain prized possessions of the families who own them. They are symbols of commitment and loyalty to the past, pre-serving a sense of the former glory of the ancestors of the families. The paintings continue to play a meaningful, though greatly attenuated, role in maintaining the protocols of those lineages and clans wishing to keep alive the values of the past.

The sentiments of a senior elder I once interviewed give a sense of the emotion engendered among the few families possessing a house screen. The late Mildred Sparks, a Tlingit woman of the Raven House at Klukwan, shared her thoughts as she and I lunched together one day in February 1968. I recounted how visitors both American and foreign with hushed voices and reverent demeanor stood and read the memorable passages emblazoned on the walls of the Lincoln Memorial in Washington, D.C. With thoughtful countenance she listened, then responded:

We don't feel as you and others do about the Lincoln Memorial. We have our own memorials. What you describe is what Chilkat [Tlingit] people feel about their home possessions. The screens and the carved poles inside our houses were handed down to us by our ancestors who had owned them. They are sacred to us and we hold them in deep feelings. They are our ties with the people who came before us.

NATIVE CULTURE AND THE PAINTING TRADITION

"My impression is that very little great art ever leaves a tribe. Its owners burn it or let it rot before they let strangers see it or take it. I suspect we have little idea what lies hidden in some of the most prosaic villages . . . .

"I think this was equally true on the Northwest Coast. Only chance permitted us to see truly great pieces. Many were lost in fires, others deliberately destroyed."

Edmund Carpenter
Introduction to *Form and Freedom:*
A Dialogue on Northwest Coast Art

MUCH has been written by popular writers and serious scholars alike about the Native Americans who resided along the Pacific Northwest Coast. But as the present book attests, much remains to be explored and documented about the people, their culture, and their aesthetic preoccupations. They were among the most imaginative, innovative, and exuberant artists in the Americas.

The geography of the Northwest Coast incubated and nurtured a way of life that goes back thousands of years, distinct from all other cultures in the Western Hemisphere. This narrow littoral was a region of immense physical complexity, an oceanic environment clothed in a virtually limitless forest covering the rugged and precipitous mountain ranges. Great peaks plummeted as much as 2 and 3 miles (3.2–4.8 km) to the coastline below; countless islands studded the emerging shorelines; pounding surf and immense tidal fluctuations harbored a veritable treasure of sea creatures as well as avian travelers.

This geography was and remains to this day a seascape of awesome and intimidating power except to those who through accumulated experience have mastered its secrets. The region is an immense symphony of churning ocean, occasionally becalmed but never tranquil, seemingly countless inlets and impregnable fjords, and mountain chains, one following another mantled in a dense forest of red cedar, spruce, and hemlock. The geologic and biologic forms all converged in a sustained and intimate interaction. The sea itself was not only the seemingly infinite source of nourishment for its settlers but also the highway employed by strangers and friends communicating with ally and enemy. Later it was the ocean highway by which momentous change swept over the people in waves, ultimately setting the native tradition on a collision course with European settlers in the mid- to late 19th century. Through the centuries the native people evolved a way of life that successfully utilized the region's abundant resources for their physical as well as spiritual needs and well-being; the region provided many of the forms the people employed as symbols for expressions of their social and spiritual traditions.

Who were these Native American or First Nations people? Their settlements were thinly scattered far and wide. Villages, typically of an ephemeral nature, might be settled for a time then abandoned for a better site, then just as often resettled again. A restlessness seemed to mark these people as they moved from one

place to another in pursuit of both seasonal subsistence and locations to establish longer-term settlements. Over the course of generations the people came to understand the subtleties and fundamental characteristics of their environment. They learned which resources they could utilize only seasonally by contrast with those having no distinct cycle of life; which materials and foods from the adjacent coast and forests were useful; and where food could be harvested in an abundance exceeding all need—all which assured them not only of survival but also in some cases virtual opulence.

Within the geographic boundaries of the region, well-defined Native American groups emerged to occupy and control specific areas along the coast, areas they came to zealously protect and to claim as possessions for their descendants. Such possessions included, among many things, the exclusive use of particular rivers and streams that were spawning grounds for the species of native salmon, seal and sea lion rookeries, islands known for easy and abundant gathering of bird eggs, or secret places to find berries or camas root. All were guarded with great passion and ferocity. With passing generations the ownership of such coveted locations developed into the economic and political structure upon which tribal and family security and power were based.

Thanks to these abundant resources and a mild climate moderated by the offshore warm current the various coastal groups increased in numbers. They prospered as few other peoples in ancient North America. They evolved languages and dialects quite different from Native American groups that lived outside the

Northwest Coast littoral. The isolation of their geography allowed only limited contact with peoples beyond the riverine, coastal, and maritime orientations of the Northwest Coast natives.

Within their geography the people separated into distinct tribal and clan identities. Each group developed a principal village, some of which became so populous that extensions or smaller satellite hamlets were formed by necessity. The outlying hamlets maintained ties with the parent villages in differing degrees of intensity. The tribe included all those who spoke the same language, shared the same customs, values, and beliefs, identified a specific territory as their original homeland, and above all possessed a special sense of identity or feeling of belonging together.

Among the northernmost reaches of the Northwest Coast tribes were those peoples collectively known as the Tlingit (tlin-kit), a name of Tsimshian derivation meaning Place of Tidal Water People. Sharing a name does not in any way imply a political unity or cohesiveness among the villages. On the contrary, the Tlingit were divided into 18 groups (two of which were inland tribal entities), each insisting upon not only its special autonomy from all others but also its separate and unique origin and ancestry.

Southward of the Tlingit near what is now the border between Alaska and British Columbia was a very important and distinct territorial group called the Haida (hi-duh). They were the epitome of a maritime people, residing on the major islands that comprise the Queen Charlotte Islands located 60 miles (96.6 km) or more west of the coast of British Columbia. The Haida were divided into three groups, each of which incorporated several large and a number of smaller settlements. The Kaigani Haida established villages in southeastern Alaska at Tlingit expense in the 17th century. In the northern Queen Charlottes, centering around Graham Island, were the several settlements of the Masset Haida. Southward on Moresby Island and its adjacent smaller islets lived the third division known as the Skidegate Haida; their 14 villages were spread out along both coastlines of this large island.

On the mainland to the east of the Queen Charlotte Islands were the Tsimshian (tsim-shee-un). They also were separated into three divisions or territorial units. The Coast Tsimshian tribes settled the coast area and several nearby offshore islands. The two other groups occupied inland villages strung along two vast and swift river systems. The northern river was called the Nass and its people there known as the Nishka Tsimshian. The river 50 miles (80.5 km) southward was the Skeena and the people who occupied more than 20 villages along its banks for 200 miles (321.9 km) inland called themselves the Gitksan.

Further south into what is now central British Columbia were two groups of people, the Northern Kwakiutl (kwä-ki-ootl) and the Southern Kwakiutl. Their villages numbered 21 in all, perhaps even a few more. The term "Kwakiutl" originally referred to one tribe of four who settled around the Fort Rupert trading area of northern Vancouver Island. But the name was bestowed on all of them by late 19th-century explorers and scientists; the modern descendants assert the name does not truthfully reflect the group of tribes as a whole. In the late 20th century, descendants prefer the term "Kwakwaka'wakw," which means Speakers of the Kwakwala language, to designate all the Kwakiutl tribes of the region. The term "Kwakiutl" has become so deeply embedded in the scientific and popular books, journals, and other publications, however, that it must continue to be used in this book.

Situated between the Northern and the Southern Kwakiutl divisions was a riverine enclave inhabited by the Bella Coola (Bilhula in the earliest literature). Again some late 20th-century descendants have sought to reject this nomenclature; they prefer to be called the Nuxalk (noo-khoulk; the "x" is a gutteral sound throughout transcriptions of Pacific Northwest native words), but also due to previous precedent this book uses the term Bella Coola. The Bella Coola people resided along the Bella Coola River and its many tributaries. Here a few large communities prospered in close association with many smaller hamlets. Bella Coola people spoke a language radically different from that of their immediate neighbors, the Kwakiutl. The nearest linguistic tie is to the tribes further south who were called the Coast Salish. The Coast Salish occupied both sides of the Strait of Georgia and the adjacent island areas. They peopled 14 small, self-contained, autonomous groups.

The remaining tribal group sharing in the Northwest Coast tradition occupied the western coast of Vancouver Island. These people are identified in early literature as the West Coast tribes or the Nootka, a term which again some descendants wish to repudiate. They prefer the term "Nuu chaa nulth," meaning Mountains in a Row, referring to the topography of their region. This new name has been adopted more readily than others and is used throughout this book. They numbered 16 tribes in all, and all prided themselves on their political independence from each other.

These tribal groups of the Northwest Coast shared many fundamental characteristics only slightly modified by minor local variations. Regional specialization of food production and consumption, craft skills, trading, and entrepreneurial activities can be identified as can consequential variations in political and social organization. Instead of inventorying and explicating these variables from north to south, a more valuable exercise for our topic is, by contrast, to point out the critical differences that set Northwest Coast Indian culture apart from that of neighboring groups to the north, south, and inland.

First and foremost, the Northwest Coast tribes enjoyed a notable increase in population in aboriginal times. This growth coupled with increasing wealth led to the planning and building of larger, more substantial, and better constructed permanent settlements. The preponderance of these large, multifamily or clan houses reflected both a relatively sophisticated building technology and dramatically impressive architectural styles (Figures 3 and 4). Northwest Coast groups were set apart from their inland neighbors and those to the south by their sea oriented, maritime outlook. Their focus, with the exception of the river inhabitants, was almost exclusively outward toward the channels, bays, inlets, and the ocean itself. This orientation was readily evident in the long trading voyages undertaken to exchange specialized goods and localized resources as well as to create distant alliances through marriage.

Other equally dramatic differences include the pronounced social stratification of the Northwest Coast society. The major social class differences between clan and lineage members and between and within tribal groups were widely and ostentatiously displayed upon every conceivable occasion. Enormous importance was placed upon the rank, privilege, status, and social position of each clan and lineage. Even individual tribal members were measured and counted in the minutest shades and degrees, particularly among the ranking families of the tribes. Part of their focus on social class was the extraordinary preoccupation with wealth and the importance placed on owning and acquiring material trade goods in addition to ritualistic and symbolic properties of both a material and nonmaterial kind. Wealth of all kinds reflected favorably upon the possessor's position and status within the tribe. One form of wealth was the right to the use of secret, inherited, ancestral tribal names. Other symbols of wealth included feast dishes, costumes for various social and ceremonial events, and heirlooms such as masks that represented gifts bestowed upon the owner or his family from supernatural benefactors or spirit powers. The passion for the pursuit of wealth reached its zenith in the potlatch, an astonishing and unique social event involving the prescribed giving away of the clan or lineage's accumulated wealth to invited guests from other groups. These gatherings were week-long feasts combined with status-oriented activities.

Within this region an entrenched and highly valued artistic tradition flourished. A wide range of art forms flowered. Sculpture was the predominant form executed in a variety of media—stone, bone, and wood—culminating in the towering carved vertical columns that came to be called totem poles. The impressive ceremonial clothing demanded outstanding skill from the female weavers. Clothing with totemic crest symbols emblazoned upon it revealed social position; the symbols were inherited family crests that identified their owner's roots, ties, and family history as well as social status within the community. Crests were more important to the family than tangible properties such as houses, salmon streams, and seagoing canoes.

Painting on wood and animal hides, in fact almost any suitable material, thrived, as did the grass- and root-weaving arts. The latter together with carving were handmaidens attending the people's profound interest in theater. Dancing performances, ritual displays, secret society performances, potlatch dramas derived from historical as well as from mythical experiences, all utilized masks, complex costumes, drums and whistles, symbolic and totemic objects, and more, created for such purposes by both the general population and a large body of artists and craftsmen.

This book focuses on this artistic tradition in its relation to the widespread practice of painting totemic crest symbols on village house fronts and on the interior partitions of houses of high-ranking families. Though painted house fronts were neither commonly nor usually erected in all Northwest Coast villages, the practice was more widespread than early literature indicates. The record is opaque at best and requires further qualification. Some villages were marked by a number of house front paintings while others had few if any. Not every household within a village used them or could afford to commission them. Paintings seem to have been reserved for those families who not only occupied socially important hierarchical positions but who also enjoyed great wealth and power.

One can only speculate as to how many houses in all these villages possessed both house front paintings and house interior screens—a doubling of prestige and display of wealth. So little documentation exists relative to interior screens because European visitors aroused suspicions among the North American natives and received few invitations to enter the homes of the wealthy and well placed. My experience with Frederica de Laguna in Klukwan was a quite exceptional opportunity that had been carefully negotiated.

Though totem poles have attracted far more attention due to their size, sculptural qualities, and the mystique surrounding their meanings, house front paintings and interior screens are of great regional importance. Many clans and lineages appear to have preferred the flat-painting form of advertisement of their ancestral history and status. The comparably scant attention given flat paintings may be due in part to the differing impact of time and weather. Poles carved from rot-resistant red cedar trees were long enduring and the deeply sculptured surfaces retained their symbols for years. By contrast, house front paintings faded rather rapidly due to exposure to the elements—often they disappeared

from view within 10 years. In addition, changing fashion has greatly influenced the historical significance of the screens. Historical evidence suggests that house front paintings were more common in earlier times and that dramatic changes in cultural motivations led to the widespread ascendancy of totem poles in most villages.

The Explorers' Observations

Numerous references were made to house front and screen paintings by the early explorers who recorded their contacts with native tribes up and down the coast in the latter part of the 18th and early 19th centuries. These expeditions were mounted by the leading European powers exploring the outermost limits of what was still a mysterious global geography. England, France, Spain, Russia, and a nascent colonial America were the contending states, each seeking to establish its territorial position in this vast and still largely unexplored part of North America. There were myriad claims and counterclaims to these northwest regions, much aggravated by the already apparent promise of economic and political fortunes to be nurtured by holding possession in the region.

The European and American interest in the Northwest Coast brought both explorers to map and traders to exploit the products of the region. The first important trade commodity sought during the 40 years or so after the first Spanish trading missions in the 1770s was sea otter pelts. Contact with Native Americans started slowly then accelerated to a dizzying pace, altering the way of life of the people. These associations shattered the cultural insularity of millennia, bringing to the shores not only new goods and technology but Western ideas as well. Much of this contact was certainly beneficial, stimulating the native culture in positive ways; just as often, however, it brought confrontation arising out of the social and cultural gulf separating the Europeans and the Native Americans.

It is useful for the purposes of this book to turn to some of the observations of those early explorers, for they record the first certain evidence of a painting tradition on a monumental scale. Captain James Cook's *A Voyage to the Pacific Ocean* (1784), recounting his explorations of the late 18th century, contains several observations on the quite remarkable development of large-scale architectural undertakings and associated decorative elements including painting. At about the same time the early fur trader John Meares visited a Nuu chaa nulth village. He describes in his account two striking architectural characteristics common to the region: the massive houses in which the people lived and the widespread embellishment of those houses, which involved painted iconographic representations of supernatural beings drawn from the native mythologies (Nabakov and Easton 1989:243).

Other accounts by the growing number of explorers, travelers, and traders sparked the interest of Europeans. In his voyages of the 1790s Captain George Vancouver noted painted house fronts employing a variety of designs. He writes: "In the village located in the Johnstone Strait [Kwakiutl country] 18 of the 28 houses counted were decorated in some way on the outside." Vancouver records additional observations: "There were figures drawn on 34 of the houses in another village [Bella Bella, also Kwakiutl] each with varying degrees of designs and painting . . . . There was a village on the hillside in tiered layers of houses with several house fronts in painted designs." Captain Vancouver also describes painted house fronts in a village located at the mouth of the Nimkish River in 1792 (Kwakiutl country). He suspected the designs on these houses "probably had some kind of meaning" (Barbeau 1950:243–244).

The drawings made by the ship's artist to accompany these observations include reproductions of some of the natives seated in front of the houses or along the beach. Vancouver's European artist, unfamiliar as he was with the thoroughly unusual subject matter of Northwest Coast artistic style and design, simply represented the paintings on the house fronts with series of circles and dots.

In the early 19th century, other outside observers reported paintings on dwellings located in the lower Fraser River valley in what is now British Columbia. Simon Fraser, the renowned Northwest explorer, saw such paintings on homes in 1808 at the village of Kwatten, a Coast Salish settlement located along the Stalo River. Franz Boas, the famous American anthropologist, later compiled much of the early evidence for house front paintings from among the Coast Salish people who lived in several widely dispersed villages in the valley (Barbeau 1950:408–412).

These and numerous other examples of flat painting recorded by travelers and scientists provide critical evidence that establishes the historical fact of such paintings at these early times. The historic record becomes clearer and more detailed with the employment of photographic technology by the increasing number of explorers, scholars, and travelers curious about the nature of the region and its native inhabitants. An unknown percentage of the photographs made in the 19th and early 20th centuries found their way to archives in both Canada and the United States. Those photographs still extant dating from the mid- to late 19th century depict many superb painted house fronts in the coastal villages. They convey the sense of a well-established tradition replete with a full-blown and settled body of symbolism, technique, and organization of many design elements. Such a tradition must have required a century or more to develop.

Along with greater understanding of the art of flat painting, the photographic record reveals much about the culture of the Northwest Coast Indians. The pictures show many house front paintings located in specific villages, but then photographs of some of those same villages taken a short time later not infrequently picture no painted house fronts. Are the data with respect to time and place inscribed on the photographs incorrect, or did the paintings literally disappear within the space of a few years? What were the fundamental factors operating that explain their disappearance? Evidence suggests that some of these marvelous works of art were painstakingly created for a temporary occasion or display and then removed, to be stored out of sight or destroyed. Some of the paintings seem to have been false fronts, temporary props installed to serve a special purpose or celebrate a unique occasion, then, having served this temporary purpose, they

were no longer usable or needed. More on these customs will be discussed in later pages.

By the 1880s a goodly number of the paintings displayed on the house fronts had disappeared. Weathering was certainly a factor. Some of the photographs from this time reveal faded, often barely discernible patterns and designs of intriguing complexity. One example of the difficulties of and hence the questions raised by the rapid decline in house front painting is an 1873 photograph of the Northern Kwakiutl village at Kitimat, British Columbia, taken by the pioneer photographer Richard Maynard. It records a long house with a large front painting. But even with a powerful magnifying glass the design is barely discernible. Another example, a photograph taken by the scientist and photographer George Dawson in 1878 shows three houses along a terrace above the high tide mark (Plate 4). But again most of the details of each of the paintings have faded beyond recapture. This loss of detail is repeated with depressing regularity in all the villages up and down the coast.

In at least some measure the increasing disregard for house front paintings can be traced to the accelerated tempo of change in the 19th century. Even though the sea otter fur trade dominated by clipper ship trade to China had run its course by the 1820s and 1830s, the number of Europeans in the region continued to increase. The most notable agent of change was the Hudson's Bay Company which sought by establishing a continuing presence to monopolize the fur trade in the Northwest. In pursuit of this strategy the company began building a series of forts and trading posts up the coast from its base fort in what is now

Vancouver, Washington, on the Columbia River. The first post established in the northwest Indian country was Fort Nass (later Fort Simpson) in the northern region of the present province of British Columbia; then came Fort McLoughlin at Bella Bella. Fort Rupert followed near the northern tip of Vancouver Island, as well as Fort Langley on the lower Fraser River. These forts *cum* trading posts proved to be magnets attracting the different tribes and clans. The forts affected the natives more than anticipated; many of the tribes and clans abandoned their traditional nearby settlements and moved lock, stock, and barrel to the forts in order to take advantage of the numerous trading opportunities that presented themselves.

The race for the new wealth the Western world could provide was pursued by the natives with a vengeance. Goods poured into the region from Europe changing much of the native material life. An influx of settlers followed. From the Alaska panhandle to southern British Columbia native institutions and social practices were inundated with foreign goods and ideas. Tribal rivalries further stimulated trading. Spiritual and religious beliefs and practices were altered or replaced at different velocities, transforming in a remarkable variety of ways both social and cultural landscapes. In the newly established settlements near European neighbors, Western-style houses began to supplant the native architecture. The venerable interior screens, once the centerpieces of pride and status within clans and sources of identity and history, also began to disappear.

It is my view that interior painted house screens were at one time far more numerous than house front paintings; I hasten to add that I do not have the concrete evidence to support this conclusion. Photographers were only infrequently given access to house interiors. Our present photographic record does not, therefore, accurately reflect the full measure of the interior-painting tradition. Had circumstances been different or the fates kinder, our documentation would be far more extensive. The natives husbanded deep feelings with respect to interior screens, quite unlike the seemingly transitory interest in house front paintings which, once lost or faded, seem not to have been replaced. Interior screens, on the other hand, remained within the shelter of the house. Some Tlingit informants have reported that when they moved from one site to another, only a few of the most prized possessions, including the interior screens, were moved to the new location. The remainder of the dwelling and its contents were left behind. As Mildred Sparks's eloquent statement in the Introduction recounts, the screens testified to deeply held emotional ties with long-deceased but still venerated ancestors.

Other forces were at work during this transition period. Conflagrations consumed entire villages. When the cedar used to construct the houses ignited, the flames went out of control in a matter of moments. One fire after another is known to have swept through the villages with astonishing regularity. Fire was thus one of the most powerful agents of destruction of native treasures up and down the coast. In prehistoric times the villages destroyed by fire were undoubtedly slowly rebuilt along traditional lines and even more slowly refurnished with the traditional wealth goods and ceremonial contents. But in the radically changed and rapidly changing period of the late 19th century, when the native peoples rebuilt burned-out villages with encouragement from missionaries and colonial government agents they largely adopted Western-style architecture based upon smaller, framed dwellings suitable for only a single family. Thus, the native people, in a conscious effort to emulate Western models, completely altered their village landscapes and the outer trappings associated with them. The settlements took on the decided look of Western-style villages.

Only in the more remote corners of the Northwest Coast, places far less accessible and thus less exposed to outsiders, did the people attempt to ignore foreign influences. But native architectural forms prevailed for only a few more decades even in such conservative communities. Photographs taken from the 1870s to the early 1900s document the evolution of these architectural changes. Though some traditional houses remained they were modified by such practices as the installation of pane glass windows and hinged doors as well as the use of milled lumber siding. Some of these changes were only cosmetic; interior living arrangements changed more slowly. In the intermediate phase the new houses were of Western style on the outside, native on the inside.

Yet some house front paintings incongruously remained (Plates 5 and 39). Though these anomalous decorations attracted curious visitors their condition was rapidly deteriorating. In such an advanced state of disintegration, they represented the dying gasp, the final stage of collapse and disintegration of the old tradition, and the passing of a way of life representing hundreds if not thousands of years of evolution. Many of the painted house fronts and interior screens that survived continued adversity were

finally lost once the old values, practices, and spiritual associations were discarded in the contest with European culture. The most precious heirlooms of the past became increasingly irrelevant. There was no longer any assurance that screens once stored for future ceremonial uses or other social displays in those venerable long houses would ever have any value again.

Meanwhile a great enthusiasm for collecting the artifacts of dying native cultures from around the world was drawing huge endowments to the leading museums throughout the European world and to the founding of new institutions. All were building staffs of increasingly sophisticated anthropologists and ethnographers. These cadres of learned experts fanned out across the globe to preserve as much as possible of hundreds of dead and dying aboriginal traditions. So it was that in the latter 19th and early 20th centuries museum collectors swept across the Northwest Coast in search of artifacts thought to reflect the "uncontaminated" past.

The search for artifacts was undertaken with a competitive vengeance. Representatives from the major museums of the world converged on every accessible, and most of the terribly inaccessible, corners of the Northwest Coast in search of the exceptional, the peerless, and the unmatched examples of tribal art. The collectors' exuberance, even their passion, for this search is without historical parallel. Many native families could not resist the new siren's call to sell their heirlooms and accumulate yet more wealth, a desire consistent with long-standing tradition. The already jeopardized economic well-being of many families further encouraged them to sell seemingly useless baggage.

Douglas Cole's superb study *Captured Heritage* (1985) provides a detailed description of the events that unfolded in this era. Margaret Blackman, another writer describing the period, cites an incident in which two native-style houses were purchased outright from the Haida village in Kasaan in southern Alaska and shipped intact to institutions for a future international exposition and subsequent museum display (1984:159). Some of the most breathtaking examples of native paintings were acquired by museums in the course of these collectors' expeditions. After purchase, the art was transported across oceans and continents and then stored within the inner sanctums of their new owners. And there, with but a few exceptions, they have remained. Inventoried, prized, and all but forgotten. Though few in number, some of these house front and interior screen paintings represent the finest examples of the tradition; many are clearly finer pieces than most of those recorded in extant photographs.

The Geographic Distribution of the Paintings

Analysis of the flat paintings preserved in photographs or museum collections discloses a considerable disparity between the painting practices of the different tribal groups ranging from Alaska to the Strait of Georgia. At the northern apex some Tlingit groups seem to have made few house front paintings. The tribal and clan tastes instead concentrated on interior screens and wall partitions. These same groups, with the exception of the southern Tlingit, also showed a limited interest in raising large totem poles in front of their houses.

Among the southern Tlingit, house front paintings, though not necessarily interior screens, were more abundant. This finding is hardly surprising when considered in historical and geographical terms. The southern Tlingit lived in close proximity to the Coast Tsimshian, masters of two-dimensional painting. They brought the art to its highest aesthetic plane. Evidence shows that there was considerable social and economic interchange between these two groups. The Coast Tsimshian significantly influenced the southern Tlingit, whose leaders held the Tsimshian artists in high regard.

Tlingit flat paintings can be divided into three categories: traditional house front paintings, interior screen or wall partition paintings, and, as the former practices gradually disappeared, adaptations of earlier forms. These new forms appeared on screens during the early years of the 20th century.

Interestingly enough the largest number of extant examples of painted monumental art both in museums and *in situ* come from the Tlingit. A total of 35 examples of paintings from the genre were collected, 28 of which were interior screens. There is no question in my mind that many have yet to surface. This general picture of the abundance of Tlingit paintings is clouded somewhat by the fact that many of the pieces are poorly documented. Museum acquisition data simply identify the examples as Tlingit with no further information about the particular communities from which they were obtained or about the family or lineage who owned them. Some examples labeled as Tlingit seem more likely to be Tsimshian, but not in all cases can provenience clearly be assigned by artistic derivation due to the extensive interaction between the Tlingit and the Tsimshian. The documentation for Tsimshian house fronts and screens is somewhat more substantial than that for their Tlingit counterparts, but many questions relative to their origin likewise remain unanswered or murky at best.

Tsimshian paintings clearly display the culmination of skills developed through the work of several generations of peerless masters. These artists exerted a powerful influence on not only the people to the north but also those to the south, the Kwakiutl and Bella Coola tribes. The Tsimshian painters attained phenomenal heights in the medium. Their brilliance was manifest in nearly all elements of the art: in the scale of the work they undertook, in the intricate nature of the symbolism they employed, in their mastery of brush work, in their utilization of space, and in their subtle, complex, interlocking flow of lines. Many examples of Tsimshian work, located from the coast areas to the lower Nass and Skeena river regions, have been recorded in journal accounts. The late Marius Barbeau reported seeing in the early 1900s numerous paintings, most of which were later lost to fire.

I have included in this study six Tsimshian masterpieces as representative examples of Tsimshian painting (Figures 5.1 [and Plate 10], 22, 24, 25 [and Plate 2], 26 [and Plate 28], and 27). They are in a class by themselves, and these illustrations hardly do them justice. The last of these examples, Figure 27, comes from a Nass River village and is included as an interesting departure from the tradition—the color formulas usually followed were not used in this case.

Among the Coast Tsimshian, monumental painting appears to have taken precedence over totem pole carving and raising. The opposite is true of their relatives along the Nass and Skeena rivers and, as mentioned earlier, of the neighboring southern Tlingit villages. The Kaigani Haida of Queen Charlotte Island also had primary interest in monumental art centered on colossal totem poles. House screens or house front paintings were apparently seldom made or used; consequently only a few have been documented in photographs or have survived in museum collections. There are three known examples of Kaigani house screens accompanied by some documentation; two of them are now ensconced in museums. Two house front paintings are known, one from Edward Edenshaw's house in Howkan, the other near Skidegate village (Figure 29).

The surviving evidence from the Kwakiutl groups changes the assessment dramatically. These people were accomplished artists who rivaled the Tsimshian in the variety of art forms pursued. Kwakiutl artists were as expert at their craft as the Tsimshian but were less dominated by convention and more exuberant, resourceful, and given to experimenting with painting styles. Photographs reveal an extensive and widespread use of house front and interior screen paintings in the mid- to late 19th century. Painting continued to flourish well into the early 20th century despite antagonism from Canadian government agents and missionaries.

The largest number of known Kwakiutl examples is associated with the southern villages. Few examples from the Northern

Kwakiutl have survived, possibly only the result of the numerous fires that devastated nearly every village. A secondary cause of the loss of Kwakiutl examples is the consequence of considerable missionary activity among the tribes. The journals of early travelers regularly mention house front paintings in villages before missionaries arrived, but few of the pieces have survived. The Southern Kwakiutl tribes seemed less willing to adopt Western ways and more determined to maintain their traditional practices. Photographic records from the 1880s and 1890s show some villages still containing only traditional plank wood houses.

In photographs and museum holdings I have located 36 examples of large-scale Southern Kwakiutl paintings; 14 of these are house screens and 22 are house front paintings. I am convinced this is but a short list of what was once present in the villages of the Kwakiutl. Kwakiutl screens painted on wood were traditionally discarded and burned after completion of the ceremonies for which they were commissioned. As a consequence few of them remained to be collected. Wood as a medium was gradually replaced by cloth, muslin, or canvas for displaying the paintings of crest symbols. A fairly large representation of the later forms exists. The Kwakiutl also adapted their flat painting interests to memorials for the dead, of which a number of examples are discussed later in the text.

Like those of the Northern Kwakiutl, the Bella Coola paintings were either destroyed by fire or abandoned at about the turn of the century. Photographs from the 1870s onward present clear evidence of the extensive use of both house front and interior screen painting. There is one remarkable photograph from Komkotes village (present day Bella Coola) in which five huge house front paintings are spread along the terrace above the high-water mark of the river. They can be seen easily with a magnifying glass. None apparently have survived, but careful, close examination has permitted me to reproduce the huge house front on the extreme right of the photograph (Figure 31; Plate 9). Also pictured is an interior screen that was in an advanced stage of decay when the photograph was made in the early 20th century (Plate 32).

The most southern tribes, the Nuu chaa nulth of Vancouver Island and the Coast Salish groups along the Strait of Georgia, bore much of the brunt of the contact with European visitors. I have been able to find but one example of a Nuu chaa nulth house front. The changes wrought by associations with Westerners clearly had far-reaching effects on the natives. Several fine examples of interior screens have survived in museum collections, as well as seven paintings on other media including muslin and canvas, suggesting an ongoing artistic tradition growing out of earlier practices. Hardly any evidence of Coast Salish flat painting survives, only the recorded statements of early explorers and scientists. Their journals reportedly mention both house front and interior screen paintings, but I have been unable to track down a single Coast Salish screen from published sources.

In one of his most illuminating remarks, the Northwest Coast Indian authority and scholar Philip Drucker pointed out "painted facades were present at Clayoquot, Nootka, Quatsino, Fort Rupert, Owikeno, Bella Coola, Bella Bella, China Hat, Xaixais, Haisla; extending to the Tsimshian proper, Gitksan, Masset, Skedans, and Sanya Tlingit." (1950:46). This list of villages and tribes traces a continuous thread of house front paintings from the southernmost to the northernmost reaches of the Pacific Northwest Coast Indian settlements. The work of this book only confirms Drucker's earlier view of the extensive and intensive cultivation of the art of two-dimensional painting that once flowered in this region. But a new way of life was emerging for the natives, one no longer entirely of their own making and one quite different from their former vital traditionalism. The dissipation of the Native American lifestyle and its artistic tradition was epitomized in the passing of the art of flat painting.

"The house is everything. The house is more important than the people who live in it!"

A Tlingit elder in the coho lineage, raven division, at Sitka, Alaska, 1990

THE FOUNDATIONS OF THE PAINTING TRADITION

Northwest Coast Indian villages of the late 20th century are vastly different from their predecessors of the traditional past. In the late 19th century, instead of settling near abundant salmon streams, berry thickets, or hunting grounds, people relocated their villages to gain better access to lumber mills and salmon canneries, which had come to define the key economic locations in the region. The work that Native Americans found there assured their entry into the Western economy. For the first time, they were faced with participating in a currency-based economy.

In itself the transplantation of villages was nothing new. I have referred to the many groups who deserted their traditional settlements in this period in order to gain increased access to the trading opportunities associated with the Hudson's Bay Company posts. The Stikine Tlingit moved downriver to Fort Wrangell when Russians established a major post there in the 1830s. The scattered Coast Tsimshian tribes converged on Fort Simpson. The Kwakiutl representing four tribes from Turnour Island moved to Fort Rupert. By the early 20th century additional village populations had moved to other locations primarily out of economic considerations; Klawak, New Kasaan, Ketchikan, Yakutat, and Hydaburg, Alaska, are a few examples. Hoonah, Sitka, and Klukwan, all highly conservative Tlingit villages, on the other hand, were among those that remained in their homelands.

The newly established towns required the people to cross mental as well as physical barriers in order to exist in this new culture that involved quite different social and political assumptions and practices. Among the many matters that had to be faced were the necessities of learning to communicate in a different language—spoken English—and the acceptance of a different spiritual paradigm, namely Christianity.

The Village

The old, time-honored villages were impressively large even by the standards of the latter-19th-century pioneer frontier. The largest settlements contained from 30 to 40 houses lodging a population ranging from 500 to 800 or more people. Smaller settlements might contain 250 to 400 people. Photographs, in addition to the ethnographic accounts made by travelers, provide a great deal of information about the size of many of these houses and the status and position of those who occupied them. Specific villages often have a record of the names of the lineages that resided there, along with the clan affiliations, the crest names of the houses, and the crest symbols that gave the houses their special position and status within the community. All these data provided researchers with a rich harvest of information that helps explain the nature of the Northwest Coast Indian tradition.

Politically, the people of a village formed a single tribe. The autonomy of a village was recognized by rival as well as related tribes. The village was both the skeleton and the heartbeat of community life.

Each village was located on or near the place on which the first ancestors had purportedly settled. Traditional stories relate how some of these settlements were established, in many cases following long periods of wandering. Momentous events were believed to have once transpired in connection with the first village foundations: whales ascended from the ocean depths to transform themselves into human beings; grizzly bears discarded their animal garments to become human beings; a creature representing the sun descended from the sky world to become a founding ancestor; eagles and wolves, sky beings, and undersea beings assumed roles as benefactors or ancient ancestors. Such profound and memorable events were regularly recounted in tribal oral history. They were passed on to each generation, modified in each retelling as is the case in oral histories. But despite the ever-changing content, the stories provided the people a special kind of identity with their forebears. The number of such narratives runs into the hundreds. Each group and subgroup cherished as part of their spiritual possessions scores of tales relating to their distinctly different pasts.

Such tales instilled a strong sense of pride that encouraged each generation to perform deeds worthy of its ancestors.

Each village was built near a dependable source of food and other required natural resources. Most coastal settlements were situated on terraces cleared of the dense forest cover, several feet above the diurnal high tide marks, on a preferably sheltered stretch of the coastline. Each village required a beach in order to accommodate the numerous large and small dugout canoes that provided not only transport to other villages, whether for purposes malevolent or peaceful, but the means to pursue specialized subsistence activities as well. Houses were laid out in a single row, rarely in two rows, paralleling the shore line (Plates 4 and 8). Villages located inland along the larger river arteries such as the Bella Coola or the Skeena required construction on elevated embankments. Houses were built on stilts and were linked together by pathways constructed from planks of rot-resistant red cedar (Plate 9).

Some settlements such as Kitkatla, Klukwan, and Chaalth or Aldertown, the Stikine River Tlingit community, were established near strategic points adjacent to especially favorable fishing grounds or near mountain pathways known as grease trails. These primitive routes led to isolated villages in the interior of what is now British Columbia and southeastern Alaska, where the people had developed quite different folkways. Much trading was carried on along grease trails, which greatly enriched the coastal tribes located where the trails terminated. The increased wealth permitted these coastal villages to effectively dominate their rivals. The trails were therefore protected with almost fanatical resolution.

The social composition of each village was based on a number of layers of organizational structure. The relationships between these structures were exceedingly complex. Peeling away some of these layers, one after another, forms a basic picture of how the tribe functioned, unravels the power relationships within the group, and explains what motivated the people within each village, simultaneously revealing the role played by two-dimensional paintings. Every layer was intimately linked with the layers above and below it, making up the very fabric of Northwest Coast village life.

The northern tribes—villages of the Tlingit, Haida, Tsimshian, and Northern Kwakiutl—were almost universally divided into units whose complementary roles regulated the relationships between their members. Among the Tlingit people were two-fold subdivisions, essentially halves, identified as raven and wolf. One was born into the raven half or the wolf half and remained a member from the cradle to the grave. The halves interacted with and complemented each other, serving vital social, economic, and ceremonial functions; they regulated marriage relationships between members, assisted in the burial rites of the opposite half, and helped with the reciprocal activities involved in potlatching. Primarily these two major subdivisions acted as the defense and support for kinsmen against those outside the tribe; Tlingit people refer to their opposite halves as "my outer shell."

The creature designations that identified a group's members served as totemic or crest symbols. Such crests possessed a powerful emotional appeal; they were the rallying points for community sentiment and personal identity and self-worth.

The Haida employed a two-fold division of each tribe similar to the Tlingit system. Their eagle and raven halves had roles and functions similar to those of the Tlingit divisions. The Tsimshian tribes used a more complex structure of four groups—eagle, wolf, frog-raven, and killer whale or blackfish. These four served functions similar to those of the two groups among the Tlingit and Haida peoples. One Northern Kwakiutl tribe followed the lead of the Tsimshian but used six subdivisions—beaver, raven, crow, blackfish, salmon, and eagle.

Beneath the "outer shells" was a second layer of social organization made up of clans, smaller groups within the main divisions. A tribe typically contained a number of clan groupings, each under the banner of its distinctive totemic crest symbol. Some tribes were home to several clans within their organization, others to but a few. Some clans embraced hundreds of members, but others were composed of only a few families and were marked by a dwindling membership. Clanships were critical organizations that served as the foundation for the primary activities of their members.

The individuals within a clan were related through matrilineal descent to a common ancestor who might have been a human being, an animal or bird, or a supernatural creature. Clan ties bound all the members together in an intensely personal and intimate, protective relationship. Some clans included several families, each of whom lived in a separate house that was ranked under the leadership of a single, dominant house. Each of these extended families constituted the next most intimate layer of the social organization. Defined as the lineage, this group represented an even closer, more demanding emotional tie among the people. Each

individual in a village was embraced by one lineage, one clan, and one subdivision, groups layered according to emotional intensity and demands upon their members. For life, each individual was held by intricate and numerous bonds that sustained in him or her a deep sense of reverence for the past. Everyone, particularly those of high rank, acknowledged a debt to uphold the status and pride of their groups.

Village social structure was considerably different among the central and southern tribes—the Bella Coola, Southern Kwakiutl, Nuu chaa nulth, and Coast Salish. They were far more flexible and less formalized in their social organization. The clan layer of the northern tribes was completely absent. The large divisions of the central and southern villages were subdivided directly by the lineages. Among the Southern Kwakiutl a lineage was called a *numayma*. Descent within them was reckoned bilaterally rather than matrilineally. *Naynumaymos,* a term for several lineages within a village, used the names of ancestors as their symbol of identity rather than birds or animals. However, the names of ancestors were intimately linked with the crests they had handed down to their descendants, and these crests were representations of animals, birds, or supernatural beings derived from their mythologies.

Clans of the northern tribes and lineages of the central and southern tribes fulfilled much the same functions. They delineated and zealously guarded the territories, such as specific salmon streams or berry thickets, that were inherited from their ancestors. Members held property in common and shared in food-gathering activities. They disciplined, nurtured, and educated their respective members, providing them with support and protection from external threats as well as succor in times of crisis. Each group held in common ceremonial paraphernalia such as masks and totemic crests, songs, dances, and rituals. The leaders were the custodians of names and property associated with their ancestors, including the rights and prerogatives tied to using the symbols during tribal and other ceremonies. Most important of all, members shared in common the legends and myths of their history—the ancestral migrations and encounters with supernatural patrons and benefactors. They placed considerable importance on the significance of ancestral exploits, commonly thinking of their progenitors as super-human.

Leaders designated to take over the honored places within the kin groups were endowed with inherited ancestral names. Theirs was a heavy burden of responsibility to preserve the fortunes of the group and to see to its continuity and perpetuity. Each tribe employed countless ways of referring to their ancestors, terms that were used publicly during ceremonial functions: Chief Root, Grandfathers, First Root, First in Line, and Chief in Front, to name but a few.

The House Group

Yet one more layer operated within the social organization of both the northern and southern tribes—the house group—the most intimate and significant kinship unit in the lives of its residents. The demands of this unit upon its membership were stringent in the support required and the allegiance and loyalty demanded.

Each village was composed of a number of houses. The size and power of each house was dependent on its acquired or inherited status in addition to the nature of the rights and privileges of its members. A big house was not only large in size but also awe-inspiring in terms of the relative wealth it was able to command. The largest houses were therefore occupied by the most influential families. Other houses tied to it by kinship lines were of lesser rank and held less lofty positions. The Tlingit referred to the occupants of the lower-ranking houses euphemistically as "people of the house next door" (Kan 1989:99). Lesser house groups commonly acknowledged the dominance of the main house group in affairs of the village.

The influential houses possessed a magnetic appeal for their members; the house was the primary identity for its inhabitants. The survival and continuity of the house group was of paramount importance and had to be continued at all costs. Its perpetuation prevailed over the immediate welfare of its individual members. This emphasis on continuity was imbedded in the consciousness of the house leaders. The Tlingit held that the preservation of the idea of the house as a source of identity for its members was as important as the physical house, and its demands continued even if the physical house had vanished. The idea of the house lived on to occupy the modern frame dwellings that eventually replaced the traditional long houses.

Traditional houses were impressive structures. I have walked among the ruins of these dwellings, mere tilted and decaying shells left of the abodes from another age. I was awestruck by their dimensions. Several were still standing in the late 1940s and could be examined in great detail in a few places, including Cumshewa and Skedans in Haida country, as well as at Quatsino, Alert Bay, Fort Rupert, and Gwayasdums in Kwakiutl territory. Constructed of red cedar beams in the central and southern areas, and hemlock and spruce along the northern Northwest Coast, these houses were engineering marvels of their time (Figures 3 and 4; Plate 7).

The foundations were constructed of tree boles often 3 feet (0.9 m) in diameter weighing 2 to 3 tons (1.8 to 2.7 metric tons). The basic design was a variation of gable-roofed architecture. The Coast Salish were an exception, preferring a shedlike construction. These houses provided living quarters for 30 to as many as 50 or more people, depending upon the wealth and power of the house group and the lineage to which it belonged. They were generally of rectangular shape and 40 feet (12.2 m) wide by 50 feet (15.2 m) long, but some houses exceeded those dimensions by half again as much. The height of the roof beams typically exceeded 15 feet (4.6 m), but those of the great houses reached closer to 20 feet (6.1 m). One great house located in Hwa'tis, a Koskimo (Kwakiutl) village, was built over a stream that passed through the center of the house, an imaginative forerunner of a built-in water supply. These long houses, whether of conventional size or larger, when fronted by a painting of proportionate length were extraordinary sights to behold.

A house was the residence of the group leader, his wife or wives, their offspring, and one or two families of close relatives, and on special occasions more distant relatives as well. All the members of the house group dedicated themselves to the continuity of the lineage that possessed the house.

Every house in each of the villages was marked by subtle differences that denoted the place of each lineage in the power structure. The houses of the wealthier lineages tended to be located in the central part of the village, flanked on both sides by the others in descending order of wealth and status. The display of monumentally sized paintings or totem poles, both depicting the stellar crests associated with the house lineage, tended to be associated with the largest and hence wealthiest houses. Houses possessed of such means were also likely to possess interior painted screens depicting additional crest symbols, the sources of lineage pride and honor. House front paintings and interior screens portrayed the honor and wealth of the lineage and its special history. The painted crest symbols represented hereditary property. The screens and house fronts could not be loaned to outsiders or given away to be used by other houses. Here the family symbols and their importance were publicly exhibited before kin, friend, and foe.

The house leader carried a heavy burden in preserving the house, its name, and its possessions in order to pass them on intact to the next generation. The house group must live on regardless of the cost to its current residents. To the Tlingit people such a leader was called *yitsati*, or keeper of the house. He was addressed by his ceremonial name during all special occasions, was held in high regard by others of the tribe, and had considerable moral power over his lineage. Other tribes had their counterparts to the *yitsati*. The Tsimshian referred to such persons as house chiefs. To the Kwakiutl they were the *gialaxa qikamay*, the first chiefs, literally, the first to come down. The keeper of the house became the custodian of all the lineage property, its dancing costumes, masks, clan hats, and batons, which bore the crests belonging to the house.

Houses were more than living spaces for the members of the lineage. They were the repository of all the lineage treasures as well. They served as the meeting place at which critical family affairs were discussed; they were places where much of the education of the young took place; they were the center for conducting the ceremonies meant to reinforce the memory of the lineage. The house was a place where the lineage leader hosted social functions for other members of the tribe or for distinguished visitors. As such these great places were often physically transformed in order to accommodate the crowd of invited guests. The house was, in effect, converted into a theater in which were presented ritual performances planned to impress the guests. These dramatic events were aimed not only at entertaining but at re-enacting the clan and lineage legends and history. In these ostentatious displays the glory of the house lived again amid spectacles designed to awe the guests.

Other men of high status were also involved in the affairs of the important houses. Though they did not bear the most venerated ancestral names they were nevertheless highly respected people. To the Tlingit such a person was called *ahn ka war*, or rich man. Those in such a position commanded considerable resources that allowed them to host frequent feasts and potlatches. They were open-handed in their generosity, showering their wealth upon others. Such behavior accorded them yet greater respect and influence.

The wealth of a house included material possessions such as the house itself, rich and abundant salmon spawning streams, good berry- and root-gathering plots; furs and skins; coppers, shieldlike objects of flattened, cold-hammered copper which were coveted items of great prestige and value; canoes; and Hudson's Bay Company blankets valued for trade exchange and as an informal type of currency between the tribes. And there were slaves captured in raids on neighboring villages, which conferred enormous status upon their owners until the practice gradually discontinued as the natives adopted more and more of Western culture. But the most important elements making up the wealth of the house were the lineage myths and legends, ceremonial songs and dances, and crests. This spiritual wealth gave a family its prestige and influence in village affairs.

House Names

Each house had a specific name that had been handed down through successive generations and that was derived from the major crests associated with its lineage. These crests were the symbols that legitimized the ostentatious public displays so common and regular a part of the Northwest Coast Indian tradition. The crests depicted in the house front and interior screen paintings (as well as on the totem poles) were drawn from such hereditary property. The names and crests found among the Northwest Coast tribes seem almost countless in number and variety. Thus two houses may have appeared to have claimed the same crest or name, yet their symbols differed markedly in visible detail or in the legends associated with them. In his book, Ronald Olson explains, "To the

Tlingit the names of the houses are of great importance. Each house had a history back of it which accounts for or explains its name, special features that set it apart such as paintings and carvings. Only the persons residing in the house would know its details of history, reciting of these at ceremonies constituted a validation" (1967:10). This statement holds equally true for all the tribes of the Northwest Coast.

To give examples of house names, I point again to Tlingit practice. A house in one village is called Killer Whale Dorsal Fin House. Its name is derived from an unusually important crest arising out of clan history. Other village house names are Frog House, Eagle's Nest House, People of the Burned House. There is Dog Salmon House, Whale House, Wolf Bath House, Raven Bones House, Bear's Den House, Woodworm House.

The Tsimshian also named their houses after particularly noteworthy crests. The following are several names for houses once recorded but which since the turn of the century have completely disappeared: Where Stands the Bear House, Spread Eagle House, Star House, Garment of Rainbow House, and Where Opens the Sky House. The Haida also had a rich array of names varying from the monstrous to the poetic: the Monster House, (which, incidentally, was perhaps one of the largest houses on record), the House Making a Noise, Thunder and Lightning House, House of the Stormy Sea, Grizzly Bear House, and House of Contentment. But these few names and associated crests only hint at the mass of crests possessed by most houses.

Southward from these northern examples, a modest shift in the preoccupation with house names is discernible. Though the crests belonging to the houses continued to be of primary importance, house names were instead first associated with names of ancestors. Among the Southern Kwakiutl the houses had extended names that included an ancestor's name, a crest, and the legend associated with it. Some examples are: the House of Siwida, To Whom People Paddled; Yakuglas, Giving Away Wealth House; or Hamside, Giving Food House. Other names with illustrious histories include: Nimogwis, the Great Only House; Nigaytzi, Great Mountain House; and Wallas, the Great One. Southern Kwakiutl houses also used animal or bird names such as Sea Lion House, Eagle Talon House, and Raven House.

Some documentation can be found on house names among the Nuu chaa nulth (Drucker 1951:223). There was Maquinna's House, named after the legendary historical figure, and Captain Jack's House, located in Friendly Cove. Their house names did not follow the general northern vogue but were also related to crests.

The Crest System

Interclan or interlineage relations within a village or between villages were often far from tranquil. Intense competition was rampant and indeed appears to have been an institutionalized custom. Factionalism and ill will were omnipresent, simmering beneath the surface of acknowledged ties of kinship and other social relationships. Interpersonal and interlineage tensions and rivalries were endemic. Actual or assumed slights eroded the pretense of unity within the village. Jealousies, prickly pride, and covert competition dominated not only intertribal but village relationships as well. Raven clans might dominate among specific Tlingit or Tsimshian villages while wolves dominated others. Among the Kwakiutl, for example, every one of the 21 tribes held a shifting rank in a vertically oriented hierarchical structure. Wealth, status, and political ambition always bubbled beneath the apparently calm surface. In consequence the relations between tribes, clans, villages, and lineages were never static. Under various pretexts one or another group forever challenged the current established order so that they might rise to a position of greater eminence. Over time, the fortunes of houses and lineages regularly rose and fell in relative social position. To maintain the position of a lineage or a clan within the hierarchy a leader had to regularly potlatch. The unending competition for rank and status drove the people to constantly project their worth so that others might be compelled to acknowledge their superior rank.

I have alluded to the role the possession and display of crests played in the lives of the Northwest Coast tribes, but the crest system came to the fore amongst the competition of the tribes. The never-ending competition for social place depended upon the regular display of one's crest symbols and also upon the vigorous cultivation of other avenues aimed at touting clan or lineage identity.

The foundation of the crest system lay in the beliefs associated with the origin and creation of the world. It was a heritage that bestowed upon the various groups a basis for interpreting the world as they believed their ancestors had formulated it. Creation myths were set in a world very different from that in which the people found themselves. The natives' search for identity and meaning led them back to the "mythic age," a period when all living forms came into existence. Various creatures—human, animal, bird, and supernatural—coexisted and participated in a common social framework. The creatures had infinite powers, including the ability to change from one physical presence to another in this world where magical events occurred and mind-shattering transformations took place. These beings played important roles that formed the hearts and minds of their descendants. The amorphous mythic age provided the fertile background of preternaturalism out of which came the symbols necessary for explaining not only the origin of the people and their world but also the exploits of their ancient progenitors. Creatures of all manner of shape, form, and power were invented and in turn made to be benefactors bearing a stunning array of supernatural gifts, including the tribal, clan, and lineage crests along with their powers and names.

Probably in no other part of the world have totemic crests been so intimately and insistently translated into tangible material possessions as was the case on the Northwest Coast. Nowhere else have totemic symbols been so manifest and so omnipresent in the social life of the people as found in this region, save for the possible exception of the materially impoverished aboriginal Australians. Inherited crests derived from the events of the mythic age number in the hundreds. Their imagery pervaded the consciousness of the people. And nowhere else have the legends, honors, and privileges associated with crests been more intensely fo-cused than on those dwelling in the Pacific Northwest villages. Material possessions ranging from the mundane to the rarest of objects, and immaterial wealth of the most common to the most sacrosanct were tied to the crests. Crests were at the heart of the metaphysical value system of the Northwest Coast Indian life.

The social role of crests extended from the Tlingit country in the north to the Strait of Juan de Fuca. The social uses and im-portance of crests rapidly fades south of this point. Crests re-mained a factor in a diluted form among the tribes occupying the west coast of the Olympic Peninsula but were absent in the tribes south and east of Puget Sound.

Crests were reproduced by artists in countless ways, and all were considered treasures. These representations employed every conceivable shape, manner, form, and notion. This seemingly end-less variation of crest replications is without parallel elsewhere. The crests connected the past with the present descendants and were therefore vital elements in the lives of all. Crest symbols are found on bowls and receptacles made for both social and cere-monial uses, on spoons for eating, canoe prows and paddles, body tattoos, storage boxes, baskets, ceremonial garments, skin and box drums, carving-tool handles, clan hats, crest batons, the scepters of chiefly power, masks, totem poles, and, finally, on the enormous two-dimensional house front paintings and interior wall screens.

Crest representations included eagles and hawks, wolves and grizzly bears, salmon and blackfish, killer whales and the Prince of Killer Whales, frogs, Frog Woman, and flying frogs. There were suns, rainbow creatures, cloud beings, woodworms, mosquito monsters, and salmon people. In the mythic age all inhabitants of the land had ocean counterparts: sea eagles, sea wolves, sea bears, octopus men. There were also conventional sky eagles and thun-derbirds. This remarkable pantheon was peopled by innumerable ghosts and forest beings and all manner of male and female prog-enitors of individual families.

The late Marius Barbeau, an authority on Tsimshian folklore, once inventoried the crests belonging to the Gitksan division of the Tsimshian tribes. Thirty-three single-spaced pages are required to list all the crests identified with this riverine group of tribes (1950:158–191). The crests were either inherited from matrilineal ancestors, associated with quasi-historical episodes involving an-cestors, or bestowed on families through encounters with various spirits. One family created the right to a crest on the basis of be-ing the first person to encounter a white man in tribal territory. This crest depicted a male face with a beard. Every crest clearly had a story to tell. The crests and their associated stories were the bedrock of the people's identity and history, their pride and honor.

The crest system touched upon every institution, social event, marriage negotiation or alliance, burial rite, and potlatch. The want or loss of crests doomed a house to ignominy. Many ambi-tious families were driven to acquire ever more crests to enhance their power and social position.

Crests were at the base of every individual's birthright. Among the northern Northwest Coast people an individual was inextri-cably linked to the crests of his or her lineage or clan. The crests in turn could not be transferred to or shared with outsiders. They remained the exclusive property of the lineage regardless of changing fortunes. Among the central coastal groups, on the other hand, some crests could be transferred to other lineages. For example, certain highly valued crests were viewed, indeed because of their value, as negotiable sources of wealth. They were often transferred to others as part of a dowry to cement a marriage between roughly equivalently ranked families; crests and other properties given thus were held in trust as an inheritance for future children. Crests could also be transferred to another group to settle festering grudges arising out of civil or criminal disputes; such transfers served as indemnity payments and were aimed at restoring peaceful relations between the parties involved. Crests were frequently acquired by raiding parties. A leader who coveted the crests of a rival was likely to lead an assault on the other village, taking the crests by force or even killing the enemies and taking the crests as booty.

Mythology and Two-Dimensional Painting

The myths belonging to each lineage and clan provided the sources for the objects depicted in the painting arts. A painting need not have featured the primary symbols identifying a particular lineage; a house leader might choose one of his family's many crests to proclaim the richness of the lineage and the variety of its possessions. The art served to constantly remind others of an episode in the history of the family. But how were the assigned parts to be arranged and in what meaningful form of composition? How were all these elements to reflect the cultural milieu? The decisions on these matters were largely left to the artist who was given the task of determining how to render the various characters and actions recounted in the associated stories.

I have selected four paintings to illustrate the close relationship between mythology and painting. They are in part chosen because the documentation that accompanies them is relatively complete. In contrast very little or no information is available for the majority of the house front and screen paintings to help explain either the meaning of the crest or the story behind it. Most significantly, the artists are generally unknown. The collecting mandates of museums did not call for their collectors to acquire information as to the meanings of the paintings or the names of the artists who created them. Further, there is some evidence of reluctance on the part of the tribal owners to explain the myths recorded in the paintings. The Northwest Coast Indian tradition assigned all the rights and protocol in the telling of a myth to the leader or to a professional narrator from outside the lineage that owned the story. The narrator was expected to frequently mention the considerable wealth being expended upon the assembled audience. One could neither tell nor refer to these stories except within the context of giving away wealth to those witnessing the telling; in any other circumstance, lips were sealed.

The following examples illustrate the complementarity between narrative and painting. Without a story as a source for the imagery, the native artist commissioned to paint a house front or interior screen would have little to communicate through his art. Contrariwise, in the absence of a painting to reinforce its message, a story lacked the requisite visual impact upon audiences.

THE SEA MONSTER HOUSE FRONT (Plate 10)

The first painting is a house front in the classic northern style of painting employed in the early to mid-19th century. It is housed in the National Museum of Natural History in Washington, D.C., and was collected in 1875. It came from the Coast Tsimshian people residing in Fort Simpson, British Columbia. This work may just have been completed and was apparently used on but one occasion when it was purchased by the museum collectors. As a consequence it is in first-rate condition with its line and formal details exquisitely preserved. The artist remains unknown but was probably from the Tsimshian people. This house front consists of 22 vertically oriented cedar planks of uniform thickness but differing widths; all have superbly adzed surfaces. It is 38 feet (11.6 m) long and about 15 feet (4.6 m) high at the entrance but tapers on each wing to about 10 feet (3.0 m) high. This is a colossal work and certainly represents one of the finest examples of its genre in existence. Bill Reid must have had such a painting in mind when he said "it's almost like a miracle" (Holm and Reid 1975:123).

The central figure portrays a huge sea monster named Nagunaks. He is shown with fingers extended and claws on his feet. His body, arms, and legs enclose the main entry into the house. A series of five smaller faces are drawn atop Nagunaks' head and seem to serve as a crown. These have been interpreted as representing mermaid children. On each side of the central figure and outlined in solid black are two massive killer whales, or more accurately blackfish, a blunt-nosed kind of whale. Dominating either wing each blackfish faces the central figure. Their mouths are open revealing rows of sharp teeth. A long decorative tongue protrudes between the rows of teeth. Both blackfish have large dorsal fins that sweep upward to the top of the painting. Some scholars have suggested that the blackfish simply represents another physical aspect of the sea monster, as Nagunaks is portrayed as the master of all creatures that reside in his watery realm (Figure 5.1).

Separating these three black figures from the top portion of the painting is a long horizontal border in red. Above this border are 12 small figures presented in a frontal squatting position. Protruding from one side of their heads are dorsal fins. Each of these figures has hands with fingers and palms facing forward as well as other design elements positioned within the body areas. No two figures are alike. It is unknown what they represent as they do not fill a role in the story as it is known today. But they raise some intriguing questions because of their seemingly similar relationship to other screens (Figures 10, 22, 26, and 53; Plates 14 and 28). The entire work is rendered in two colors, black for the dominant formline color, red for the secondary design lines. Both colors appear to be native derived pigments.

The illustrations (Figures 5.2 and 5.3) show further details of humanlike beings protruding feet-first from the blow holes of the blackfish. These two figures are either being drawn down into the blow holes or are being blown out, as the story below suggests.

Each blackfish illustration reveals the internal body structure through the use of design elements. Each of the creatures' ribs is portrayed with different details that include a humanlike face (Figure 5.4). The blackfish on the left of the house front has four ribs (Figure 5.1), that on the right has five (Plate 10). The blackfish's inner body parts seem to be purely decorative. The large red figures on the blackfish noses and on their backs behind the dorsal fins may represent denizens of the ocean depths or merely artistic license in decoration. Little is known about them.

The myth associated with this painting is described in several historical sources. I have followed the version provided by Viola Garfield (1966:42). This story and those accompanying the other three paintings described in this chapter are presented in considerably condensed form. The narrative style employed in the Northwest Coast oral tradition is lengthy and extremely circuitous, providing many details as well as prolonged repetitions. It is said that all myths must have flesh and bones. The bones of any tale must not depart from the essential action and meaning of the story. They constitute the raw essentials of the tale. The flesh, on the other hand, is the embellishment provided by a particular narrator. As long as the bones can be readily recognized, neither the authenticity of the story nor the competence of the narrator could be challenged. I propose to provide only the basic themes, the bones of the stories.

The central character in this painting is Nagunaks, a creature who ruled over an ocean realm. He controlled fabulous amounts of wealth. A chief of the Gispudwada blackfish clan named Dragging Along the Shore and several of his men once went fishing. Their anchor dragged on the sea creature's house at the bottom of the sea, making a resounding noise. Nagunaks created a whirlpool and sucked them down into his watery kingdom. Nagunaks gave the chief and his kinsmen a royal welcome to his abode. He presided over a great feast and then gave the men many gifts. Because Dragging Along the Shore was of very high rank Nagunaks bestowed upon him the privilege of a house front painting, accompanied by many other valuable gifts. These included extraordinary powers to hunt animals. However, he cautioned the chief to never molest nor allow his descendants to hunt certain animals, including certain small fishes residing within waters controlled by the chief. After some further time spent in the watery depths the chief and his men returned to their village. In time the taboo against fishing for these small fishes was forgotten and subsequently violated. Some men of the chief's lineage caught and kept some of the forbidden fishes while on a fishing expedition, whereupon they were sucked into a giant whirlpool and returned to the house of Nagunaks.

THE THUNDERBIRD SCREEN (Figure 6)
The second example is of considerable personal interest to me. The screen's story and the illustration of the screen were collected by the research team of which I was a member in June and July 1949. Though this screen is not of the classic northern style of painting but rather of the late 19th-century style, it is clearly in the direct line of descent of the classic northwest tradition. As

many of the customs and practices associated with the Northwest Coast Indian tradition gradually faded and many of their physical reminders were acquired by collectors, painted screens were still viewed by the people as important expressions of their clan history. They were replaced after being sold or left behind, a fact highly significant considering the rapidly changing culture of the time. The affiliations felt with the past and the need on the part of the people to express those ties through the crest system continued unabated despite the disappearance of most traditional beliefs and practices. The Thunderbird Screen then is an example of this kind of effort to maintain some connection with the past.

The Thunderbird Screen was located in the Drum House, which belonged to the Teqwedi clan in the *shinkukedi* or wolf half of the Tlingit who resided in Yakutat, Alaska. Our research team made contact with the screen's owner, a man named Frank Italio (1870–1956). He gave me permission to reproduce it in drawings. Figure 6 is the final result of that effort. We learned the story associated with it through the interpreters of Italio's narrative. Italio explained that he had inherited the screen from his maternal uncle in keeping with the custom of matrilineal descent observed by the Tlingit. He eventually sold it to the Alaska State Museum in Juneau in 1950.

This screen had originally decorated an interior wall of the first tribal house that was built in the present Yakutat village after the tribe had moved from S'us'ka, or On the Turnstone, their long-established homesite at Khantaak Island. A Tlingit leader named Jack Peterson dedicated the new house with an appropriate potlatch (de Laguna 1972:27). The screen was made from commer-cially milled tongue-and-groove planking and was completed in 1898. It is 10 feet (3.0 m) square. The paints were commercially manufactured. The background is a washed grey or off-white color.

A Tlingit artist of the Tluknaxadi raven clan from the wolf half of this tribe made the painting. He lived in Douglas, Alaska, and his name was In Everybody's Arms Father. The charge for the painting was $400, a considerable sum in 1898, but no worthy leader would have been willing to pay an inconsequential amount for such a work.

The screen is dominated by a centrally placed figure representing the thunderbird. It stands out from the board because it was carved from a separate piece of wood subsequently fitted on the flat surface of the screen. The wings were also carved in wood and secured to the bird's body. Below both wings are two identical anthropomorphic figures with ribs and vertebrae clearly defined in the bodies. They are boys representing a Tlingit youth named Qwachna. Though Qwachna is presented on both sides of the screen there is but one boy in the story. Italio explained that the extra figure was included by the artist for purposes of balance.

Above the bird's wings are two large flat figures, each with two eyes. They represent clouds. The faces strung out along the top border also represent clouds. The two pairs of designs on each side of the outer borders, resembling slippers, are raindrops. The small human faces on the thunderbird's wings are mainly decorative. Below these faces are wolf heads in profile. When the thunderbird flaps its wings in order to create thunder and lightning the wolves become silent. The prominent face on the chest of the thunderbird represents its rib cage. On the boy's arms and legs are designs meant to represent the beginnings of feathers growing on his body. He is in the process of undergoing a transformation from human being to bird creature, the turning point in the story.

Qwachna is one of the ancestors of the wolf half of the tribe. His people were migrating by canoe from the interior and traveling down the Alsek River in what is Alaska today. They were moving towards the sea. During the voyage the people came ashore to rest. While they rested Qwachna climbed a nearby mountain. Upon reaching the top he laid down and fell asleep. Meanwhile his people resumed their journey not noticing the boy's absence. They came to a glacier where they decided to camp. As they unloaded the canoes they realized the boy was missing. The Alsek is a very swiftly flowing river. It takes only one day to travel from the mountain to the glacier, but to return to the place where the boy was lost would require a four-day journey. The people held a council and decided they could not go back to search for him for in all probability he was already dead.

Meanwhile Qwachna awoke and returned to the river only to discover that he had been left behind by his people. A thunderbird chanced to fly overhead and quickly made out the boy's difficulty. He flew down, picked up Qwachna, and brought him to his, the thunderbird's, home. The boy stayed with the thunderbird for some time. With every passing day he became more like a bird. Pin feathers began to grow out of his shoulders and his knees. Seeing his slow transformation, Qwachna pleaded that he be allowed to return to his people. The thunderbird agreed to not only let him go but to convey him to his people who had ended their journey and established a new village. Upon their arrival in the village the boy's family was overjoyed that not only was he still alive but returned to them. A council of the elders was held at which it was agreed the people would pay honor to the thunderbird by building a great house in the village.

THE BEAVER SCREEN (Figure 7)

The third painting examined here is another interior screen. It comes from the same time period as the Thunderbird Screen. It is also from the same village. I completed the drawing of this screen in July 1949, after receiving permission from the leading members of the lineage to do so. I recall to this day how cold the house was and how often I had to warm my fingers to complete so intricate a piece. It was a day-long assignment.

The Beaver Screen belongs in the Wolf Bath House, a lineage of the Kagwantan house in the wolf division of the tribe. Yakutegy Jack, the elder Tlingit man, installed it at the building of the house in 1890, and in 1905 he gave a potlatch at which the screen was dedicated. Its dimensions are $10\frac{1}{2}$ feet (3.2 m) high and 9 feet (2.7 m) wide. It was painted by a man named Daniel S. Benson, a Tlingit of the Teqwedi lineage of the wolf half of the tribe. This information was provided by members of the house who owned the rights to the screen and the story associated with it.

The central figure depicts a beaver eating a willow branch held in its paws. Its tail is crosshatched and portrayed as turned under and resting against the animal's belly. There are many cattails on each end of the willow. The beaver sits on a beaver dam, represented by the larger pattern with the eye designs on it. Below the beaver dam are two wolves that face each other and probably represent the figures from which the house takes its name. The holes in the center of the dam are entrances into the beaver's house.

Along the upper portion of the screen is the artist's rendering of the milky way or sky world. At the left is the hero of the story, Akaxankw. He wears fringed hide garments reminiscent of clothing found among interior Canadian subarctic tribes. He has snowshoes on his feet for the sky world is a place of frost where it is necessary to wear them in order to travel. The snowshoe tracks of the hero are at the top center of the screen. He also holds a bow with an arrow notched into the string. He wears a feathered war bonnet, which is not associated with Northwest Coast dress and so is a genuine anomaly. Akaxankw is looking out across the milky way to the muskrat on the extreme right of the screen, which he shoots. There are several versions of this tale that de Laguna and I collected during research in the village. All are probably genuine as they represent separate episodes of a longer narrative; I again provide only the following "bones."

The hero, Akaxankw, in the company of his three older brothers, has many adventures. They made their way into the sky world by shooting arrows into the sky, each sticking into the notch of the previous arrow until a chain or rope formed. The brothers then climbed the chain into the sky. They encountered harrowing experiences including the slaying of many monsters. They killed a brown bear with two heads and another that was half animal, half human. Akaxankw's pet dog accompanied the boys. Late

in their adventures the dog ran off to chase some clouds and became lost. The boy spent much time searching for his pet but to no avail. Following some further adventures the brothers decided to return to earth and their village, but they were unable to do so for they could find neither their arrow chain nor another way down. Soon a bird came to them and assured them that it knew a way that involved climbing down a chain of mountains that reached up to the sky. Boulder by boulder, stream by stream, they followed the bird until they finally arrived at their village. They told the people where they had been and of their many adventures. It was from this expedition that the people learned of the nature and inhabitants of the sky world.

THE THUNDERBIRD AND WHALE SCREEN
(Figures 8.1 and 8.2; Plates 11A and 11B)

The final example included to convey the complimentary character of lineage legends and house front and interior screen paintings comes from the southern Northwest Coast region. This particular painting differs from the previous three in several important ways. It is really two screens joined rather than one. Interior screens were used to wall off the quarters of the leader and his family from that of other members of the lineage residing within the house. Neither part of this screen served as a permanent element of the interior. It was installed and displayed only at times of potlatch ceremonies or other special social occasions. This screen is also markedly different stylistically from those previously illustrated. It is of an important substyle found along the Northwest Coast. The photograph shows the placement of each panel: that in Figure 8.1 is positioned clearly on the left side of the house, Figure 8.2 on the right side. Lastly, both boards are rare Nuu chaa nulth paintings; few from this region have survived.

The screen comes from the Hopachisat tribe of the Nuu chaa nulth. It probably dates back to the middle of the 19th century and is now housed in the American Museum of Natural History in New York City. The panels are made from split and carefully adzed cedar boards about 1 inch (2.5 cm) thick. They are 9½ feet (2.9 m) in width and 5¾ feet (1.8 m) in height. The combined length of both boards then is about 19 feet (5.8 m). The painting is in two colors, black and red. Both paints are of native manufacture.

Double screens are not rare. Several other examples are known but they are more typically of the Tlingit groups in Alaska, the most famed being the Killer Whale Screen at Klukwan (Figure 1.1) and the marvelous Raven Screen from Hoonah, Alaska, now in the Denver Art Museum (Figure 15; Plates 18A and 18B). There are others. These will be reviewed in more detail in the chapter that follows.

The Hopachisat were inland dwellers residing at the confluence of the Sproat and Somass rivers near Port Alberni in south-central Vancouver Island. The screen comes from the house of Chief Kuan Tough in the village called Moohoulth, a place long since abandoned. The leader residing in this village was a man named Tatoosh who told the story to George Emmons (1930: 288–292). There is no mention of the artist in Emmons's notes.

Each board portrays as the central figure a great thunderbird called Tooksuquin. The thunderbirds' wings are shown extended in flight. Each is holding a great whale secured in its talons. Whales were thought to be the favored food of thunderbirds, who would pluck them from the sea and carry them to their sky abode to consume. On each board both a lightning serpent called Haietlik and a wolf named Kanattle are pictured. Both the lightning serpent, considered the servant of the thunderbird, and the wolf were important magical symbols among the Nuu chaa nulth tribes.

The story, not recorded in great detail, tells of the clan leader's encounter with supernatural creatures while he is checking his salmon traps. One summer long ago when the sockeye salmon were beginning their journey to spawn, a chief named Sin-set of the Hopachisat people went to check his fish traps. They were secured near a waterfall where some of the salmon, having to pass over the falls on their journey to spawn, would jump and fall back into the traps. When Sin-set stepped down on a trap it collapsed under his weight and he fell into a deep pool. In the water two whales approached him, calling his name. They beckoned him to follow them.

After a long journey they came to a place called Moohoulth, near a large river. Here the whales left him saying they would return. Sin-set soon saw two beautiful women named Ohk-sis and Pay-tles, who were mermaids. Sin-set was smitten by them and he beckoned to them to come near. He asked them to run away with him but they refused; however, they agreed to visit him each day. After they left Sin-set constructed a large trap in which he hoped to trap them and carry them to a place where he could have their company. When they reappeared the next day they fell into his trap. He thereupon took them up the river to the vicinity of Sproat Lake. Here he crossed over to the far side of the stream where he heard the sound of the thunderbird's flapping wings. The thunderbird called his name, "Sin-set, Sin-set." The giant bird directed Sin-set and the mermaids to go to the wolf's house on the far side of the lake where they could get food. Standing before the wolf's house they heard a voice crying out, "What do you people want?"

Sin-set looked about but saw no one. While he was searching for the source of the voice both mermaids disappeared. He was suddenly returned from the watery world to this world and realized that he was living in the wolf's house. The thunderbird and the lightning serpent then appeared to tell him the whereabouts of the whale that lived in the lake. He pursued it but without suc-

cess. After further adventures Sin-set returned to his people and related his fabulous experiences.

These stories lie at the base of what the artist recorded in these two Nuu chaa nulth screens. The characters depicted became the crests inherited by Sin-set's descendants, preserved by them down through the generations in both story and paintings.

This review of the principal lineaments of the social organization of the Northwest Coast Indian tribes and the paramount place of possessions, both material and other-worldly, in their conception of the world, leads to an understanding of the driving forces not simply of the society but of its symbolic representations as well. And further, this understanding forms a sound foundation from which to examine the great painting tradition that is given visual expression by way of the manipulation of crests and symbols.

THE NORTHERN STYLE

"These things are what we are and who we are."

Eva Carlick, wolf clan
Stikine Tlingit from Telegraph Creek, B.C.
(Grandmother of artist Dempsey Bob)

THIS and the following chapter examine the major house front and interior screen paintings from the Northwest Coast, beginning with the Tlingit tribes of what is now Alaska and proceeding south through the many Tsimshian tribes of British Columbia. The range of the artistic tradition is presented, in the broadest terms, through examples that are particularly representative or historically significant. This analysis is founded on the photographs and illustrations reproduced in this book.

Various types of monumental paintings were found along the Northwest Coast: foremost was the house front, seconded by the interior screen. Both types can be further divided into subcategories based on different regional practices and temporal patterns of expression. This chapter focuses on the characteristics and uses,

49

and the changes, of the numerous traditional paintings of the northern tribes—the Tlingit, Tsimshian, and Haida.

The changes weathered by the art comprehend the obvious variations in the paintings' social functions; the changes resulted from and reflect the different forces that affected clan and lineage associations and identity. As house front paintings fell away there emerged among some groups what might be called house emblem paintings; they were smaller versions of the traditional house front painting that showed the people's continuing search for accommodation within the conflicting circumstances of their lives. House emblem painting was one of the new customs developed along with the adaptation of Western-style architecture. At about the same time in several tribes, screens appeared that were constructed with milled lumber purchased from commercial outlets. The uncertainty associated with rapid and continual social change appeared in the substitution of trade cloth paintings for the traditional wood panels. Interest in funerary and graveyard art was renewed. Following the eventual disappearance of the tradition of house front painting, a revival began in the mid-20th century, one that was associated with the natives' efforts to resurrect some element of their traditional past.

House Front and Facade Paintings

House front paintings were not employed by every tribe along the Northwest Coast. The northern Tlingit, for example, did not utilize house front paintings, but the southern Tlingit, residing in closer proximity to the Coast Tsimshian, did. Historical evidence suggests the Haida possessed few house front paintings, but the presence of house front paintings among the Nass and Skeena river Tsimshian was recorded by a variety of researchers.

In the case of the Coast Tsimshian, painted house fronts were not an entrenched practice until the early 19th century. The evidence is strong that the painting of house fronts and screens reached its apogee among this group. Some writers claim every house in one Coast Tsimshian town, later Fort Simpson, boasted a painted house front (Nabakov and Easton 1989:280). Though this is probably somewhat of an exaggeration, it is certain that many impressive paintings derive from the Coast Tsimshian tribes, more perhaps than from other tribes during this time period. Coast Tsimshian leaders were wealthy beyond measure, politically powerful, enormously competitive, and brimming with pride. Such an exuberant display of status as that in Plate 2, drawn in Figure 22, seems only fitting.

The art of house front painting spread south from the Tsimshian to the Bella Coola and Southern Kwakiutl tribes during the mid-18th and early 19th centuries. Beyond these limits, however, an occasional screen was recorded or preserved but the tradition did not take root. At that same time, some of the southernmost tribes bore the most forceful confrontation with the new settlers, which made it difficult for them to wholeheartedly support the tradition of house front painting.

A variation of native painting practices emerged during the course of my research for this book. Some house front paintings were substantial constructions but others seemed to be quite fragile and hence elusive to track. I ultimately discovered an alternative design of construction, one that reflected a difference in use. Two types of house front construction were commonly used in the same village at the same time. One served a temporary end and the other was designed with a long-term objective. The more permanent type of painting was done directly on the front walls of the house itself and was limited in size to the dimensions of the house. The more transitory type was painted on boards attached to the house and was larger than the front of the house. Essentially a facade, it hid the actual house from view and gave people coming in from the sea a false notion of the size of the house (Plate 12). The facade was an architectural deception that exaggerated the size of the house far beyond its original dimensions (Blackman 1984:187). Figures 9.1 and 9.2 show the sizes of two house fronts relative to the dimensions of their facades. The facade was built in such a way that it offered a more extensive flat surface on which to display the painted crest designs.

Facades were particularly common among the Tsimshian tribes along the north and adjacent coasts; the largest percentage of the paintings that have been recorded from the mid- to late 19th century were found among them. Facade construction was the dominant architectural style of the Tsimshian, Southern Kwakiutl, and Bella Coola villages and was sporadically employed elsewhere. Few Tlingit houses had facades, and Chief Gold's house near Skidegate is the one documented Haida example (Figure 29).

The permanent house front painting assured that the house and its crests remained recognizable to visitors year after year. Once painted, the house and painting did not change significantly in appearance over the years, despite the inevitable weathering that slowly eroded the detailed features. In contrast, facade paintings were of a passing nature. They were raised by the house leader for a specific occasion to serve a specific end. Once these objectives were realized the paintings were typically dismantled plank by plank and stored for possible use on another occasion. In some instances, however, facade paintings were destroyed following the occasion for which they had been created. By chance some facades that would have been destroyed were acquired by collectors; they have been and continue to be viewed as among the most important holdings in the museums of the world.

Facade paintings were never intended to be permanent features of the houses. They were props, status symbols aimed at flaunting the owners' wealth and privilege. Knowing of the facades helps clarify the mystery surrounding the appearance and disappearance of particular houses in the documentation of consecutive periods within the 19th century. But most importantly, the nature of facade use constitutes a critical ethnographic fact revealing the breadth and depth of the search for status that constantly drove the people in this society.

When a leader bent on broadcasting the social position and wealth of his lineage added a false front to his house, considerable expenditure was required. Both the workers who felled the cedar trees and made the broad planks and the artists who painted the crests had to be paid. Such a project also required long-term planning. For example, the painting of a crest of the magnitude seen in the Bella Coola facade (Figure 31; Plate 9) or that of the house at Fort Simpson (Figure 22; Plate 2) must have involved months if not years of work, beginning with the crest plan and continuing through the manufacture of the boards, the executing of the painting itself, the raising of the facade, and ultimately, the mounting of the potlatch to commemorate the event.

Published accounts occasionally refer to facades that were both carved and painted. Philip Drucker attempted to document the existence of carved facades (1950:250); however, I have not succeeded in discovering a single example of a carved facade painting dating from the 19th century to the mid-20th. Plate 13 shows one traditional example of a carved house front of considerable complexity, but it is not a two-dimensional painting. The house incorporated four vertical carved columns, essentially totem poles. Attached to the front of the house was a larger horizontal sculpture extending across the top of the facade to connect the four vertical columns. The figure represents a two-headed serpent crest. The doorway leading into the interior is also painted and employs a circular design with a human figure within. The house is one of several that once stood in Tsatsichnukwomi or New Vancouver village near Alert Bay (Plate 40). The village has since disappeared.

Interior Screens

In contrast to house front paintings, interior screens served very different ends. There was a firmer and more deeply felt emotional attachment to them. The house screen frequently was considered a revered constituent of the holdings of the lineage or clan. Though other properties might be sold or traded to outsiders over time there was much greater resistance to parting with the screens. Far more interior screens have survived and even remain intact in settlements than house front paintings.

House screens formed an integral part of the interior of the house and offered daily reminders of family history and position. Even the less powerful lineages possessed crest screens and displayed them within their dwellings. Screens served to separate the household into spaces for its different families or for restricted areas, inner sanctums, or chambers for special purposes. The screen walled off the section of the long house in which the leader of the house and his wife or wives resided. Such screens were erected 10 feet (3.0 m) or more from the rear wall of the house to provide uniquely separate quarters for lineage leaders. In the case of the Tlingit, for example, the *yitsati*, the keeper of the house, slept behind the screen. But the space represented more than living space. It was a sacred repository where the clan and lineage treasures—ritual and ceremonial possessions of various kinds associated with the group history—were stored in numerous cedar chests and boxes. These treasures were carefully guarded. They were removed from this sanctuary and displayed only for high social functions. As private space reserved for the leader and for the safe-keeping of lineage possessions, even few members of the household were permitted entry. Tlingit vocabulary reflected this division of the house: the front, the much larger area, was called the feet and the rear was called the head (Kan 1989:93).

Additionally, momentous events were staged before the lineage house screens. The ceremonies ranged from the induction of the young into the ways of the house to social affairs involving scores of guests from other tribes. When a leader died among the Tlingit, for example, his body was placed in a sitting or reclining position before the screen while members of his clan and their opposites reviewed his life and paid him honor. Food was placed in the central fire pit in front of the screen so that the deceased could partake in all these proceedings (Oberg 1973:53).

Interior screens were of two types. One was the permanent wall partition that divided the leader's private quarters from the rest of the household. The second was a temporary screen that separated the interior space used by ceremonial performers from the space occupied by the spectators and guests. The temporary type gave symbolic representation to the separation between the two different worlds of native myth, the mundane and the supernatural. These temporary screens appear to be more characteristic of the central and southern Northwest Coast tribes than of the northerly groups. These screens will be discussed in greater detail in the following chapter.

Among the northern tribes—the Tlingit and Tsimshian especially—the interior screens were far more elaborate and complex in design than those found southward. Some employed painted surfaces only, paralleling the practice followed in the making of the exterior house paintings. In sharp contrast, others were both painted and carved in shallow relief sculpture.

Among the Tlingit, interior screens were of two forms of construction. First, two flanking screens were separated from one another by a taller vertically oriented sculptured figure. This fig-

ure often included a doorway through which the sacred space was entered or left (Figure 11; Plate 1). The three elements of this form were carefully joined to form a solid wall, as partially evident in Plate 1. The alternate form was constructed as a single large screen filling the entire width of the house (Plate 3). The passageway through such screens was typically centered in the lower part of the screen.

The entry holes are a distinctive feature of the northern style of house screen and may be seen in the illustrations cited throughout this chapter. Entry holes were usually circular or oval in shape and required a person to stoop, enforcing this sign of respectful humility. Entry holes compel several interesting hypothetical questions and have prompted much speculation among anthropologists as to their function. Did they, in fact, possess some esoteric religious or social meaning, or were they simply passageways leading into and out of the quarters reserved for revered clan leaders? In most cases the bottom edge of the hole in the screen was located at knee level or slightly higher and the top was well below head height. They cannot, therefore, be construed as simple doorways for ready passage because they are much too small. It is, in fact, difficult to imagine an adult navigating through these holes with anything approaching ease. A large teenager would have difficulty entering and exiting this way; it is even more difficult to envision leaders or elders, who tended toward both corpulence and arthritic ailments, navigating such constricting passages during ceremonial functions while maintaining an aura of dignity and formality, which both their station and the ceremony demanded.

Joan Vastokas advanced the view that the oval doorways in Tsimshian interior screens represented the point of passage between profane and sacred worlds (1973:129). This hypothesis coincides with views expressed by some Kwakiutl informants. George MacDonald also concurred with this view, calling them thresholds or zones of transition (1984:27). He went on to liken the entry holes in Haida interior screens to symbols of the vagina and rebirth, making them zones of transition from one state of being to another (1984:228). There are too few Haida screens to draw any reliable conclusions. Aldona Jonaitis has advanced an alternative hypothesis, likening entry holes in Tlingit screens to the orifice leading to the belly of the crest figure (1986:134). That such holes may indeed have symbolic meaning is likely enough. That they represent the vagina, a birth canal, or a passage to the belly is something else again. Not all entry holes are positioned convincingly to suggest any of these hypotheses. Also, the hole may once have been an entryway of larger proportion that was gradually reduced to a smaller, symbolic size over time. Possibly, there was another doorway that led into the living quarters of the leader of the house, one that gave easier access than through the confined central opening.

The same constricted circular or oval opening sometimes served as the passageway through house fronts as well. Some of the same symbolism very likely applied to them; at least, they required the same humbling, bowed position from entrants. Many house fronts, however, had large, rectangular openings, large enough for erect persons to pass through. Such openings were sealed off from the elements by hanging animal hides or installing wooden doors.

Tlingit Screens and Emblems

First, I will survey Tlingit painting, then the Tsimshian and Haida art. The following chapter will focus on the central and southern Northwest Coast tribes. The examination is possible in most cases only through historic photographs, but a few photographs can be compared to the actual boards. In this book, the illustrations accompanying the text are intended to help highlight both the details within the paintings and the color formulas the artists followed.

The Tlingit of the most northerly distribution did not employ house front paintings. They produced only interior screens. Such screens provided their owners a social status comparable to what totem poles provided elsewhere. It is among these people that some of the most notable examples of interior screens can be discovered along the entire length of the Northwest Coast.

KLUKWAN

Among the Tlingit residing at Klukwan village, the interior screens reached their finest flowering in the Rain Wall Screen of the Whale House, the one example that most epitomizes the art form (Figure 10; Plates 14 and 15). A truly astonishing fact about the Whale House screen is that it remains in its original location, despite the many vicissitudes visited upon it since the early 1800s.

Numerous skirmishes have been fought over the years by various parties aspiring to acquire this famous screen. Museum and art collectors, worldwide, have schemed after it. There is enough intrigue surrounding this prime clan possession to fill a tension-gripped drama of deception, rivalry, duplicity, greed, and personal tragedy. A short account of the conflict revolving about this treasure appears in Chapter VI.

The Whale House is probably the single most famous Tlingit house in all Alaska. It was first seen by an outside observer who recorded its existence in 1885. That visitor was George Emmons, who devoted a monograph to it in 1916. The original plank-constructed house was roughly rectangular, 49 feet (14.9 m) in width and 53 feet (16.2 m) in length. It gradually fell into disrepair and was abandoned in 1899. A Western-style house of two stories was designed to replace it, but it was never completed. During construction, a potlatch was held by the owners to celebrate the new edifice. But finally, the clan treasures were placed in temporary housing to await improved clan fortunes.

The screen belongs to the Ganaxtedi clan of the raven half of the Chilkat tribe. It measures 20 feet (6.1 m) by 9½ feet (2.9 m) and is referred to as the Sukheen or Rain Wall Screen. It is made of thin, split, red cedar boards of varying widths, carefully fitted and sewn together with twisted spruce-root fibers. The front of the screen was smoothed to take the painted and carved designs, which are set in shallow relief sculpture. Plate 14 shows the screen in its original setting before the historic Whale House fell into ruin. It is flanked by two interior house posts incorporating intricately carved figures. Before it are other clan treasures consisting of masks, ceremonial hats, storage boxes, a feast dish, and other ceremonial regalia. In Plate 15 a close-up photograph taken in 1943 shows an unidentified clan elder sitting before the screen. This photograph permits a closer view of the surface carving as well as some of the design details. Note the serious cracks that have opened. The drawing of the entire piece in Figure 10 gives a better sense of the exceptional detail employed in the painting of this screen. The skill of the artist is clearly evident, being constrained to the highly conventionalized presentation of the figures while attending to proportions between the black outlines and the other color elements. The entire screen is a masterful composition and one by which to measure other Northwest Coast screens.

At the time Emmons first came upon the Whale House in 1885, a tribal leader named Yehlh Koh, or Raven Odor, was the owner. Raven Odor reported that the partition boards were made by a chief named Ka-te-tsu who built the house in the early part of the 19th century, perhaps as early as the 1830s. The painting was reputed to be the work of a Tlingit artist named Skeet-la-ka, but this fact remains uncertain. Others asserted the painting was done by a Tsimshian artist. There may be some truth in this latter contention as there are many elements in the design, particularly the handling of the border areas, that indeed tie it more closely to Tsimshian practice than Tlingit. I will return to this issue later when dealing with Tsimshian paintings.

Filling the top and side borders of the Rain Wall Screen are a series of 13 figures frontally positioned, nine of them with both arms and legs placed in a traditional stance with elbows close to the knees. This arrangement of limbs is called the hocker position and appears in many house front and screen paintings of the Northwest Coast tribes. These 13 figures represent the rain drops from which the screen takes its name.

The central dominating figure is a creature with a huge head and projections extending from each side, which can be interpreted as feather designs. It has huge, outstretched arms, each of which has two winglike projections extending outwards. The body cavity is a large oval form that encompasses the opening through the screen. The creature's feet are drawn up in a squatting position, with knees approaching the upper arms. The toes are represented by terminal claws or talons. The eyes are actually figures similar in shape to the 13 rain drop figures in the borders of the screen.

There is considerable controversy as to the identity of the central figure or what it represents. That it is a mythological or crest symbol is not disputed. Some scholars have identified it as the mythical spirit called Gonakadet, a being conceived as rising out of the ocean to bring power and wealth as well as good fortune to those fortunate enough to see him. This interpretation parallels the Tsimshian story of Nagunaks who rules the sea. An alternate explanation, which I support, holds it to be the embodiment of Raven, the culture hero of the northern tribes whose myths assign him as the creator of the world. In support of this view it should be pointed out that the raven was the dominant crest of the lineage that owned the screen. The outstretched arms that appear to have wings attached to them, the talons on the feet, and what can be taken to represent a beaklike design positioned

below the eyes on the head all support the raven hypothesis. And Aldona Jonaitis notes that Raven was the bringer of rain during the creation period as he flew around the world changing things (1986:114).

Locked within another house in the same conservative village once renowned for its wealth and power is another masterpiece. Inside the Killer Whale House, once owned by a powerful chief named Kudenaha, is the screen that de Laguna and I had the unprecedented opportunity to observe in July 1949 (Figure 1.1; Plate 1). It is little known, however, as few outsiders have been admitted to this venerable place. The matriarch permitted us a brief look under the most stringent conditions. It belonged to the Kagwantan clan within the eagle-wolf half of the Chilkat tribe.

This complex flat painting is sheltered within a Western-style frame house that replaced the original long house years ago. The screen was once divided into three parts: two separate painted screens were placed on either side of a vertical sculptured screen of low-relief carving. The central piece represents a smiling, upright brown bear (Figure 11). The bear is in a frontal position with fore- and hind limbs encircling a rectangular doorway. When the screen was moved to the Western-style house the lower quarter of the bear's limbs was sawed off to fit the space available in the house. In its original setting the entire screen must have inspired awe upon the viewer's first step into the lineage house.

When de Laguna and I were allowed to visit the Killer Whale House the central brown bear figure had been set aside. Only the two flanking screens were mounted in the single large room of the house. They were positioned on opposite walls to the left and right of the front door and had been secured with nails to the studs of the unfinished interior. Each screen consists of three horizontally oriented cedar boards of unusual breadth fitted neatly together to form a smooth painting surface. The screens are each about 12 feet (3.7 m) long and about 8 feet (2.4 m) tall to the top of the projecting dorsal fins.

Each screen depicts in profile a huge killer whale painted in black (Figure 1.1). A myriad number of secondary creatures painted in red—strange-looking figures, eye patterns, humanlike faces, all kinds of forms of bewildering complexity—surround the principal figure. The first thing I noticed upon entering the room was the vibrance of the colors and how well they were preserved. Both killer whale panels faced the rear of the house. Though I had seen one photograph of the left-side screen (Plate 1) I had never seen a single photograph of its counterpart, probably because both appear to be identical in design and execution. The colors are the same, the design elements positioned within each whale and the creatures that surround them are all the same. The two screens are in effect mirror images.

Most attention-arresting of the many features in this superb painting is the prominent dorsal fin thrusting so obviously upward from the top board of each screen (Figure 1.2). Tufts of hair of unidentified origin were inserted within the rear portions of both dorsal fins. The mouths of both killer whales are open, revealing prominent tongues and rows of flat-topped teeth. Large ventral fins, male genitalia, and flukes are other clearly identifiable features. Within the body cavity of the whale on the left side is a series of ribs, each with a distinctive face in profile, as well as the

artist's visualization of the other internal organs (Figure 1.3). A sea creature or perhaps a rendering of ocean spray is flowing out of the blow holes (Figure 1.4). Other denizens of the sea are positioned under the whales' jaws (Figure 1.5), above the noses (Figure 1.6), and on their backs behind the dorsal fins (Figure 1.7). A smaller killer whale is in the lower part of each screen between the ventral fin and the flukes.

De Laguna and I had agreed not to ask questions but I was so overcome by this experience that I lapsed momentarily to ask a question about the diminutive whale. Surprisingly, the matriarch responded by explaining the small whale did not suggest a baby whale or even the idea of a pod. The artist who created this masterpiece simply ran out of space and portrayed the second whale in a smaller scale. When I then asked who the artist was the response was stony silence.

With the minutes fleeing and with so much to observe about the paintings themselves, to say nothing of the other clan possessions inside the house, I scanned first one screen, then the other, trying to determine what differences—if any—there were between them. If there were no discernible differences, why had the artist painted two identical screens? Back and forth I went from one screen to the other. Then suddenly I spotted the difference, so cunningly incorporated that only careful, minute comparison would reveal it. The panel on the left contains a dead seal lying within the stomach cavity of the killer whale (Figure 1.8). The killer whale's stomach in the screen on the right side of the room depicted not a dead seal but rather a seal skeleton. Did the screen convey a warning message aimed at those who might threaten the people who resided within the Killer Whale House? And would their fate be similar to that of the dead seal if they tried? Here was surely a visual statement of enormous significance, a play on symbols and meaning about which outsiders could only speculate. The explanation was not to be learned from the matriarch. Probably only a few within the lineage were permitted to share the secret locked within those panels.

A third notable screen from Klukwan village once dominated the Frog House, the house of a lineage within the Ganaxtedi clan (Figure 12). It represents the raven crest and is constructed of five vertically placed spruce planks adzed to a smooth surface. The raven is frontally positioned, its head filling almost half the space of the screen. Dominating the upper portion are large wings, inverted so the gaze of the double-eye designs on each wing is fixed towards the top of the screen. The center element represents the bird's body and encloses a round entry hole. The tail feathers appear below the entry hole. This board is painted in solid black formlines with red and blue-green colors highlighting the remainder of the carved and painted surface. This screen dates back to the early decades of the 19th century and is now housed in the Seattle Art Museum.

TAKU

One of the rarest of all Tlingit interior screen paintings comes from the Taku Tlingit tribe. They once occupied the region between Auk Bay and Stephens Passage but migrated to Juneau early in the 20th century. The only evidence of the screen's existence is a single historic photograph taken in the now deserted village.

The caption attributes ownership to a chief of the Taku Tlingit named Taku Jack (Plate 16). It is a massive example of Tlingit painting, roughly 38 feet (11.6 m) in length and at its peak about 10 feet (3.0 m) in height, but tapering to about 6 feet (1.8 m) high at the sides. The photograph was made in the latter part of the 19th century, but the painting must date to the mid-19th century or even earlier. It is a tantalizing morsel of which little is known. The photograph does not provide a clear image of the figures within the screen, but a delicacy of line and subtlety of curve is sufficiently evident to place it in a class of its own. My efforts to extract details of this painting from the photograph proved a formidable task that ended in a mixed result (Figure 13).

The central part of this screen is dominated by a human face positioned above a round entry hole. Small animal-like figures crouch in profile on the left and right sides as well as in the lower portions of the painting. These are outlined in black and filled with numerous eye designs and secondary red lines composed of ovoids and U-shaped designs. Edward Keithahn asserts that the design represents a killer whale and cost Taku Jack the sum of $600 to have painted. The making of this screen led to a feud with another faction within the village, who contended that Taku Jack had no rights to the use of this particular crest figure (1963:135). Unfortunately, further information about this impressive work and its present fate is unknown.

WRANGELL

One of the memorable treasures ensconced in the Denver Art Museum is the Brown Bear Screen, the interior partition board from the house that once belonged to Chief Shakes, a leader of the Stikine Tlingit near Wrangell, Alaska (Figure 14). Shakes was in the 1880s one of a line of chieftains bearing that name. He was leader of the Nan yan-yi clan of the *shinkukedi* or wolf half of the tribe and is reputed to have hosted eight potlatches during his lifetime, an unprecedented number that reflected his enormous social stature and wealth.

This particular prize is constructed of red cedar planks that were placed in a vertical orientation and is both carved in low relief and painted. It probably dates back to the early 1840s or before and is 15 feet (4.6 m) high and 9 feet (2.7 m) wide. It depicts a massive brown bear—but a friendly looking one—the crest of this famed Tlingit lineage. It memorializes a clan myth describing an ancestress who was captured by a bear and taken to its forest abode, where it mated with her. She provided the bear with children, part human, part animal. It is interesting to compare the bear on this screen with the one on the screen that was housed in the Killer Whale House at Klukwan (Figure 11; Plate 1).

Fortunately, this superb screen possesses exceptional documentation. It has been photographed intermittently over a period of years in the Shakes house. The earlier photographs were taken inside the dwelling where it fronted the *yitsati*'s quarters. These early photographs also picture all manner of clan properties—masks, carvings, ceremonial garments. It was clearly a symbol of grandeur and power. The screen was removed from the interior of the house during the early part of the 20th century and positioned in the front of a Western-style frame home between two separate entryways (Plate 17). In this photograph two of Shakes's mortuary poles are also included containing the ashes of his parents and brother. The one on the left represents Natsilane, the mythical ancestor who created the killer whale people. The pole on the right shows a grizzly bear and commemorates an episode when that creature befriended ancestors and led them to a mountain top for safe haven during their migrations.

Following Chief Shakes's death in 1916 his widow attempted to keep the heirlooms together. In keeping with Tlingit custom, these possessions should have been passed on to the highest-ranking nephew on the chief's sister's side. But unknown circumstances led to another outcome. Perhaps there was no rightful heir, or if there was he had insufficient resources to mount a potlatch of appropriate magnificence to support his claim to the vacant leadership position. The screen was finally placed on sale in 1933 and was purchased by an Alaskan antique dealer named Walter Waters. This was a time of great and genuine privation for the native peoples as the Great Depression impacted their livelihood as adversely as it did the wider world economy. Waters subsequently sold the screen in 1939 to a Mexican artist named Wolfgang Paalen. Paalen in turn sold it to the Denver Art Museum in 1950 (Feder and Malin 1962:30). Several copies of this particular screen have since been made, but none can match the quality of the original.

Former Denver Art Museum curator Norman Feder has pointed out that two-dimensional art was the Tlingit forte. The monumentality, frontal symmetry, and elaborate utilization of images within images in this particular example makes it unsurpassed in quality and vitality.

HOONAH

Another gem housed in the Denver Art Museum is the Raven Screen (Figure 15; Plates 18A, 18B, and 19). This screen ranks among the finest of the classic northern-style painting. If ever there was a convoluted tale filled with quirks, vagaries of fortune, and just plain luck it is the provenience of this screen. Museum records disclose it was purchased in Sitka, Alaska, after museum collectors saved it from certain destruction as the Tlingit owner was cutting it into a pile for either firewood or fence posts. Indeed, one of the boards already bore the chewed-up marks of a saw blade when the negotiations began that resulted in the sale (Feder and Malin 1962:30).

According to Peter Corey, curator at the Sheldon Jackson Museum in Sitka, who has researched the incident in detail, it did not happen quite that way. The screen was, in fact, transported to Sitka in the early 1930s for the purpose of making it available for sale. It came from the conservative village of Hoonah located on the north side of Chichigof Island. It is first recorded in history as owned by a man named Henry Moses who purchased it in Sitka. It is Corey's belief that Moses rather than the Denver Art Museum intervened to save the screens from almost certain destruction. Moses was well known to the Tlingit people. He was called Mink's Father because he bought furs and curios from them. Moses had spent many years among the Hoonah people and spoke their language fluently. According to Corey, Moses witnessed the preparations to destroy the screen. He offered to buy the owner enough wood to last him the entire winter in exchange for it. In one swift stroke the boards were saved, preserving for posterity a superb example of early to mid-19th-century two-dimensional painting. In 1938 the Denver Art Museum was able to acquire the screens.

There is no information as to who the native owner was, nor the name of the person from whom the boards were purchased, nor what house they came from, nor who the artist was. Whatever our ignorance, it is certain that the artist was a master among masters.

The Raven Screen consists of two large panels that apparently were used as side partition boards. Plate 19 is a photograph of these boards as they were displayed out-of-doors in either Sitka or Hoonah. No identification data accompanies the photograph but by virtue of other evidence it can be dated between 1900 and 1938. A large central screen often accompanied boards such as these, similar to those noted in the Killer Whale House (Plate 1) and the Shakes Brown Bear Screen (Plate 17).

Each of the two panels of the Raven Screen is constructed of three planks joined together and carefully fitted to form the painting surface. Each panel is of cedar wood, about 14 feet (4.3 m) in length and $5\frac{1}{2}$ feet (1.7 m) in height. There is no entry hole in either panel. Two ravens in profile are painted on each panel, all facing the center. The birds on both panels are separated by a solid vertical band of red (Figure 15). The talons hold creatures from the sea on the left panel only, the raven on the left a sea urchin, on the right a fish. Each raven portrays a specific episode, it is believed, in the extensive mythology built up around the figure of Raven. It was Raven, the creator and trickster of the mythic age, who conceived and executed an exhaustive array of natural phenomena to benefit human kind: the appearance and fluctuations of the tides, the emergence of the sun, moon, and stars, and instructions in the art of procreation, to name but a few.

ANGOON

From the Hutznuwu, or People of the Brown Bear, Tlingit village called Angoon on Admiralty Island an interior screen with both painted and carved low relief sculpture is preserved in the University of Pennsylvania Museum. It was once a possession of the Desitan clan of the raven half of the tribe. It was collected for the museum in 1923 and is a superb example of the screen-painting art (Figure 2). It consists of 10 boards placed vertically with the largest being 16 inches (40.6 cm) wide. It is 14 feet (4.3 m) long, stands 7 feet (2.1 m) at the center and gradually tapers to 4½ feet (1.4 m) at the ends. Plate 3 shows this screen set in a changed home environment, the wall of a Western-style frame house. There is more than a touch of incongruity to this photograph. Though the screen still functioned as a reminder of the clan's ties, it no longer served its earlier design of separating spaces. It is installed against a solid wall with floral-patterned wallpaper behind it; the entry hole remains but leads nowhere.

It is called the Beaver Screen but this name seems to me to refer more accurately to the crest name of the house rather than the creature depicted in the screen. The central figure appears to me to be not a beaver but raven. When viewed as a whole, the screen does not easily show the form of any creature due to the complexity of the overall design. But if the viewer focuses on the individual elements of the painting with an eye to identifying particular characteristic features and then isolates these features from the other competing design elements, the primary figure begins to emerge. The composition of the screen is extremely complex and hence readily misconstrued—but it is decipherable.

If the central figure were a beaver it would carry recognizable beaver characteristics such as the incisor teeth, the forepaws, and the aquatic tail with the cross-hatching pattern on it. Some combination of these conventional patterns was always used to define the beaver's features in Northwest Coast art. If on the other hand the central design were meant to represent a raven, one can confidently expect an assortment of birdlike features.

How does one tease out the image of a bird or a raven from the melange of faces, wing patterns, and eye designs delineated on this screen? In the central part of the screen a black form can be readily identified. The large head has two eyes, and between them nostrils (Figure 16.1). Below the nostrils one can see a body and to the left and right are wings on which large inverted eye designs have been imposed. Below the body is the entry hole characteristic of screens of this type. On each side of the hole can be seen a leg ending in talons. Below the entry hole are the feathers, obviously tail feathers in this case, split into two parts with one part depicted on each side of the screen. Putting together all of these clues in the form of conventional patterns, the viewer can readily conclude that a bird is intended.

By isolating each color the viewer can track the progression employed by the craftsman to organize the total composition. In the basic black formlines (Figure 16.1) the identity of the creature is revealed; they make the raven recognizable through the use of several of the conventional raven characteristics. The secondary formlines are denoted in the color red (Figure 16.2). This second set of formlines adds other design elements to the composition.

This screen's use of black as the primary formline and red as the secondary color is a convention basic to painted designs on interior screens and house front paintings. However, a third color is also used in this screen. The tertiary blue or blue-green color in Figure 16.3 is used to identify a third group of elements within this complex composition. Superimposing the third color onto Figure 16.2 shows a complete recapitulation of the design elements employed in making this screen (see also Figure 2). Each of these colors is assigned a particular function within the composition. These three colors also represent the fullest and finest use of color in northern-style painting tradition. In addition to this example, the Frog House and the Whale House screens in Klukwan also utilize all three of these colors.

The fullest explanation of this screen does not stop, however, with these observations. The other design elements within the screen—both the other faces as well as the eye and wing patterns covering the remainder of the surface—all contribute to the symbolic meaning of the screen. A detailed understanding of the significance of these elements is needed to assuredly identify their meaning. Only the artist and the contemporaneous viewers could have understood their symbolism in its full detail. These various presently undefinable parts might be associated with the story or might merely be generalized symbols or embellishments employed to fill the empty spaces. A traditional compulsion to leave no areas vacant within a composition has long been understood to be a defining characteristic of all Northwest Coast representations. Equally well understood has been the range of freedom to improvise beyond the primary figure or figures. These elements may simply be examples of artistic license.

Eye designs are among the most important space fillers in all Northwest Coast paintings. They are also the single most readily recognizable feature within Northwest Coast tradition. Every creature, animate or inanimate—beings, spirits, or natural objects or forces—required elaborate conventionalized eye designs. Eyes were used to represent power beyond the ordinary. A creature endowed with great power had many eyes. Eyes also represented extraordinary powers to transform. They were used to represent the very soul of a being. The extraordinary number of eye designs with their various shapes and other external characteristics are discussed in more detail in Chapter V. But in the context of this analysis of the so-called Beaver Screen, I can only note their extraordinary number and the absence of any certainty as to their meaning.

SITKA

Several paintings from the Sitka Tlingit tribe demand attention. This village had a rich and complicated history. Its people probably contested the advance of European civilization more fiercely than any other Northwest group. Growing out of this resistance, the history of the extant house front paintings and interior screens is shrouded in secrecy and is difficult to interpret.

A particularly fine Sitka house front emblem—a later form of the house front painting modified by the influence of Western culture—of the early 20th century once belonged to a leader named Anahootz, whose English name was James Jackson (Figure 17). The emblem is on loan to the Sitka National Historic Park where it is on display in the visitor headquarters. It is an impressive, arresting painting. Anahootz was the chief of the Kagwantan clan of the *shinkukedi* or wolf half of the Sitka Tlingit, whose major crest was the wolf. Anahootz was interviewed by a U.S. Army general in 1898 who recorded the meeting. The chief was very cordial but of a dignified mien. He was dressed in a soldier's coat and hat. According to archival data in the Alaska State Library Anahootz was a kindly man who attempted to resolve the conflicts between his people and the Western settlers and administrators of the territory.

The central part of the Anahootz emblem is dominated by a frontal view of a large female wolf. Wolf cubs are presented in profile on each side of the screen. To the left and right of the mother wolf are symbols representing the cliffs that surrounded the creatures' den. Along the base is a continuous series of eye designs and human faces representing a stream that flows through the wolfs' homeland. According to the U.S. Park Service records there are 20 wolves in this screen, meant to represent the time when clan numbers outgrew their former clan house, prompting a move to a new house.

This is a fairly large house emblem, approximately 22 feet (6.7 m) in length and 7 feet (2.1 m) or more in height. It is narrow at the top, being at the most 2 feet (0.6 m) wide. It is constructed of seven horizontally oriented boards made at a sawmill. The painting is rendered in three traditional colors: black, red, and blue. There is no relief carving. The emblem was photographed in the early part of the 20th century secured to the upper portion of the outside of a two-story Western-style frame house. The emblem was used to identify the house as that of Anahootz. It must surely have experienced some weathering over time but the colors are still bright and clean. Therefore, it seems certain that the emblem was repainted with modern commercial colors. Neither the family nor the park service possesses any information as to who the artist might have been.

While researching painted screens in Sitka in 1990 I had the good fortune to meet a Tlingit man, who must remain anonymous, who arranged for me to gain a glimpse—and no more than a single glimpse—of another screen, one that had long been hidden from outsiders. The strategies invoked to assure my entry into the house had all the qualities of a cloak-and-dagger plot one reads about but rarely encounters. A silent entry into this lineage house was arranged, and once inside I was guided to a room in which one large wall was curtained. The curtain was drawn and there, exposed at last, was the Eagle's Nest Screen (Figure 18).

I was given five minutes to view this prized clan possession. It had been carefully shielded for decades so I believe I was among the first outsiders permitted to see it. I was not allowed to photograph it but I was able to remember the forms and the colors associated with each part of the design and imposed the colors on my illustration (previously published, P. Miller 1967:221). It is approximately 12 feet (3.7 m) long at the base, about 7 feet (2.1 m) in height, and constructed of six or seven boards of tongue-and-groove or shiplap commercial planks. It was probably made around the turn of the century.

The eagle is one of the crests of the Kagwantan clan within the wolf half of the Sitka Tlingit tribe. This screen is dominated by a large golden eagle with black-and-white wings spreading symmetrically to each border. Its yellow beak is poised in profile to the right of the screen. The eagle stands over a nest rendered in a wide face pattern with gigantic eye designs. Tree branches radiate from the nest to both left and right. An eaglet is nestled to the left of the mother eagle. Both birds' breast feathers are painted yellow. The background is a solid white, highlighting the two birds so they stand out prominently from the boards. The screen showed evidence of having been recently repainted with acrylic paints. The entire surface had a glossy appearance.

YAKUTAT

Another striking house screen painting belonged to the Kwashkwan clan (or the Humpback Salmon People) from the Moon House in Yakutat, Alaska. It is located in the Sheldon Jackson Museum in Sitka and is known as the Raven and the Coho Salmon Screen (Plate 22). It is 6 feet (1.8 m) high and about 10 feet (3.0 m) long. De Laguna described a very similar screen which she called Raven Made King Salmon Come Ashore Screen (1972: 324). She may in fact have been referring to the same screen. George Emmons mentioned it in a 1930 article in *Natural History Magazine* (p. 288). He contended that it belonged to the Kos-ke-di family in Sitka, but there is some confusion as to origin. Andrew Johnson, a Kiksadi Tlingit man, has asserted that it is of Hoonah Tlingit origin as most of the Kwashkwan clan who owned it resided in that settlement.

This particular screen is roughly similar to the two paintings from Sitka in that it too was mounted inside one of the smaller Western-style frame houses that supplanted the traditional long houses. The story recounted by this screen deals with Raven and his cunning plan to lure the coho (or king salmon) ashore by convincing it that a green stone had insulted it (de Laguna 1972: 304). When the salmon, finally convinced by Raven's trickery, comes ashore, Raven, of course, kills and eats it, revealing once again the guile and avarice characterizing one side of the trickster's nature.

The raven is the dominant figure in the painting, presented by the artist in a frontal position in a split image (Figure 19). The raven's wings partly envelop a large black figure in the center. This captive initially appears to be a bear or an otter but is, in fact, neither. Rather, it represents the green stone central to the story. The raven has used the stone to lure the coho ashore to its destruction. No identifiable salmon is in fact even portrayed in the painting; instead there are an assortment of eye designs, feather patterns, and a proliferation of assorted faces none of which have any role in the story but add decorative embellishment.

This screen is representative of most Northwest Coast flat painting in that it requires considerable knowledge of both a story plot and of the nature of the mythic characters in order to see the artist's intentions. Paintings such as these make great demands on the viewer's understanding of the traditional painting conventions involved while requiring a discerning eye capable of picking out significant elements in the work. The wide range of colors employed—orange, green, yellow, as well as the traditional black and red—reveal the efforts of later artists to experiment with and come to terms with the vastly augmented supply of colors introduced by European civilization. This screen appears to date back to 1898 and was possibly painted by the Teqwedi artist Daniel Benson, the same person who painted the Beaver Screen in the Wolf Bath House at Yakutat (Figure 7).

Several other Yakutat screens have survived. Two are now in the Alaska State Museum in Juneau. Of special interest is the Kadjuk or Golden Eagle Screen (Plate 23). The kadjuk is a mythical bird similar to an actual eagle or hawk; it has also been compared to the thunderbird save that when it flaps its wings there is no thunder. I was told the screen came from the Drum House where it was installed around 1905. It belonged to Nate Dakteen of the Teqwedi clan within the wolf half of the tribe. As with the paintings from Sitka and Yakutat already described, this example also appears to be from the late 19th or early 20th century. It is the work of the Tlingit artist Yehlh Nawu, or Dead Raven. The Alaska State Archives has a photograph in their files of Yehlh Nawu working on this very painting, brush in hand, paints nearby. It has a 1905 date penciled on it but that may not truly identify the date the screen was painted.

The kadjuk dominates the central space. Its wings with massive eye designs are outstretched. The animal figures facing each other at the top left and top right corners as well as others placed at the feet of the bird are identified as groundhogs or marmots. The base of the screen with two massive eye designs and a central frontally oriented face is intended to identify the mountain central to the story. The two small faces at the top margin represent the spirits of daylight. The arrangements of these various figures parallel those seen in the Wolf Bath House.

The myth tells the story of the kadjuk bird hunting for marmots. While engaged in the hunt it inadvertently dived into the side of the mountain and broke both wings. Badly injured, it began singing its death song. Some hunters chanced to hear its plaintive cry and went to investigate. They climbed the mountain and reached the bird. They splinted its broken wings and saved its life. In gratitude the kadjuk vowed to protect the hunters and their descendants, all of whom were of the Teqwedi clan of the Yakutat tribe. Thus the kadjuk became the crest of this particular clan.

Housed in the National Museum of Natural History in Washington, D. C., is a series of four house screens that apparently were initially conceived as a unit. Although no village is designated as their origin they are labeled as Tlingit. All are similar in size and each portrays a grizzly bear (Figure 20). Each panel is about 8 feet (2.4 m) in height and approximately 7 feet (2.1 m) wide and is constructed of six or seven horizontally oriented boards.

All four grizzly bears are portrayed frontally with elbows and knees meeting in a hocker position in the lower quarter of the screen space. The body is portrayed with stylized ribs and large eye designs. Their massive heads cover over a third of the vertical dimension of the screens. Secondary formlines are developed in red but seem to have been repainted. Holes for fiber lashings are evident to hold the boards securely in place one above the other. Another trait is particularly noteworthy about this assemblage of screens. In contrast to the enormous bear head, the eyes are uncharacteristically small. Each eye is a salmon-trout design, a convention commonly used among the northern tribes.

Tlingit House Front Paintings

The appearance of house front paintings among the more southern Tlingit tribes is a distinct departure from the single use of flat painting to make interior screens among the more northern tribes. And yet, few house fronts were painted, although probably more than the records disclose. The paintings are neither complicated nor are they the equals of those from the Tsimshian in the complexity of the design elements or in the scope and detail of the subject matter. Comparison of the two traditions leads to the unassailable conclusion that the Tlingit were the recipients of the screen and house-front-painting tradition from their Tsimshian neighbors, rather than the other way around.

ANGOON

The northernmost employment of house front painting was among the Angoon Tlingit tribe. Only two examples come from Angoon; they are from the late 19th century and thereafter. Two distinguished house front paintings were displayed on Western-style, two-story frame houses, but there may have been many more a century earlier. Their antecedents may go back even further, but no evidence exists of earlier painted house fronts so far north. The Angoon house front paintings are not of the kind to be found southward among the Coast Tsimshian; the forms are more representational in concept.

Both paintings in Angoon depict killer whale crest themes. The first is from the Killer Whale Dorsal Fin House (Plate 20). It belonged to the Daqlawedi clan of the wolf half of the tribe and once was owned by a man named Peter Kanash. According to informants I interviewed, the exterior boards were painted in 1896 by a man named Yehlh Nawu, or Dead Raven, who belonged to the Desitan clan. He was paid $500 for the painting. The protocol governing such undertakings were strictly followed; the artist had to be chosen from among those belonging to the opposite half of the tribe rather than from among the patron's half. One informant further advised that all the members of Kanash's clan helped defray the screen's cost. Following its completion the *de rigueur* potlatch was mounted.

According to Barbeau the two whales on the house front depict a myth associated with Natsilane, a clan ancestor (1950:291–292). Natsilane is said to have been the creator of the first killer whales. He carved eight whales from yellow cedar wood and sang songs that instilled power in them. Gradually their lifeless forms took on movement. He showed the whales how to swim, and after many unsuccessful tries they were able to begin foraging for themselves. Since Natsilane is the ancestor of the people, they regard the killer whales as their primary crest and often speak of themselves as the Killer Whale People. Eye designs cover the body, fins, and flukes of both whales in this house front painting. They represent, according to my informants, the ocean water running off the whales' backs. Water shines at night as if it was composed of sparks, they explain.

The second house front painting in Angoon is a profile view

of a ferocious killer whale pursuing a hair seal (Figure 51; Plate 21). With the whale's open mouth about to devour its victim, the painting presents an intimidating scene and must surely have advertised some social meaning. It is of approximate turn-of-the-century vintage. In the 1930s and 1940s the house belonged to a Tlingit man named Robert Jamestown, Sr. It had survived a major fire that swept through Angoon in 1922. Only vague information about its symbolic meaning is now available. According to Jamestown's widow, the painting had almost been whitewashed out of existence in order to spruce-up the village for expected visitors and to give it a "modern look." The visitors may have been the delegates of the 1929 Alaska Native Brotherhood Association conference. A model of the house front was later made from plywood. This copy was placed inside the house where I had the opportunity to examine it in detail (Figure 52).

An odd assortment of colors were used, ranging from black for the formlines of the whale to grey and brown for the seal. Green and yellow colors were also used for small anatomical parts of the whale. The four eye designs across the whale's back may represent ocean waves akin to the symbolism natives attribute to the Natsilane painting. No explanation was given for the four additional faces, two of which are positioned below the whale's body, or for the figure placed to the right of the flukes. The people of Angoon showed a marked reluctance to share with visitors information about their society and its practices. As a consequence little is known of their painting and other artistic activities. Garfield has suggested this painting may be another rendering of the Natsilane myth (1948:81–82).

TUXIKAN

The old Tlingit village located at Tuxikan had one house front painting—and it was a good one (Plate 24). This tribe, the Henya, from the first days of European contact occupied Prince of Wales Island in Alaska. But they abandoned their traditional winter village at Tuxikan in 1904. Most moved to Klawak while some settled in other villages such as Ketchikan. George Emmons first photographed the house front painting in the late 1880s and early 1900s. It was last photographed in June 1930, surviving for several decades before the boards were purchased by the Heye Foundation for the Museum of the American Indian in New York. It is presently displayed in the New Customs House Museum in New York.

The Dog Salmon House, the original owner of the painting, belonged to Tecumseh Collins, and its occupants were known as the Dog Salmon People, or Anxa'khitan Hit. Their crest commemorated the adventures of an ancestor who belonged to the raven half of the tribe. The painting is a large profile of a dog salmon covering the entire front of the house. A raven's head projects out of the fish's top fin. A similar raven head can also be seen to the left, near the salmon's tail. Both heads symbolize the raven clan as the owners. The salmon's body is shown with a series of stylized ribs; its mouth is filled with rows of large curved teeth.

The story associated with this painting is one of the more haunting tales that have come from Northwest Coast mythology. Usually titled "Moldy End," it is a widespread myth and one to which several different lineages have claimed rights. As might be expected of so well known a tale there are several versions with variable accounts of the events of the story.

After a chief's young son and his companions had been playing near a stream for a time he became hungry and asked his mother for food. She gave him a piece of dried salmon but it was moldy so he threw it away. As he did so a gull appeared and pulled him into the stream, where he immediately disappeared and was carried out to sea. The boy soon found himself in an undersea village occupied by salmon people who, as it turned out, sent the seagull to fetch him to their village. The salmon chief's house bore a painting of a salmon on the front of it. But the boy did not know he was among the salmon people because they looked like human beings to him. They called him Moldy End recalling his disrespect for the piece of salmon his mother had given him to eat.

The salmon people gave him a small stone to keep in his mouth so he would never become hungry. But one day Moldy End lost the stone and instantly his hunger returned. One of the salmon people showed him how to club one of their children and roast it—as it really was a fish. But before consuming the fish he was admonished to observe the unforgiving law of returning all the bones into the water. If he did so all would go well; if he did not untold misfortune would overtake him. But while eating the meal he misplaced some of the bones. Almost at the instant he had completed his meal he fell desperately ill. Several of the salmon elders quickly associated the missing bones with the illness and recovered and returned them to the water. Immediately the boy was restored to full health.

Soon thereafter the salmon people prepared to return to the streams of their origin to spawn. Setting out on this journey the chief of the salmon village took the boy with him. The two headed for the very stream beside which Moldy End's village was located. It so happened that the boy's mother was one day standing beside the stream thinking of her lost child when she saw a large dog salmon swim by. She called her husband who quickly came to the riverbank and speared the fish. The chief then brought it to her to clean. When she slit its belly a child emerged from the salmon's body who was transformed before her eyes into her missing son. He had miraculously returned to the place of his birth. That evening the boy told his family of his supernatural visit to the home of the salmon people and their teachings of how to respect and care for the salmon by caring for their bones. His descendants took the dog salmon as their special crest. The house front painting in Tuxikan purported to be a copy of the painting the boy had seen on the salmon chief's house in the undersea village (Garfield 1948:145, 147–148).

GASH

One house front painting is known from the Cape Fox Tlingit village called Gash. The Sanya Tlingit tribe that inhabited this village were in relatively frequent contact with their close neighbors, the Tsimshian. The house adorned by this painting was photographed during the Harrison Expedition to Alaska in 1899 (Plate 25). In addition to the house front painting, the clan had raised two totem poles that can also be seen in this photograph. The owner and the clan that occupied the house remains unidentified. The painting depicts a grizzly bear with bared teeth centrally positioned over the front doorway. Two appendages extending above the roof line represent the bear's ears. The body is split bilaterally so that each half of the bear is seen in full side view on left and right parts of the painting. This symmetrical division of bodies is a common convention in Northwest Coast art, and the more southerly the tribe the greater was its use of the convention. The bear's ribs are suggested and the fore and hind paws are clearly defined.

This house front was purchased from the Tlingit owners before the turn of the century by the New York Zoological Society where it was reconstructed in 1904 and mounted in Bronx Park in New York. In 1942 it was turned over to the Heye Foundation, the Museum of the American Indian, where it was installed for a time.

SAXMAN

Concluding this survey of the highlights of the flat-painting tradition among the Tlingit is an example near Saxman in the vicinity of Ketchikan, Alaska. The little available record of this house suggests it once belonged to a family known as Na-hut-de who lived at Saxman village. (Conflicting sources, however, conclude that the painting comes from the village of Tuxikan.) The house seems to have been built on stilts with a set of steps leading to the front doorway. The only date I can certainly associate with it is 1899. The house is reported to have been destroyed by fire.

This clan crest shows a halibut presented in profile extending across the entire width of the house (Figure 21). Its head with its rounded eyes is at the extreme left side of the house and the tail extends to the extreme right. Twelve small faces painted in a line are intended to represent the halibut's backbone. Designs suggesting scales are drawn on the upper and lower sides of the body. Ribs radiate outward from the faces of the backbone.

Several other house front and screen paintings belonging to the Tlingit are known, but among them are fragments of screens or reconstructions of screens based upon fragments. One such example, now in the collection of the Portland (Oregon) Art Museum, has been reconstructed from a single board said to have come from the Coho House in Sitka (Plate 26). The third vertical board from the right side is the original fragment of spruce wood; the remainder was reconstructed by Steve Brown of the Seattle Art Museum in the 1970s. This single board is $11\frac{1}{2}$ feet (3.5 m) in height; the overall dimensions of the screen are impressively large. The face in the reconstruction may represent a bear with two dog salmon designs centered at its base. Brown suggests it may be Gonakadet, the Tlingit ruler of the undersea realm.

Tsimshian Background to Painting

Coast Tsimshian territory held the very heart of flat painting; all historical sources point to this part of the Northwest Coast as the very center of house front and interior screen painting. It was here that this monumental art form reached a fever pitch in the first half of the 19th century, specifically the 1840s to late 1860s (Munro 1988:69). It was in this region that the final masterpieces of the form were created in one brief explosive period. Then all house front and interior screen painting came to an end. The gravest misfortune is that so little of this outpouring has survived. The few examples that remain tell a story of a remarkably resonant period, short but intense, where both artists and paintings flourished in a mushrooming social economy.

When the Hudson's Bay Company established its trading post at Fort Simpson in 1833 to advance their commercial interests, nine Coast Tsimshian tribes abandoned their established winter settlements and converged on nearby sites. Each group staked out specific boundaries near the Fort and constructed new dwellings. Here the people had easier access to the flood of trade goods that ranged from metal tools and woolen blankets to firearms, manufactured clothing, distilled spirits, and exotic foods.

In 1857 the population of Fort Simpson was reported to include 2300 Tsimshian natives living in 140 houses located outside the boundaries of the fort (Duff 1964:93). Each of the nine Coast Tsimshian tribes was organized into four different clans represented by the totemic creatures blackfish or killer whale, raven, wolf, and eagle. Their close proximity in this new settlement brought increased tensions as jealousies and rivalries between leaders grew. Each leader tried to gain dominance not just in trading position but social standing. The competition heightened during this changing period as chiefs laid claims to exclusive trading rights and social prerogatives—all of which propelled them into more vehement acts of economic and social aggrandizement, including the time-honored *sine qua non* of tribal competition, pot-

latching. Potlatches between rivals intensified as the most powerful vehicle for the domination of rivals. During this brief period the Tsimshian world was rapidly, radically, and irreversibly changed.

With the wealth accumulating from the Tsimshian role as middleman in trade between the Hudson's Bay Company and other Indian tribes, it was possible for the Tsimshian clan leaders to finance the building of larger and larger, increasingly ostentatious houses. Such houses required, indeed demanded, house front as well as interior screen paintings to visibly prove to all the rank, social status, and privileges of each of the clan leaders. Every chieftain of every lineage and clan that was congregated around Fort Simpson sought to outdo every other chieftain by commissioning the biggest and the best paintings (Garfield 1939:332). George MacDonald has speculated that there may have been 50 or more house front paintings produced in Fort Simpson during this volatile time.

But eventually it all came to nothing. The late Marius Barbeau wrote that in the course of his extended research spanning the period from 1900 to the early 1940s he personally witnessed the loss of eleven painted house fronts. All the killer whales with copper plates adorning their bodies, the eagles and ravens, the cranes and wolves, the halibut and blackfish with rainbow and sun symbols— to mention but a few—that he had recorded in his field notes vanished without a trace (1950:773). Fires and flooding, and that scourge that devoured whole villages within a fortnight, smallpox, all had a hand in this inexorable decline. Barbeau also made detailed records of the crest paintings within the houses that he observed (1950:780–782). All that he had seen were swept aside by not just natural disasters, but also the radical shift in views and values of the Tsimshian.

The fundamental change in world view among the Tsimshian, the new value system that ended the flat-painting tradition, came about through the corresponding instrumentalities of missionaries and settlers who flooded into the region. Probably more than by fires and floods, paintings were purposely destroyed by the natives themselves, growing out of the new-found religious zeal that swept across Tsimshian territory. The massive conversion of the Tsimshian to the Methodist and Anglican faiths in the 1850s and 1860s utterly altered the nature of Coast Tsimshian society within the space of a single generation. Wilson Duff graphically comments, "The missionary Father William Duncan [the driving force in this conversion] transformed one of the most rank conscious class systems of Native American culture into a new society where rank and class were abolished—ergo, no need for symbols of rank or class as revealed in the traditional crest system" (1964:93).

The significant difference between some, but not all, Tlingit tribes and the Tsimshian groups was their respective responses to missionizing and Western forces. Most Tlingit groups accommodated but held firm to certain cherished practices. But the Tsimshian around Fort Simpson for the most part swiftly and enthusiastically embraced the new spiritual and ethical values in a wholesale rejection of their past. Deep factional splits emerged resulting from intense bitterness between those who became Christians and those who vehemently opposed doing so, in turn further devastating tribal society.

Tsimshian Paintings

What then is left of the Tsimshian painting tradition from that competitive and eventually artistically destructive period? Explorers and scholars, collectors and settlers managed to preserve a sampling of evidence that gives a sense of the greatness of Tsimshian house front and interior screen painting. The best examples, in my opinion, are presented in the photographs and drawings of this text, all of which were derived or selected from museum collections and photographic archives.

By far the most elaborate house front paintings on the Northwest Coast were created in Tsimshian country. In both size and sheer number no other group is their equal. Furthermore, in complexity and the broad sweep of design, in the extraordinary surface detail, in the variety of brush strokes, in the range of faces and forms associated with the various figures, Tsimshian examples stand alone without peer. Their paintings reveal a mastery of detail as well as an elegance of form unmatched elsewhere. All these qualities were captured by a handful of Tsimshian artists—whoever they might be—during the fleeting middle of the 19th century. Tsimshian prestige was great in those few decades, both in terms of wealth and their use of art to proclaim that wealth. Neighboring tribal groups were profoundly influenced by them and spent enormous resources in trying to emulate their social practices.

FORT SIMPSON

One truly prodigious house front comes from mid-19th-century Fort Simpson. It was part of the Thunderbird House and belonged to Chief Sqagwet, also called Chief Ledyard, of the eagle clan within the Gitando tribe. It is pictured in Plate 2, a photograph thought to have been made in 1879. The house was so large and its totem pole positioned in such a way at the front that it can also be located in the 1870s photograph of Fort Simpson village in Plate 27.

The house front is said to have measured 50 to 60 feet (15.2 to 18.3 m) wide and about 20 feet (6.1 m) high at the apex. At least 25 separate boards set vertically were employed in its construction. Some idea of its great extent in both vertical and horizontal dimensions can be ascertained by comparing the house front with the three adults in Western-style clothing standing at the left. The height of the house can be judged also by comparison with the immense totem pole just to the right of the round opening that served as the house's front entryway. The entry hole was clearly more than adequate in size to admit ready passage by erect adults—a marked departure from the tiny entry holes described previously for interior screens. The upright planks projecting behind the top of the painting at each corner suggest this is a facade. Both the photograph and my illustration (Figure 22) give some idea of the width of each plank in this painting, the largest being in excess of 2 feet (0.6 m). The upright figure on the

totem pole portrays the beaver crest of the resident clan.

The primary black lines of the house front painting define the central figure as a thunderbird in a frontal position. At each end of the house the artist has placed a profile view of a smaller thunderbird. Though both of the smaller bird outlines are similar their secondary red lines within the wings and the body cavities proclaim different meanings. I have not been able to clearly delineate all their differences in my drawing due to various obstructions; vegetation and a picket fence obscure the lower right side of the painting and a wooden platform obstructs the lower left side of the design.

One element of this painting is missing in all the photographs, however—a great beak appendage that projected forward from the front of the bird's head. Evidence suggests it was installed some time after the painting was completed. The beak is reported to have been at least 20 feet (6.0 m) in length, requiring the support of a vertical plank positioned several feet from the house wall. Eventually it collapsed and was not reinstalled.

A substantial border in red spreads across the top of the house front and defines the immense design below it. The primary thunderbird head takes up almost half the space of the entire painting. Its mouth and nostril designs incorporate numerous intricate patterns but they cannot be identified with any degree of certainty. The designs suggest subtle details were used to decorate them. Each of the central bird's eyes is unique, enclosing three small figures that mirror the 11 figures marching along the upper border of the painting. Each figure in the eye pattern possesses individual facial expressions as well as variations in the palms of its extended hands. Attached to the body of the bird are two legs with formidable talons in red.

The 11 border figures and eye designs are reminiscent of those in the house front painting of the Sea Monster House (Figure 5.1; Plate 10), held in the National Museum of Natural History in Washington, D.C., that records the Nagunaks myth recounted in Chapter II. Both paintings come from Fort Simpson within the same time period. Notice in both paintings the left sides of the heads of the five figures on the left side and the right sides of the heads of the five figures on the right side. They suggest dorsal fins but whether that was so intended remains a question. What they do strongly convey, however, is that the same artist may have worked on both these paintings.

The symbolic figures painted on the Thunderbird House front are so precise and detailed that much of their intricate patterning is lost in the photograph, which had to be shot from a great distance in order to include the entire painting. One can be certain that what was captured in the photograph is but a small part of the complex figuring incorporated into this particular house front.

There is no record of the fate that befell this house front painting, if any part of it survived or if it was burned. There is no record of the myth associated with the crests, no explanation of the protocol governing the contracting for the artist's services, nor a report of what he was paid for this prodigious effort. In all probability a painting of such magnitude must have involved an enormous payment because quibbling was beneath the dignity of a wealthy and powerful leader among the prideful Northwest Coast tribes. Those retained to make such socially important artifacts might ask virtually any price and be so paid. The society expected a person of high rank to pay far more for services than a person of lower rank even if the services performed were identical in time and difficulty. In a kind of conspicuous consumption, the greater the fee paid, the greater the social prestige earned. Commissioning and possessing a work on this scale must have elicited open paeans of admiration, suppressed groans of jealousy, and sighs of envy from friends and rivals alike.

Another striking house front from the Coast Tsimshian was installed in 1992 in the Canadian Museum of Civilization in Hull, Quebec (Figure 24). It is an almost full-scale reproduction employing designs of the original plank painting. The remnant boards on which this new model was built had been stored for years in the University of British Columbia Museum of Anthropology in Vancouver. They were acquired by a medical missionary named George Raley some time in the late 19th century. The surviving planks were hand-split cedar boards, the largest measuring over 3½ feet (1.1 m) in width. They date back well into the early part of the 1800s. Few other details have been preserved about their history or the circumstances surrounding their purchase.

This reproduction of a house front painting is nothing short of spectacular, and the story of its discovery and reconstruction is almost equally compelling. Various bits and pieces derived from what seemed to be two distinct sets of boards and fragments of several others ultimately were pieced together. Careful analysis and comparison over several years led to the conclusion that the fragments did indeed make up a single complete house front painting (Forrest 1982:12–19). H. R. MacMillen, the Canadian lumber magnate, purchased these several separate sets of boards together with other artifacts in 1946 from the Raley family. He donated them to the university in the same year. The immense value of this assorted batch of old boards was not then understood; they simply lay in storage for years, covered with dirt and grime. The solid black formlines that defined the basic crest symbols were dimly recognizable, but the secondary lines painted in red could hardly be distinguished. The collection seemed virtually worthless and badly abused.

The discovery of what was hidden beneath the dirt and grime centered around the insights of Bill McLennan, a photographer at the University of British Columbia Museum. He was involved in a project photographing the painted and carved boxes and containers in the museum's collections. As a part of this project he tried infrared film to pick up and clarify the bruised and faded painted surfaces on these items of daily use. He discovered that the secondary designs painted in red, barely distinguishable in black-and-white or color film, jumped out of the photograph with sharply legible clarity in infrared. George MacDonald of the Canadian Museum of Civilization suggested McLennan try the infrared film technique on the boards of the old Raley collection in order to determine what might be learned from them. The result was the beginning of the resurrection of a Tsimshian masterpiece. This house front stands together with other newly constructed Northwest Coast houses as part of a tour de force exhibition in the Grand Hall of the museum in Quebec.

This Fort Simpson painting represents the epitome of the Tsimshian cultural flowering of the mid-19th century. The reproduction is about 39 feet (11.9 m) long and about 16 feet (4.9 m) high at its apex. Its dominating central figure is a great bear flanked on both sides by bear cubs. The bear's head is enormous, covering fully half of the length of the house. Its body surrounds the narrow oval door. Both the bear's front and hind limbs are positioned around the doorway. Its body area is decorated with a series of secondary red designs suggesting ribs. The complex design above the bear's nostrils and between the two large eyes is a proliferation of secondary designs that center around what appears to be a human figure. The human face is presented frontally and its hands and legs extend on either side of the bear's nostrils. The bear's ears are filled with secondary formline designs. Its mouth is open revealing four large canine teeth and a long row of smaller teeth along the upper portion. The smaller bears on either side of the painting are shown in profile and face the central bear. Claws on both fore- and hind limbs are readily distinguishable as are the elaborate series of secondary designs around the tails, ears, and noses. The bear cubs' body cavities enclose further secondary designs suggesting ribs and other body parts.

I do not know the amount of freedom the renovating artists had in reproducing those areas of the painting that were unidentifiable or entirely missing on the original boards. But the overall effect is stunning. The complexity and scope of the details are impressive. Few extant paintings have comparable secondary details displayed on such a grand scale. Notice in Figure 24 that there are 33 individual renderings of a single type of eye design—the salmon-trout pattern—a significant element of Northwest Coast design. And there are 14 individual human profile or frontal figures replicated in the painting (see also Figures 23.10 through 23.15).

KITWANCOOL

A Tsimshian interior screen of considerable merit was collected from the Gitksan village of Kitwancool in the upper Skeena River region (Figure 25). It also is on display in the Canadian Museum of Civilization in Quebec. It provides solid evidence that such paintings were present among the inland Tsimshian tribes as well as those residing along the coast. The Kitwancool screen is almost 5 feet (1.5 m) in height and 10 feet (3.0 m) in length. It was probably one of two boards used for interior screens but this is the only one that has surfaced. It is constructed of four horizontal boards each smoothly surfaced and painted in the usual red and black colors. Shrinkage of the planks has caused some warping. The brush strokes reveal a master's work: they are fluid, controlled, and highly refined. Though superficially both sides look similar, there are subtle differences between them.

Marius Barbeau, who acquired the screen for the museum in 1923, calculated its creation as mid-19th century. The central dominant figure had a huge, projecting beak carved in wood and attached to the face. It was not a part of the original board, however, but was added by the owner in the 1890s. This painting represents one of the few surviving examples of house fronts or screens with added appendages. It lacks the central entry hole so common to some of its counterparts.

Barbeau suggested the principle figure was a dragonfly and

was, therefore, a decorative rather than a crest figure. This assertion, however, runs contrary to the central place crests played in this art form. It is doubtful that any chief or lineage leader would commission an expensive design on an important clan possession that was not tied in some way to that group's history or crest symbolism. Further, if it is indeed a dragonfly, it would necessarily have to exhibit some of that creature's known attributes to remain within the general scheme of Northwest Coast symbolism. Such characteristics as a segmented body, patterned wings, and large circular eyes were used elsewhere and were clearly within the accepted tradition. But those attributes are not found on this particular screen. I contend that the central figure represents the mythological Raven. The straight and narrow beak is one of Raven's most commonly represented features. Other conventional characteristics include its large wings, legs with distinct talons, and the clearly defined tail feathers—all readily evident in this painting.

The raven plays a key role in Tsimshian folklore. Not only did the bird represent a clan crest, it also was a dominant figure within the vast body of oral narratives. A scholar named Henry Tate recorded hundreds of tales dealing with Raven. They were edited by Franz Boas, one of the leading Northwest Coast ethnologists, and then published in a 1000-page volume entitled *Tsimshian Mythology* (1916).

Four humanlike figures are depicted on this board, one located in each of the four corners surrounding the central figure. They are undoubtedly symbolic ancestors. All are positioned frontally, their heads outlined in black, their bodies in secondary red.

Their hands are raised, palms open. The elbows meet the raised knees in the commonplace hocker position. The expressions of the two on the left are similar; those on the right differ in minor details around the nostrils. Notice the use of eye designs in the bird's body, as well as the stylized face profiles on the wings and at each corner of the bird's head. Also, double eye designs are used on the bird's face, and salmon-trout patterns across parts of the bird's body, the wings in particular. The beak appendage is reported to have had red cedar bark decorations attached to the lower part of the jaw.

GITLAHDAMSK

Two additional distinctive house front paintings come from the Nass River Tsimshian, upriver from the coastal tribes. The Nass people raised a large number of totem poles before the turn of the century and thereafter that have been well documented. The same does not hold true for their interior screens and house front paintings. Though it is true that the upriver Tsimshian did not enjoy the wealth inundating their coastal cousins in the 19th century, the few flat paintings that have survived bespeak the shared artistic and social traditions.

Gitlahdamsk once boasted a large number of clan houses before which stood a jungle of totem poles but few flat paintings. One of those few house front paintings belonged to a clan leader named Minesqu. Though nothing remains of the house, a number of photographs of it were taken after the turn of the century. Plate 28, dating from 1903, gives a good sense of the house. A 60-foot-tall (18.3-m) totem pole stands at the edge of the stairs leading to the front entrance of this spectacular lineage house. The painted wall was a facade and is 45 to 48 feet (13.7 to 14.6 m) wide and at least 20 feet (6.1 m) high. It is dominated by a birdlike creature with a great wing spread. The photograph reveals an enormously long and slender beak projecting at least 40 feet (12.2 m) from the face (not shown in the accompanying drawing, Figure 26). Near the creature's face the appendage carries in printed roman letters the English version of the leader's name, Minesqu. It was supported in part by the pole at the foot of the stairway and by additional scaffolding about 20 to 30 feet (6.1 to 9.1 m) from the roof.

This birdlike creature covers three-fourths of the house front space. Its body is suggested by the European-style double doorway, but little more. Its great wings, each with four lengthy feather designs, spread out on each side of the body. Feet and talons are seen at the lower edges of the doorway. Above its head are a series of 10 figures, five to each side. Each figure has a clearly defined face and is in a squatting position, its hands and feet in the familiar hocker position. To either side of the central figure are similar but smaller figures, each birdlike, having long and thin beaks projecting outwards. Other figures were painted below each of these secondary figures but weathering eroded them to the point at which they can no longer be distinguished with any degree of accuracy.

The mystery is what this creature represents. Many elements of the design suggest a bird but it is not a thunderbird as its beak is too slender, long, and narrow. Absent any record of what these three creatures represent I venture that they do not, in fact, represent birds, but rather monsters from the mythic age. Among Minesqu's lineage crests, I suspect, was that of a long-nosed monster who was the progenitor of mosquitoes. Tsimshian oral tradition does include a narrative in which these long-nosed, menacing figures play a signal part in a terrible ordeal that was experienced ages ago by Minesqu's ancestors during their migrations. The noses of these terrible beings were made of crystal or glass and were used to eviscerate their victims. Minesqu's Tsimshian ancestors had encountered and were attacked by this tribe of blood-thirsty killers. The ancestors chose to flee the village where the monsters lived. After many harrowing battles the people ultimately triumphed. They then set the monster leader's body on fire. What emerged from the ashes were mosquitoes destined to harass humankind for all eternity.

Note the similarity between Chief Sqagwet's house front in Fort Simpson (Figure 22) and this particular painting. Minesqu's facade, however, does not possess the refinement and subtlety of brush work and composition seen in the other. The 11 figures at the top border of Minesqu's house front are similar to those on Chief Sqagwet's, and to those in the Nagunaks painting (Figure 5.1). These concurrencies lead to the interesting speculation as to who influenced whom. All three paintings share a number of similarities, which suggests that the Gitlahdamsk artist was inspired by what he had seen in Fort Simpson and attempted to emulate many of the same features, but not fully successfully.

Another Gitlahdamsk house front painting of the same historical period demands our attention. All documentation is lacking save for a photograph taken by the ethnologist and museum collector George Emmons, who photographed the house in the late 19th century. It was called Killer Whale House as the entire painting portrayed a double-headed killer whale with two dorsal fins (Figure 27). The whales face outward from the center and are joined at their backs. Their mouths are open revealing rows of sharp-edged teeth. The curved dorsal fins rise almost to the roof line around a humanlike face. Simplified eye designs along the shared body cavity suggest ribs.

A particularly unusual feature of this painting is in the primary formlines. As they are recorded in the black and white photographs, they completely reverse the accepted color conventions governing the northern style. In this particular instance—and this house front painting is virtually unique—the primary formlines are red rather than black. And, contrariwise, the secondary formlines are black rather than red. A thin line or "light" black formline surrounds the two killer whales. A thick band of red bounds the bottom length of the house just above ground level. As the accompanying drawing indicates, no doorway entry was provided in this house front. Emmons's caption simply reads "Old house at Gitlahdamsk."

Haida Paintings

The third group of tribes employing the northern style of flat painting were the Haida, who occupied the Queen Charlotte Islands. But examples of their art are few. I have located only a handful of records of large-scale flat paintings despite extensive search. Photographers and observers thoroughly blanketed the scattered villages in Haida country during the latter half of the

19th century yet few house front paintings were recorded. By contrast totem poles repeatedly appear in both photographs and written documents. The Haida tradition centered on carved totem poles; they made a great many which are among the finest on the Northwest Coast. Also, their carved and painted maritime dugout canoes were sought after by all the other coastal dwellers. The limited number of house front and interior screens reflect these people's primary interest in and preoccupation with other forms.

I am aware of only two Haida house front paintings. One of them belonged to Chief Gold, or He Whose Voice is Obeyed. He was the leader of the raven division in Haina village. Located near Skidegate, a major center of Haida culture, the Haina settlement dated back to only the mid-1850s. It consisted of a row of stately clan and lineage houses along the waterfront, before many of which stood immense totem poles. Most of the poles were subsequently acquired and displayed by the world's ethnographic museums. When I explored this site in 1948 all the poles as well as the houses had vanished. All that was left was an eerie silence and a fleeting history (Malin 1986:163).

Chief Gold's house was called the Moon House and was constructed with a facade, a rare structure along this portion of the Northwest Coast (Figure 29). Although the precise dimensions of this house are unknown, Chief Gold was a very rich man; his house most certainly must have been large and impressive. The planks of the facade were vertically oriented across the entire front of the house. According to George MacDonald (1983:121) it was the only painted house front standing on the Queen Char-

lotte Islands in the 1880s. By 1900 only the frame remained and by 1912 everything, including the painted house front, for all practical purposes had disappeared. My drawing is based on a photograph taken in 1884 by Richard Maynard.

The central face on the lower three-quarters of the house front represents a thunderbird with its mouth open. Inside the mouth a humanlike figure, the man in the moon, is painted in red. Its face and hands surround the top and sides of the oval entry-way and its lower limbs are clearly delineated to the sides. The thunderbird's ears rise to the red border at the rim of the roof. Along the center band of the thunderbird's head are two large eye patterns (stylistically resembling those in Figure 23.7). The two smaller thunderbirds are poised in profile at each end of the house.

The arresting part of this house front painting is the large, rounded sculpture—a sort of plaque—that is secured at the peak of the house. It represents a thunderbird or hawk's face resting on a disk that symbolizes the moon. The moon was reportedly painted a gold color and the bird's face was painted blue. These colors, naturally, soon faded but they were employed to confirm Chief Gold's high rank (Barbeau 1950:353). Marius Barbeau, quoting James Deans's 1899 Haida tale, refers to the crests as part of the following myth denoting the origins of Gold's ancestry.

A woman, who somehow miraculously survived an epidemic that had extinguished all the others in her village, fled the disaster still in a feverish daze. She wandered aimlessly for some hours but eventually fell to the ground exhausted and slept. When she awoke a stranger stood before her. He told her he had come from the moon in order to keep her company until her kin joined her.

They stayed together for many months and, as no others from her village appeared, she finally succumbed to his entreaties and agreed to accompany him to his home in the moon. There she in due time gave birth to a son, who grew up and returned to the earth in search of his people. Finding them gone he then founded a new ancestral family.

HOWKAN

Two screens are known to have been painted among that group of northern Haida commonly called the Kaigani. One is from Howkan village, located on Long Island off the southern coast of Prince of Wales Island in southeastern Alaska. The screen was inside the Eagle House and is in the classic northern style dating to the mid-19th century (Figure 28). It is about 12 feet (3.7 m) in length. The Canadian Museum of Civilization in Quebec now owns this superb painting.

This house screen displays an eagle crest in nearly mirror images on each side of a large human figure, presumably an ancestor, who occupies the center above a round entry hole. The human's legs encircle the entryway. The eagle design characteristics on either side are among the most abstract compositions in the entire genre. It recalls, due to the many similarities, the superb screen from Angoon, the Tlingit village some distance directly north of Howkan (Figure 2; Plate 3). Both were painted in three colors, black, red, and blue-green. Both have round entry holes. Both employ shallow relief carving in addition to painting on all symbolically significant surfaces. The Angoon screen, however, is of larger dimensions.

The human figure in the Howkan screen is placed frontally, its hands raised at its sides. The eagle crest design on the left side is similar to that on the right, but differences are evident on closer examination. The beak of the bird on the left contains six teeth, that on the right seven. Some small anatomical features are subtly modified between the two figures. The surface patterns are also marginally different along the lower parts of each side of the screen. The eye patterns below the eagles are said to represent rocks. The artist did not strictly adhere to the rigid conventions governing formline and secondary line colors; some formlines are red rather than black. And a relatively large proportion of space in the composition is reserved for the blue, tertiary color. The surface of the five vertical cedar boards has a very finely adzed texture. The area below the entryway in the bottom border is finely adzed in an alternatively attractive stippled effect. A great deal of careful attention has been paid to the aesthetics of the wood itself in this example.

KLINKWAN

Another house screen is known from Klinkwan, a Kaigani Haida village in very close proximity to Howkan. The house belonged to a man named Harry Edenshaw in 1901 when C. F. Newcombe took the photograph reproduced in Plate 29. But it was, as the photograph shows, in an advanced state of collapse. Two large boards with both carved and painted surfaces were lying on the ground. Both boards still bore evidence of shallow relief carving as well as detailed painting. But the boards were too weathered to attempt to draw them for illustrative purposes. The designs alternate between abstract figures similar to those prominently used on Haida storage chests and representations of coppers with crest symbols painted on the upper surfaces. The copper designs alternate on vertical and horizontal planes. With the aid of a magnifying glass the carefully stippled textures on both boards can be seen.

Coppers were distinctive shield-shaped objects, the originals of which were flattened from cold-hammered copper nodules. They were used in the social economy of all the Northwest Coast tribes and were of great value, generally considered surrogates for slaves. Coppers had names and often possessed long and complicated histories. The surfaces of some were engraved with what are presumed to be abstract patterns of human, animal, or bird figures associated with the crests of their owners. Other coppers were simply painted in black. They were generally owned only by highly ranked people.

Though these examples disclose more than a mere presence of painted house fronts and interior screens among the Haida, they remain an exception in the Haida tradition. This account of Haida screens concludes the examination of the northern-style house front and interior screen paintings. The following chapter discusses the flat paintings of tribes residing southward, which in some ways depart significantly from those of the northern tribes.

THE CENTRAL AND SOUTHERN TRADITIONS

"Among the Kwakiutl the most prestigious privileges claimed by powerful leaders were painted house fronts depicting creatures of mythology."

Bill Holm
"Northwest Coast Indian Art,"
Handbook of North America, Volume 7

DURING the 19th century the painting of house fronts extended southward from Tsimshian villages in an everwidening arc, incorporating numerous stylistic variations. Though there were some geographic and cultural differences between the maritime and river dwellers, house front paintings in this more southerly region became a vigorous and well-documented practice. The enthusiastic reception of this new mark of social status ultimately resulted in an explosion of house front paintings, particularly among the Southern Kwakiutl tribes. Large-scale paintings were provided in growing numbers as this vogue established itself as an acceptable mode of embodying lineage position and prestige.

Later, the collapse of such displays was accompanied by the gradual abandonment of many of the traditional village sites.

These joint marks of degeneration appeared in conjunction with the decline in numbers among all the tribes. Some of the Western world's most profound effects were experienced by the Coast Tsimshian and their southern neighbors who lived along the British Columbia coast. Not only were these regions inundated by new settlers and strange customs but the native populations were radically reduced by disease to virtually unsustainable lows, resulting in the near extinction of several of the region's tribes.

Northern Kwakiutl Paintings

The coastlines and islands just south of Tsimshian territory were richly dotted with native settlements by the early 19th century. These numerous but distinct villages were identified collectively as the Northern Kwakiutl but the term belies both their independent destinies and their separate bodies of folkways. Subtle shades of variance in social customs set one village aside from those contiguous. Historically, the Tsimshian and their southern neighbors carried on considerable contact. The Tsimshian groups made their influence felt in a number of ways. Intermarriage with tribal neighbors and trade exchanges led to imitative social organization and practices, among them crest systems and prerogatives, artistic symbolism, and subsistence practices.

Northern Kwakiutl people have traditionally been assigned to one of two groups, the Haisla and the Heiltsuq. The Haisla tribes occupied two winter settlements, Kitimat and Kitlope. The Heilt-suq included several tribes known as the Haihais, Bella Bella, and Owikeno peoples. Those tribes residing further south have commonly been known as the Southern Kwakiutl. The impact of Western culture on the Northern Kwakiutl was in many respects far more devastating than that experienced by the Southern Kwakiutl, because the latter's response was more determined and consequently more resistant to cultural change.

There is significant evidence of the presence of both house front and facade paintings among the Northern Kwakiutl, but sadly the number of examples is not impressive. In village after village from Haisla territory to Bella Bella villages, from the Bella Coola valley to the Southern Kwakiutl groups, evidence points to an extensive use of monumental paintings in the early to late 19th century. Captain George Vancouver during his explorations wrote in the 1790s that the village he identified as Bella Bella had 34 houses with painted designs.

KITIMAT

A photograph taken in 1872 at the Haisla settlement of Kitimat reveals several house fronts with painted symbols. This village is geographically close to the Skeena River and Coast Tsimshian tribes. The photograph was made by professional photographer Richard Maynard who produced much valuable documentation of numerous Northwest Coast villages. The unfortunate element here is that all the paintings were by that time badly weathered; they are insufficiently clear to reveal the details. Like the Vancouver observations, the presence of these paintings in settlements immediately south of the Tsimshian positively establishes their use among this group of people.

KLEMTU

Another house front painting in Northern Kwakiutl territory was documented in the village known as Klemtu or Kitasoo. Klemtu was located on Swindle Island near Milbanke Sound, about 150 miles (241.4 km) south of Fort Simpson. In the early 1870s, in addition to the native settlement there, a cordwood station was built by Westerners to supply steamboats with fuel. Both Northern Kwakiutl and Coast Tsimshian moved to Klemtu and for a time made their homes there. But this occupation was short-lived. The town was gradually abandoned after 1875. Some of the inhabitants, Kwakiutl and Tsimshian alike, settled in other Kwakiutl villages, such as Bella Bella (Olson 1955:344). Kwakiutl and Tsimshian families commonly intermarried and stimulated fruitful exchanges of social practices and customs. One such exchange was the use of house front paintings. Plate 5 reproduces a forlorn example, a facade, from Klemtu. In Figure 30 I have undertaken to extract as much of the details of this painting as can be read from the Richard Maynard photograph. The owner is unknown and no information about the painting has survived. The house has long since crumbled and disappeared.

The Klemtu facade painting portrays a large bird figure positioned over the doorway. Its wings extend outward to each side of its body. On each side of the main figure is a single bird figure in profile; they probably represent ravens. Their beaks are large and straight, characteristics usually associated with ravens. The faces on the lower parts of the left and right birds represent joints between the birds' bodies and the tail feathers, which have been obliterated by weathering. It is interesting to examine the central bird figure. If it were split down the middle into two equal parts, the two images that emerge appear similar to the profile views of the birds positioned on either side. Each bird has been endowed with several eye patterns, most are of the salmon-trout design. The colors used are black and red.

This Klemtu painting is reminiscent of others used by the central tribes that clearly speak to Tsimshian influences. This particular example is of a modest scale, but its appearance is significant.

BELLA BELLA

A short distance southward from Klemtu was Bella Bella, a village occupied by the Heiltsuq Kwakiutl. This place came to play an increasingly important role in the southward and eastward expansion of northern tribal influences along the Northwest Coast, because Bella Bella was the site chosen by the Hudson's Bay Company to locate a trading post called Fort McLoughlin. As such it became an almost irresistible magnet drawing trade and social customs from much of the coastline. In turn, it became the hub for intertribal trade as well as the scene for social and cultural exchange between native and non-native people.

Bella Bella became the prime focal point for the meeting of Northern and Southern Kwakiutl tribes and so played the principle role in the spread of northern social beliefs and practices beyond their place of origin. Northern painting style took root in Bella Bella together with some of the associated northern ceremonial activities, rituals, social events, and art—all conspicuous in the powerful presence they gained within a short period of time following the establishment of Fort McLoughlin. A strong Tsimshian influence was clearly evident in the vicinity of the fort soon after its founding. The genius of the Kwakiutl in this setting was the welding of ideas from the northern tribes with their own creative energies, leading to new and different ritual and ceremonial activities that became distinctive to the Bella Bella–Fort McLoughlin settlement.

The original Bella Bella village had been settled by six smaller tribes who united to form a single political unit early in the 19th century. In midcentury the increasingly influential Methodist missionaries urged the people to set up another village some 3 miles (4.8 km) distant. Eventually all the Bella Bella people abandoned the old site and moved to the new one. During this period Fort McLoughlin, established in 1833, began to founder and was entirely abandoned several years later. By the early 1870s most of the populace had completed the move from the former traditional residence. The former village with its many long houses, totem poles, tribal arts, and house front paintings—all reminders of the native past—was forsaken (Olson 1955:320). Bella Bella's population turned away from their past in the same way as the native people gathered around Fort Simpson had done earlier when they moved with Father Duncan to Metlakatla in Alaska.

A photograph in the Canadian archives depicts the new Bella Bella village from the late 19th century. It confirms the presence of one house front painting. Unhappily, its main features were largely obliterated before the photograph was made and only the barest outline of the figures can be made out. What is most significant about this 1880 photograph, however, is that seven old-style long houses still remain intact near the water's edge. Close by them, at scattered points located on higher ground, are an assortment of Western-style cottages. It is possible any one of the seven long houses was adorned by a house front painting.

Bella Coola Paintings

East of Bella Bella is a remote and nearly inaccessible part of the Northwest Coast, the Burke Channel. It circuitously leads into the Bella Coola valley. Here numerous small enclaves of native people were established along the various tributaries and channels. There were once 27 small villages scattered along different inlets in this part of the interior, but only a few were long-term settlements. Komkotes, now called Bella Coola, was a permanent village as were Kimsquit and Talio. But Talio was totally deserted by 1900.

The Bella Coola people were never large in number. They spoke a Salish language in contrast to their Kwakiutl neighbors to the west who were Wakashan speakers. The Bella Bella Kwakiutl occupying the coastal regions to the west maintained exchanges with their Bella Coola neighbors. These exchanges either introduced or maintained many of the common Northwest Coast tribal practices, including potlatches, secret society ceremonies, masked performances, raids on rival villages, and raising totem poles or flat paintings as symbols of wealth and prestige.

KIMSQUIT

Kimsquit village continued to be occupied for some years after Talio was abandoned. But in the early 1900s the remaining residents moved to Komkotes. The latter settlement later became the premier village of the Bella Coola, boasting a population of several hundred.

Photographs dated 1881 point to two Kimsquit houses with painted fronts (Plates 30 and 31). None are known from Talio. Both Kimsquit house fronts employed several circular designs with figures painted within the circles. The figures appear to represent human forms accompanied by other symbols not readily identifiable. Both houses have facades and employ a tripartite architectural style, a trait exclusively of the Bella Coola. In other words, the facades were constructed of three distinct sections: the mirror-image left and right sections flanked a taller middle section. Usually, the boards of the center section were vertically oriented and the others were horizontal (Figure 9.2). The hand-hewn cedar boards employed in the Kimsquit facades were enormous. Judging from the height of the adults standing in the photographs, the boards were in excess of 30 to 36 inches (76.2 to 91.4 cm) wide and probably 2 inches (5.1 cm) or more thick. Unfortunately, neither house front painting has survived, nor has the meaning of the crests displayed on them.

Bella Coola house front paintings have a distinctive flavor that sets them apart from the tribes farther north. They depend upon similar design elements such as the crude renderings of the salmon-trout designs, the frontal face patterns, and the X-ray effect used to portray the internal skeleton and organs of the figures; but overall they lack the forcefulness associated with the northern standards.

KOMKOTES

Plate 9 is a Richard Maynard photograph taken in 1873 portraying a strikingly powerful scene. The number of painted house fronts in this one village is far greater than in all but a few other locations recorded on the Northwest Coast. This is Komkotes village. Five of the six houses are standing in a row with crest symbols painted in an expansive scale upon their facade fronts. All were constructed of enormous wood planks in tripartite form. Only with the aid of a magnifying glass do the details of the paintings stand revealed, save for the closest house front at the extreme right. Since such a large group of paintings would not have been raised under commonplace circumstances, some special event must have taken place in Komkotes shortly before Maynard took the photograph.

The painting on the fourth house from the right appears to make no sense whatsoever. It must have been assembled very hastily to result in a meaningless jumble. Bill McLennan of the Museum of Anthropology in Vancouver, B.C., and I have speculated about this strange painting and concluded that all these house fronts were hastily erected to commemorate some special occasion. The family occupying the fourth house must have been unable to raise the facade correctly in the short time before the event and simply put up something to create a grand effect, figuring the visitors were unlikely to be knowledgeable about the proper ordering of a facade painting. We propose that those attending the occasion were the Westerners posed in the forefront of the photograph. The party, which includes Israel Powell, the Canadian Commissioner of Indian Affairs, was possibly on a fact-finding mission mounted on relatively short notice. All these house front paintings probably were raised to impress the commissioner on this special occasion. It was an effort never to be duplicated again.

I have drawn the house front painting shown at the extreme right in Plate 9 to provide the reader with a close-up view of its complicated composition (Figure 31). It is an impressive example of Bella Coola painting and reveals strong similarities to Coast Tsimshian roots. Tsimshian influences are recognizable in the shape and elaboration of the house front, its size and scope, and the dominant use of northern-style formline features. Further, eye designs proliferate across the entire surface of the painting, a thoroughly Tsimshian trait.

The central crest symbol in this painting is an immense thunderbird frontally oriented. This figure takes up fully three-quarters of the space of the central portion of the house front. The two lateral panels of horizontal planks depict two thunderbirds, each of a smaller scale than the central figure and presented in profile view. This painting contrasts sharply with the two house front paintings from Kimsquit (Plates 30 and 31).

The dominant thunderbird's wings spread to each side of the panel surface, its talons, merely suggested, are balanced on each side of the doorway. The thunderbird's head dominates the upper space and encompasses a proliferation of complex patterns that suggest head feathers. Eye and face designs are shown in profile. The beaks of the two secondary thunderbird figures are both prominent and sharply curved downward, with mouths open and design elements suggesting tongues. Their wings are large and formidable. The wings of the bird on the right consist of three large downward-thrusting wing feathers, each of which contains numerous circles, simple as well as complex eye designs, dots, and other formline features. The strong formline quality is also seen in the frequent use of salmon-trout designs. Note the number of these salmon-trout eye patterns that have been rendered in an upside down fashion; besides showing the artist's license to innovate, I believe they are meant to signify an artist's ability to "see" in all directions. Each thunderbird undoubtedly was originally painted with tail feather patterns that have been obliterated by weathering. Over the bird's forehead is a small design, commonplace in such paintings, of a frontal view of a humanlike face with palms of the hands to each side in characteristic northern-style presentation. It is decorative rather than symbolic in intent. Also, in the top left hand corner is a small silhouette figure in realistic human proportions, but its significance is unknown. Perhaps it was the artist's signature but no similar signature design is known in any extant paintings.

The extraordinary detail within the various eye patterns, the wing and face designs, and the rhythmic flow of wing patterns, circles, talons, and U-forms in this particular painting suggest Tsimshian stylistic roots. Not all the design elements in this painting were sufficiently clear, so there are gaps along the lower border in particular. Of course, as is the case of many such paintings, no information about it is available.

Notice the vertical poles at both left and right sides of the house front, as well as those to the right of the doorway. These poles supported the boards, stabilizing the planks that sat one atop the other. The poles were tied together with sinews or rope to provide further stabilization.

The Bella Coola were known to have used painted interior screens in their lineage houses. This knowledge derives from the work of the early 20th-century anthropologist T. F. McIlwraith who thoroughly documented the ways of the Bella Coola (1948) He noted that a chief might well use wall paintings rather than totem poles to publicly display and validate his claims to crests connected with his people's ancestral history. The archaeologist Harlan Smith, working in the Bella Coola valley between 1920 and 1924, documented a number of the people's material objects and their uses (Tepper 1991). He inventoried, however, only a single example of interior screens. The people may well have destroyed the numerous screens recorded in earlier accounts, a practice also found among their neighbors to the south.

The one interior screen that survived for a time in Komkotes village is pictured in Plate 32. It graced the interior of one of the respected lineage houses in the early 1900s, belonging to a leader named Clelamen. At the time the photograph was made, around 1920, the screen was in an advanced state of disrepair. According to Smith's notes it was torn down and part of it reused, but the remainder was lost. The original colors are not discernible from the photograph.

The large face in the painting represents a grizzly bear. Its mouth is menacingly wide open, revealing rows of flat-edged teeth that surround a Western-style rear doorway. Notice the knob on the right side. Eyes appear at the corners of the painting above the mouth. Barely perceptible at the extreme right is what appears to be a limb that extends upward toward the house beam. A paw is suggested with an eye design at its center. Five sharp claws extend outward toward the edge of the panel.

Clelamen's house was of an aberrant architectural style in that a number of small animal and human figures and topographic features representing mountain peaks were carved as separate pieces and secured atop the roof. Although Clelamen died at the age of 50 in 1893, he was considered an important figure because he had successfully mounted eight potlatches—a truly amazing accomplishment.

Southern Kwakiutl Paintings

The paucity of examples of house front paintings that survived into the 20th century changes dramatically within Southern Kwakiutl territory. The numerous surviving examples suggest a people's exuberant involvement in displays of not only house front painting but other forms of flat painting as well. Various explanations have been advanced to interpret this florescence. Most notably some have pointed to such factors as: (1) the improvement in reporting techniques, including photography; (2) far easier accessibility of southern sites to Western explorers, anthropologists, etc.; (3) the late arrival of the painting customs among the southern tribes; and (4) some combination of these factors leading to more extensive documentation. It seems to me, however, that the spirited cultivation of customs and practices that originated in the north is the best, most convincing explanation for the abundance of Southern Kwakiutl painting.

Southern Kwakiutl settlements were established in a variety of settings, ranging from remote and precipitous fjords, to island specks that dot the coast and the waterways of the northern quarter of Vancouver Island, to more accessible locations on the mainland and Vancouver Island. Among these scattered sites house front painting not only took root but actually became a primary vehicle to publicly proclaim chiefly status. Both house front and interior screen paintings flourished within a vigorous social life fueled by overweening pride in extended lineage family origins, privileges of inherited rank, and extraordinarily powerful competitive motivations. A heyday of painting, the likes of which has not been documented for any of the more northerly tribes, developed in the mid- to late 19th century.

Despite the efforts by missionaries and provincial administrators in the late 19th century to repress native arts, several villages continued to utilize them for traditional social and ceremonial occasions. The tribes potlatched publicly or sub rosa, they raised totem poles, and they also decorated their house fronts. To endeavor to encompass this remarkable explosion in creative output

I have drawn from 11 of these Southern Kwakiutl communities in order to map the breadth and depth of their practices and activities. Other villages might just as readily have been selected, for all of them joined, more or less exuberantly, in this flowering of flat painting.

HUMDASPI

One of the most impressive series of paintings was found at Humdaspi on Hope Island, off the northern tip of Vancouver Island. Here was a village occupied by a people known as the Tlatlasikwala. Humdaspi was a typical Southern Kwakiutl village situated in a sheltered cove on a forest-cleared terrace, several feet out of reach of the high tide. An 1880s photograph depicts five houses in a row, showing but a part of the village. Four houses have facades and three of the five bear painted fronts.

The large house at the right of the photograph employs three bold figures, the largest centrally placed over and around the doorway (Plate 33). It depicts a figure enclosed within a large circle. Two animal figures occupy the space on the left and right sides of the facade. The entire front is similar in its positioning to the house fronts from Kimsquit (Plates 30 and 31). The immense central oval in this house painting represents Galoyaqame, the moon, and the figure painted inside it is an ancestor known as Lelnakula Gilakaso who was taken to the moon by Galoyaqame (Boas 1897: 375). The hands of the figure are humanlike and its feet froglike. The moon crest belonged to the mother of the house leader, whose origin was the Goasila tribe located in Smith Inlet to the north. The house had belonged to the Gigilgam lineage within the Tlatlasikwala tribe. The figures on each side of the painting represent bears, crests the family acquired from an ancestor named Kwexagila. Both bears are similar in posture, the front and hind limbs coming together in a hocker position. Ears are raised in alert stance, claws clearly revealed, and teeth bared.

The third house front painting from the right in Plate 33 is badly weathered. Enough is recognizable to reveal two large eagles or thunderbirds facing each other. A third figure between the thunderbirds cannot be identified. The birds' wings are outstretched and the faded designs associated with them suggest a northern formline practice.

The second house from the right in Plate 33 demands closer scrutiny (Figure 32). Above the doorway are two large signs printed in English. The top sign simply reads "cheap" emblazoned in bold, capital letters. The message in the lower sign announces to visitors that the head chief of this village resides therein and English-speaking visitors can get information from him. It is an unambiguous example of the many instances of entrepreneurial enterprise in which the Kwakiutl people sought to gain wealth from their relationships with Westerners.

This house front painting is executed with sensitive skill. Central to the composition is a large, humanlike face. A lengthy figure extends outward in both directions from this face. Each end of the long figure terminates in a profile face suggesting a sea monster or supernatural creature, perhaps a two-headed serpent known as the sisiulth. This serpent is a treasured crest possession shared by several lineages among the Southern Kwakiutl. The creature's body is composed of a series of delicately executed formlines

with various eye designs, which can only be suggested in my drawing because the sign is so weather-worn that only the boldest elements are discernible even with a magnifying glass. Virtually all of the detail is too faded to provide basis for a complete reconstruction.

A later house front painting from Humdaspi is reproduced in Figure 33. It is a facade whose relative modernity is betrayed by the fact that the boards are the product of a commercial sawmill. This painting portrays a fearsome-looking face representing a whale or sea monster. The whale's mouth is open and positioned around the doorway leading into the long house. Its teeth are cut from wood panels and arranged around the top of the doorway. The head covers the central two-thirds of the house front space. Its eyes are simplified dot and circle designs peering out from the wall. The nose is humanlike and aligned directly over the doorway itself. There is no information about the crest or its mythological associations.

FORT RUPERT

A pivotal Southern Kwakiutl center in the late 19th century was located at Fort Rupert, near the modern community of Port Hardy. The tribal group occupying this town called Tsa'his were the Kwagiul. The Kwagiul people actually consisted of four confederated groups that earlier in the century had resided on Turnour Island located to the east. These people migrated from their traditional island homeland to occupy Fort Rupert sites in 1849. The four groups making up this newly formed assemblage were the Kwagiul, or Smoke of the World; the Qomoyue, or Rich Ones;

the Qomkutis, or Rich Side; and the Walas Kwakiutl, or the Great Ones (Boas 1897:330).

The reason underlying Fort Rupert's importance was the Hudson's Bay Company trading post built there in 1849. Access to the goods produced in the Western world was the primary motivation for the natives' move. Numerous facade house fronts once dominated the shoreline, and the place was the scene of intense tribal competition including intertribal raiding of rivals, potlatching, and related forms of overt aggression. Though it was for most of its existence a major center of carving, mask making, and winter ceremonies, Fort Rupert saw few house front paintings. On four different visits to Fort Rupert between 1946 and 1950 I saw a few well-executed mortuary paintings on model-type screens as well as a number of finely carved totem poles, but no house front paintings or interior screens.

The only photograph of this village of which I know records but a single house front painting (Plate 34). Interestingly, the painting was not done on an enlarged facade as was usual among the central tribes. The photograph was taken in 1880 by George Dawson of the Canadian Geological Survey. A raven is portrayed as the central figure and is shown within an enlarged circle. The circle probably represents the sun, as the mythical Raven was conceived as a great benefactor to mankind by bringing the sun to the present world. The raven's wings spread out beyond the circle, the large individual feathers being readily apparent. The beak is turned to the right in a profile view and its legs and tail feathers are positioned at each side of the entrance.

This raven painting is flanked by mirror images of bears, their heads upright, paws extended toward the raven figure. Bill Holm has identified this work as a classic example of northern-style painting and confirms that the unknown artist was thoroughly familiar and comfortable in that style (1990:611). The eye designs, profile faces, and mouth patterns within the raven's head practically cry out "northern-style Tsimshian" as the place of inspiration if not necessarily origin.

The painted elements of this particular photograph are gratifyingly clear. Sharp, crisp, and well-defined, they betray no trace of weathering; therefore, it must have been completed shortly before the photographer's arrival. Fort Rupert is hardly an ideal place to establish a settlement as it is utterly unprotected from storms and gales which, during the winter months, are unrelentingly fierce. This suggests the painting was made in 1880 or shortly before.

ALERT BAY

Fort Rupert's fortunes gradually ebbed in the early 20th century following the closing of the Hudson's Bay Company trading post. Its decline prompted the rise of a rival Kwakiutl village called Ee'lis, or Facing the River. The Nimkish tribe occupied this site in the middle of the 19th century. It was located on Cormorant Island and is now called Alert Bay. The Nimkish ranked second to the conglomerated Fort Rupert tribes in the hierarchical order of potlatching and in the region's wealth. Alert Bay has become a center of the Southern Kwakiutl cultural renaissance, but it began from far more humble origins.

The Nimkish tribe moved to Alert Bay from a settlement near

the mouth of the Nimkish River on Vancouver Island's northeast coast in the mid-19th century. An 1862 photograph provides a panoramic view of the newly established settlement (Plate 35). There was a row of 10 newly completed long houses positioned along the shoreline at exactly the spot where the village still stands. Each of these houses was constructed with a facade. Neither totem poles nor house front paintings are to be seen at this date.

In 1873 Richard Maynard, in turn, photographed the village (Plate 36). His pictures document a magnificent house front painting, among the very first of a series in this community. The impressive painting on the Thunderbird House represents a gigantic thunderbird holding a whale in its talons (Figure 34). The painting is remarkable as it is among the first paintings to which a perpendicular appendage was affixed to represent the beak of the thunderbird. An 1881 photograph made by Edward Dossetter reveals the beak was still attached to the painting, but a few years later it fell off and was not replaced.

This magnificent, impressive painting was the imposing crest of a man named Tlah go glas. He was an important leader within this village and was considered a great man thanks to the many potlatches he hosted. His totem pole memorial stood in the village graveyard for many years and was, among others, a major tourist attraction.

The bird's gigantic wings are clearly revealed with its strong feather designs spreading across the entire width of the house front. The feathered wings include profile eye designs and frontal face patterns to represent the thunderbird's wing joints as well as its awesome power. Its legs and talons are minuscule by comparison, seemingly inadequate for the Herculean task of grasping the whale, which also spans the entire width of the house. The whale is painted in profile, its tail and flukes on the left side of the house, the enormous head on the right. Take note of the small blow hole positioned behind the whale's head, identified by the inverted small face design. The doorway splits the whale's body into two parts. The body is painted so that its internal construction can be seen in detail, an example of the X-ray presentation commonly found in Northwest Coast paintings. With graphic clarity the artist has painted eight large rib bones and the associated vertebrae of the whale's backbone. The surface boards of this house appear to have been whitewashed prior to the painting of this impressive figure.

Even though many house front paintings were raised in Alert Bay, totem poles were the predominant status symbol among the Nimkish people. At one time at least seven large columns stood along the single path that ran through the community in the early 20th century (Plates 12 and 37).

Another famous house front painting from Alert Bay was combined with a tall totem pole; the status of the house owner thereby geometrically increased. The Talking Stick Pole, the principal feature of the house, was placed directly in front of and attached to the Raven House. The pole was modeled after the staff bearing crest symbols that chiefs held when speaking at potlatches and other ceremonial functions.

The Raven House was first photographed in 1881 when the pole was already in place. No painted crest had yet been applied on the facade, nor do the several photographs of the house from the year 1889 to 1890 show any painting. The next photograph of what is in essence an historic sequence was taken in 1911 and shows the recently painted raven figure clearly portrayed on the lower half of the facade (Plate 37).

The Raven House was named after the crest bird that dominated the series of figures on the pole (Figure 35). According to Barbeau, the owner was Chief Wakias who traced his family line to both the Owikeno and Nimkish tribes. Wakias's mother was a Nimkish woman of high status. The raven crest belonged to Wakias's father who was an Owikenoan (1950:673). The carved raven had a huge movable beak that opened and closed by means of ropes running into the house, so that it could be manipulated by family members. Guests entered this great house through the raven's mouth when the lower beak was dropped. The opening was so restricted that guests were required to make a low bow upon entering the house, surely a sign of humbling as well as deep respect for the power and status associated with Wakias. It was a novel exercise in creative imagination for it was the talk of the town up and down the island coast for years.

The house facade was built of horizontally aligned milled lumber and was eventually whitewashed to provide the background for the painting. The raven's wings spread out on either side of the totem pole with the bird's legs and talons positioned below them. Tail feathers are displayed behind the carved figures on the totem pole. The original colors were black and red with green and yellow accessory colors.

A third house front in Alert Bay was so atypical in style and content as to represent a stunning departure from the traditional form but one absolutely in keeping with the function of the native tradition (Figure 36). The painting was clearly meant as a paean to the owner's wealth and generosity. The symbols employed are not the traditional crests derived from sea and sky beings but rather crude depictions of the property the house leader had distributed as gifts to humble his guests in the many potlatches he had mounted. The house front is covered with poorly executed outlines of dugout canoes, blankets, and coppers arranged in columnar form. My drawing is based on a photograph taken by James Swan, a professional artifact collector, during the 1870s.

An 1881 photograph by Edward Dossetter discloses that this and the Thunderbird House front (Figure 34; Plate 36) were the only flat paintings in Alert Bay at the time. Furthermore, there was only one tall totem pole with a single figure sitting at the top of it in 1881.

HWA'TIS

Located along Quatsino Inlet on the north coast of Vancouver Island, a short distance from Fort Rupert, was a village called Hwa'tis. It was situated near a perilous narrows called Tza'tsen, or Place of Swift-flowing Water. It was the winter village of the Koskimo tribe. I had the good fortune to do ethnographic research in this village and its environs for a 10-week period in 1950. Hwa'tis had once been a community of 400 or more people containing 24 lineage houses, some of which were of colossal size.

Two house front paintings were seen here in the late 19th century. One was photographed from a considerable distance offshore so the details are obscure. The second house front is portrayed in far greater detail from a close-in photograph (Figure 37). The house once belonged to Skookum Jim, a Klaskino Indian from the west coast of Vancouver Island. After his death in the late 19th century the house passed to his son, Quatsino Sam. Sam had an enormous reputation as a shaman. He also carried the social ranking and title of *gialaxa qikamay*, meaning the first to come down from the sky world. He was chief of the *ne aynsxa* division of the Koskimo tribe. Informants reported that this great house contained an enormous number of symbols of wealth including carved screens and totem poles decorated with many crest figures. After Sam's death, an agent of the provincial government in charge of local Indian affairs named William Halliday ordered that the house be burned, destroying the means to verify those reports and, if true, to document the inventory of possessions and their possible meanings.

The house front of Skookum Jim and Quatsino Sam as drawn here represents a thunderbird and whale. There are credible similarities to the example located in Alert Bay discussed earlier (Figure 34; Plate 36). The subject matter is the same. The thunderbird is painted in profile with spread wings and talons grasping the whale. The whale again is divided into two parts by the house door and has eight sets of ribs and vertebrae in X-ray presentation. It was, however, not as masterfully painted as the Alert Bay example.

GWAYASDUMS
The Kweksutenok tribe lived in the village of Gwayasdums situated on Gilford Island, a short boat journey eastward from Alert Bay. At Gilford, the Kweksutenok built a substantial community with a number of imposing houses. Not to be outdone in the competitive race for recognition and prestige, the Kweksutenok sought to surpass, and so humble, the Nimkish. The village contained a number of imposing interior house posts though few totem poles were erected. A number of excellent house front paintings were mounted. Five are known to have existed in this village in the late 19th century, all decorating house facades.

One of the five depicted a sea monster; indeed, it was part of the Sea Monster House. A gigantic face peered out from the front of the house (Plate 38). The house belonged to Johnny Scow and was photographed in 1900 by C. F. Newcombe. The painting was refurbished before 1917 to offset weathering and to restore it to its original condition.

Figure 38 shows a second outstanding house front painting from Gwayasdums. It was also a facade and was constructed of milled lumber. The painting represents a raven crest. The bird is similar to the thunderbird from Alert Bay (Figure 34), but its wing feathers and other features have not been duplicated with the same degree of skill. The legs and talons of the raven spread out in a fashion similar to that of the raven at Alert Bay (Figure 35), suggesting a direct, if crude, imitation.

At one time an enormous wooden beak was attached to the house and projected from the front of the painting (Figure 38). This appendage in turn was once supported by a carved vertical figure representing a man dressed in Western-style clothing, which I have not included in this drawing inasmuch as it has long disappeared. Again there is a similarity to the Raven House at Alert Bay in the appendages that were both added at a later date. However, the Gwayasdums beak was positioned above the doorway so did not serve as the entrance, and furthermore it was not movable.

A third significant painting in Gwayasdums belonged to Herb "Copper" Johnson. An impressive carved figure stood in front of the house and depicted one of Johnson's family crests (Plate 39; see also Plate 6). This was Tzonoqua, a mythical woman of the forest, who was believed to bring wealth to those fortunate enough to encounter her. Indeed, the sculptured column announces the wealth she brought to Copper Johnson in the form of the two copper symbols the figure holds in her outstretched arms and the third copper attached to her head. This is a supremely blatant message signaling the enormous wealth possessed by Copper Johnson. According to Edward Curtis (1915:296) the hands are outstretched in order to receive the property the owner's wife is bringing as part of a marriage contract. An indication of the size of this humanlike totemic figure is that a person of 5½-foot (1.7-m) stature or thereabouts would reach the knees of the Tzonoqua. The overall height of the carving exceeds 20 feet (6.1 m).

Behind the Tzonoqua figure is a painted house front displaying some of Copper Johnson's crests. The central figure surmounts the front entryway and again represents a copper. The face painted on its surface is accompanied by a pair of hands positioned below it. At the left, and probably counterbalanced on the right, is the outline of a whale.

The fourth example from Gwayasdums (Figure 39) is vastly different from the preceding three. In this case an immense circle representing the rainbow surrounds a group of traditional figures.

The design includes a number of circle and dot designs, none of which I have attempted to include because the only extant photograph of this painting is in such poor condition that I could not be sure of their internal relationship nor their relation to the total composition. Nor have I tried to draw the faces reported to have been included at the base of the circle near the doorway representing the two-headed serpent or sisiulth. Symbolically, those who enter the house of the double-headed serpent are swallowed up, and so humbled by the host's awesome crest. Within the circle is a bird representing a loon. This crest was derived from the owner's mother who was from the Mamalilikulla tribe residing at Memkomlis on Village Island (Curtis 1915:264). Several faces shown in profile, three on each side of the circle, appear along the outer border and probably are decorative elements only. In this instance they resemble whale dorsal fins. The two eye designs that face each other at the top of the circle directly above the loon represent the two faces of the double-headed serpent. This house and its painting ultimately collapsed and were lost.

TSATSICHNUKWOMI

A native village in the general vicinity of those just discussed but on Harbledown Island slightly south had the name Tsatsichnukwomi, meaning Those of the Inlet. It was later called New Vancouver and was photographed in April 1900 by C. F. Newcombe. The approach from the sea presented a view of several houses with extremely ornate painted and carved house fronts. Though it was not a large village, it surely contained some of the most unusual house front paintings. In addition, two of the houses had raised a series of large totem poles to further decorate their facades. Pride and status thus multiplied.

Two of the painted house fronts are featured in a remarkable photograph (Plate 40). The painting on the dwelling at the left depicts not only a human figure but five coppers and two animals as well. The dominant figure positioned above the doorway represents a human with arms and legs extended. The body design encloses vital organs represented by eye designs. The coppers bear painted designs and might replicate designs engraved on the owner's actual coppers. There is no recorded data describing the house leader's intended meaning for the symbols portrayed on this house front. The blatant display of coppers suggests an aggressive pursuit by the chief of domination over rivals.

Among the Kwakiutl, intertribal rivalries often depended upon the casual destruction or giving away of coppers. In this way coppers became weapons of social control or intimidation. While conducting research at Fort Rupert in the 1940s, I heard native chiefs, in an effort to convey the enormous social value of several coppers, liken them to loaded shotguns sitting in the closet. Some particularly prized coppers were assigned monetary value amounting to many thousands of dollars. Coppers were a metaphor to be used as a weapon not only to counter any threats directed against a family by other ambitious or rival families but also to engender dominance over the same families. That a leader owned five coppers attests to the immense economic and political power he possessed. Displaying the wealth so explicitly on the house front advised outsiders to consider the risks involved in any attempt to intimidate such a chief or his people.

The identification of the two animals located on the periphery of the painting is ambiguous. These creatures may represent a form of rodent and their position relative to the coppers may suggest they are associated with rivals who might attempt to gnaw at the owner's wealth.

Stylistically, this house front is an anomaly. It has none of the features commonly associated with classic Northwest Coast painting. It seems more pictographic and may represent an earlier strata of painting arts that eventually gave way to the more engrossing northern style with its vast array of stylistic features.

The painting on the house at the right in Plate 40 is of a sea monster, possibly a whale or a bullhead. Its mouth is bisected by the doorway. The eyes are large. The painting shows signs of weathering as the numerous smaller decorative elements that were added to enhance the surface appearance were virtually extinguished at the time the photograph was taken. Notice how closely this painting resembles that of the house belonging to Johnny Scow in Gwayasdums village (Plate 38). At the apex of the roof a sculptured three-dimensional figure is in a squatting position. The head has nine projections radiating from it representing the sun crest of its owner. A copper is attached to the slim pole at the center of the photograph. As in previous examples, these advertisements signal with a vengeance the owner's wealth and achievements.

H'KUSAN

One more noteworthy painting comes from the southernmost group of Kwakiutl residing near Cape Mudge. This tribe occupied the Salmon River area on the northeast side of Vancouver Island.

Their principal village was H'kusan. The facade painting is notable not for its superior execution but for its impressive dimensions (Figure 40). It has been estimated to be about 18 feet (5.5 m) tall and 40 to 45 feet (12.2 to 13.7 m) wide. This house was known as the Whale House and was owned by Weklakalas, Potlatch Gifts Too Heavy to Carry. The whale was his hereditary crest, which was eventually passed to his son, Johnny Moon (Sismey 1961:25). The first known photograph of this house was made in 1905 at which time the painting was in the process of composition. A large scaffold had been raised to accomplish the task. The name of the artist was Kiadexsegila. By 1919 H'kusan was abandoned, and by the time the last photograph was made in 1923 only the main beams of this enormous house were still standing. The painting had disappeared.

The painting depicts two large whales in breaching mode. They are mirror images facing each other above the central doorway. Their flukes curve inward toward the doorway. A series of ribs and vertebrae drawn as bars and simple eye designs traverse the length of each whale's body. The dorsal fins are small in contrast to those found on most paintings of killer whales or blackfish, suggesting that these figures were intended to represent grey whales.

Photographs document a number of painted house fronts in neighboring Southern Kwakiutl villages, but unfortunately none of the images are suitable for reproduction or redrawing due to the extreme degradation of either the paintings or the photographic positives. These numerous additional examples from Kalokwis, or Crooked Beach, on Turnour Island, Tzawatainuk village in Kingcome Inlet, Ba'as at Blunden Harbour, and other associated villages, along with those paintings discussed above, all confirm the widespread use of house front paintings among Southern Kwakiutl village leaders. But more importantly they attest to the importance attached to this social practice as a tactic in the larger strategy of claiming and assuming superior social status.

Marius Barbeau wrote that a house front was taken intact from a Kwakiutl village and installed at the World Columbian Exposition in Chicago in 1893 (1950:782). Somewhat earlier Franz Boas sketched a house front painting he saw in Humdaspi and included the picture in his invaluable book *The Social Organization and the Secret Societies of the Kwakiutl Indians* (1897:376). Though the sketch was crudely drawn and depicts but a part of the entire composition, the subject appears to be one and the same as that exhibited at the Chicago Exposition. In comparing the Boas drawing and the Chicago Exposition photograph I cannot but feel the painting exhibited in Chicago was not the original but rather a reproduction; the Chicago version simply lacks authenticity and appears an improvised imitation. I have sought to refine Boas's rough and incomplete illustration in an effort to depict the house front as it must have looked in its pristine, newly completed state (Figure 41). The lines and the colors may not precisely replicate the actual historical work, but save in matters of minor detail Figure 41 is a faithful reproduction of the house front painting Boas once stood before to sketch.

The painting shows a thunderbird positioned over a doorway. A large sun symbol is depicted on each side of the house. The thunderbird possesses bifurcate limbs comprised of human hands above avian wings. Each hand was given five clearly visible fingers. This juxtaposing of hands and wings was not an uncommon feature of Northwest Coast Indian art. The combination of characteristics from different species on a single creature was used to symbolize its dual character, human as well as animal or bird.

Hands frequently mirrored obtuse but nevertheless significant meanings. In the ceremonial dances they provided a silent but certain message to viewers that helped to unfold a story. Dancers used hand gestures to impersonate a character's journey into or from an ethereal world; they symbolized the groping for supernatural power. The hands were employed as a necessary part of a continuous drama of communication used by the dancers, synchronized to the dance steps and the chorus of singers narrating the events within the performance. Gestures included covering the face with the hands, moving the hands over the head, pawing the surrounding space, all showing a search for the hidden secrets that would unlock the powers of transformation. The dancers often moved in circles during potlatch proceedings, coming from behind the back screens and advancing to the front entrance of the house and then back again. The sun circles in the painting in Figure 41 may well represent such dance circles and suggest that the performer was traveling on a journey in search of the gifts associated with supernatural power.

The two sun symbols in this Humdaspi painting I have drawn in red. They are among the most ornately conceived images seen on house front paintings. Each has four rays emanating from its inner circle. An inner smaller disk encloses a diminutive human-like figure with outstretched arms and legs in the hocker position. This particular sun crest was historically associated with a lineage of the Smith Inlet people north of Blunden Harbour. Note the use of the salmon-trout eye designs in all eight of the sun's rays. They appear to be either copies of the northern-style salmon-trout designs poorly understood by the original painter or the unhappy consequence of Boas's untrained and casual drafting skills.

In the justly famed study entitled *Primitive Art* (Boas 1955: 246–254) seven detailed illustrations of house front paintings were reproduced from Kwakiutl originals. Among these drawings were two killer whales, two thunderbirds, a whale, a beaver, and a profile view of a raven. All were attributed to George Emmons, whose drawings made in the 1880s were turned over to Boas for his research (Carpenter 1975:16). Though there is no question as to Emmons's scholarship and veracity, he failed to note from which village each painting was derived. I have searched through hundreds of photographs in museum archives in what has proved a fruitless effort to find any supporting information that might identify the time and place of the originals that Emmons reproduced.

It can be safely concluded that house front painting was not only a widespread social practice among the Southern Kwakiutl, but it possessed a sustaining dynamism of its own. What explorers, traders, and anthropologists have been able to document and analyze is likely but a small part of the meteoric rise and fall of flat painting among these native peoples. Despite the probable gaps in the record, the productions of the Kwakiutl artists were and remain impressive to behold.

Southern Kwakiutl Variations in Painting

The northern Northwest Coast tribes utilized screens as an integral part of house interiors whereas those used by the Southern Kwakiutl were installed only as temporary accessories. These transient features were made of wood planks and utilized as room dividers or curtains to seal-off special spaces for specific ceremonies, most usually in connection with potlatch events. Like those of their northern neighbors, the screens symbolized for the Kwakiutl the separation of the two worlds that constituted the Northwest Coast native reality, the mythic world of supernatural beings and forces and the profane, present-day world of mere mortals. However, and unlike the northern practice, when the symbolic purpose for which the screens were constructed was served, the Southern Kwakiutl dismantled and destroyed them. Only a few, late in the screen-making tradition, were collected and saved by museums; even fewer have survived in native hands.

By the middle of the 19th century the northern tribal influences had relatively thoroughly infiltrated Southern Kwakiutl territory by way of Bella Bella. This northern influence brought new vigor to the flat-painting arts in the central region. The use of painted wood screens among the Southern Kwakiutl generally antedates this northern thrust but particular northern stylistic characteristics appeared with increasing frequency. Such elements as the formline features and various eye designs were interpreted by the Northern Kwakiutl artists with greater innovative freedom than before Tsimshian influence (Holm and Reid 1975:250).

Interior screens formed the backdrop for ceremonial performances designed to bring guests from near and far to witness the spectacle of social status, wealth, and inheritance of the chief mounting the event. Some, though not all, screens were constructed with holes in the painted boards to allow entry into and egress from the back portion of the house. The space in the rear of the long house served as a private room where preparations for the performances could be made. This off-stage room was used for donning costumes and adjusting the single- and multiple-faced masks, or for rehearsing the movements of the dramatic dances. It was also a place where the performers could conjure up the mental state appropriate to the portrayal of supernatural beings.

I know of one interior screen photographed in Hwa'tis, a Koskimo village, just after the turn of the century that provided no means of passage from a "green room" to the stage (Figure 42). This particular screen was small and did not apparently extend the full width of the house into which it had been installed. This screen was in the Sea Lion House at Hwa'tis village. Unfortunately, the photograph from which I drew the painting was taken in extremely poor light and only the barest of features are recognizable. The single face presented is the sun symbol, portrayed as a large human face set on a round disk. Four rays decorated with eye patterns project from the disk.

The Sea Lion House belonged to a man named Tza'kyus of

the Koskimo tribe. It was still standing—its magnificent sea lion interior columns intact—when I was doing ethnographic research in the region in 1950 (Figure 4). The screen, however, was nowhere in sight. When Tza'kyus died the house was passed on to Chief Johnny and through him to his daughter, constituting a part of her marriage dowry. A few of the remaining columns in this house were later acquired by the University of British Columbia Museum of Anthropology.

The bulk of the evidence for the use of painted interior wood screens comes from the research recorded by numerous scholars, with the cooperation of elder native informants, during the late 19th and early 20th centuries. Their joint efforts brought to fruition two major exhibitions in the 1920s, each shown in one of the two most prestigious institutions of higher learning in the United States at that time: the Chicago Museum of Natural History and the U.S. National Museum in Washington, D.C. These stunning exhibits introduced to the wider public the secret ritual dramas that formed the central focus of Franz Boas's writings. The exhibitions consisted of a number of sequential tableaus depicting a secret society initiation rite performed by the *hamatsa*, or cannibal dancer, during the Kwakiutl *tsetseqa*, or winter dances (Plate 41). Both exhibitions shared a number of features. Both employed mannequins dressed in authentic robes made from red cedar bark, and set the figures in replicas of long houses. Cedar bark rings denoting rank and place within the secret societies were draped around their necks. Eagle down that had drifted from above to alight on the bodies of all the participants symbolized peaceful coexistence. A mannequin at the extreme right in Plate 41 beats

a box drum. In the Chicago example a large log was placed horizontally in front of the figures who made up part of the chorus of singers. The crest painted on the log represented the double-headed serpent or sisiulth. A log was used in actual performances by the chorus to tap out a cadence with sticks, their rhythms timed to the performer's movements.

A role was defined for each mannequin to reflect a particular part in the actual performance. The drama reaches its explosive climax when the dancer, impersonating the *hamatsa*, makes his entrance through the hole in the screen. The *hamatsa* enters the long house in a trancelike state, returning from an incredible journey that took him to the house of a terrible power, the cannibal spirit, who resides in a supernatural realm. Being in an altered mental state, he must be kept under control, guided by assistants, such as those seizing him by his neck rings, who keep the *hamatsa* from running amok. The character must be calmed and reassured that he is no longer in the cannibal's house and at his mercy but rather has returned to the human world. This awakening then unfolds in the subsequent dance sequence.

The *hamatsa*'s gradual return to a full sense of his humanity proceeds by way of his description of his fantastic journey, employing a ritualized series of dance steps accompanied by the chorus. The verses sung by the chorus inform the audience in great detail of the events taking place before their eyes. With body movements and eye and hand gestures the dancer communicates all he has endured during his fantastic journey. The chorus and their accompaniment beat out the music and rhythms associated with the reenactment of this extraordinary spiritual odyssey.

The seated mannequins portraying the chorus in the Chicago exhibition were much too youthful in appearance to be participants in such a drama. This honor in their traditional context was reserved for male elders who had themselves long since undergone the initiation rite and who had seen this performance repeatedly so when finally selected to perform they knew all the nuances of song, dance, melody, and words that were integral to the ritual. These veterans alone possessed the status to participate in such an awe-inspiring undertaking. Both museum exhibits unhappily set the mouths of the mannequins in a closed position, for the chorus would actually have been in full voice at this heightened moment of the *hamatsa*'s return. One can indeed imagine the explosion of drumming and singing at the moment the *hamatsa* escapes the mythic world and leaps into the world of mortals.

These exhibitions illustrate the critical ceremonial and spiritual function of interior screens. They were absolutely essential elements in the dramatization of the prerogatives belonging to individual leaders, to having lineage status, and to secret society membership. It was the individuals in those groups and social classes who made up and maintained the power structure within Kwakiutl society.

The Southern Kwakiutl artists were not content, unlike their more northern counterparts, to steadfastly stick with traditional materials. They adopted other media whenever it became available to better serve the needs of the rituals. They responded quickly to new and different materials in a positive way, which led to a whole new level of artistic achievement as canvas and other cloth and commercially purchased paints in an assorted range of

colors became available as trade goods. The artists began at once to utilize them. These newly available products of Western commerce were probably used to their fullest potential in the winter dances. Cloth paintings could be more quickly and more cheaply made and raised than traditional wooden screens before the potlatches or winter dances began. They were also substantially easier to store afterwards. With this change the traditional hole in the screens was no longer used as a staging device but was replaced by side curtains.

Some of the finest examples of flat painting on cloth evolved in the early 20th century. Figures 43 and 44 are my drawings of two such cloth paintings that served as backdrops for potlatch proceedings. Many other examples are extant in both museum collections and among the possessions of various living family descendants. Every tribal division as well as every lineage aspired to possess its own screens reflecting its crest prerogatives. Clearly, such a numerous assemblage of screens cannot be illustrated. Only those few that are particularly typical or unusual were collected as part of the research for this volume.

Figure 43 shows a two-headed raven standing on a box containing a humanlike face. Interestingly, the raven is given some eagle characteristics including the wings and tail feathers and the talons. Notice the meticulously painted broken lines in the wing and feather areas of the bird, which are rendered in red against the contrasting black primary lines. This particular painting was used in ceremonies photographed by Edward Curtis in the early part of the 20th century, perhaps before 1915, at Blunden Harbour (1915:176). Raven, the culture hero, was purported to possess incredible powers including the ability to transform himself from a bird into a man. That the man in the box is a transformed raven is indicated by the feathers hanging to either side of the face. Note the mouth in the face on the raven's abdomen. It signifies the insatiable appetite assigned to Raven in traditional mythological tales.

The man who owned this screen was known as Siwit, the chief of a lineage of the Awaitela tribe who resided on the west side of Knight Inlet. Eventually these people moved to Tsatsichnukwomi, later New Vancouver, located on the northern part of Harbledown Island. How the screen eventually came to Blunden Harbour is not documented.

Figure 44 is a backdrop screen prepared for a major potlatch hosted by a man in Alert Bay in 1965. The central circular disk enclosed a human figure whose arms and legs are in the traditional hocker position. On each side of the circle a raven is painted in profile with its wings outstretched. Its legs and tail feathers parallel the lower part of the circle. Is this the mythical Raven again, setting free the sun for mankind at the time of the beginning of the world? The disk suggests the sun. Note that the human figures in both screens are gesturing in the same way, as a secondary feature in Figure 43, but a focal point in Figure 44.

Another painting from this genre is redrawn and reproduced in Figure 45. This screen was reportedly collected by the Museum of the American Indian in New York in the early part of the 20th century. It is attributed to Willie Seaweed, a Blunden Harbour artist possessing chiefly rank who was also renowned as a carver, dancer, and raconteur extraordinaire. This cloth screen is more than 10 feet (3.0 m) tall and 14 feet (4.3 m) wide. It represents two whales positioned around a circular symbol. The whole central figure may represent the sun or the circle may symbolize the cave in which the inner face, a grizzly bear, resides. The grizzly was one of Seaweed's family crests (Holm 1983:81). The figures were painted in black on white muslin. It is a wonderful example of this emergent art form.

Another kind of two dimensional painting was employed in later Kwakiutl theatrical performances. These were flats of commercial plywood with special esoteric crests depicted on them. They were of two types: the first was a stage prop known as *mawihl* or *mawitl*, and the second were referred to as temporary totems. The *mawitl* panels most usually were raised near the curtain separating the performers' preparation area from the audience section of the long house. The temporary totems were, on the other hand, raised in front of a leader's house for brief periods. Little is known about the use and meaning of either of these types of paintings; few were collected by the museums. These flat paintings remain an intriguing question for future research.

The *mawitl* were first described early in this century by the photographer Edward Curtis, and some of the best photographic images of these pieces were made by him. Philip Drucker, on the other hand, who wrote extensively on Northwest Coast cultures, does not mention them in his various publications including his definitive *Kwakiutl Dancing Societies* (1940), which deals with Kwakiutl theatrical performance practices. *Mawitl* boards vary in height from 6 to 9 feet (1.8 to 2.7 m). Following completion of the performance for which they had been prepared the boards were discarded or burned (Curtis 1915:175).

Mawitl boards were apparently raised on the stage area at particularly dramatic climax points in the winter dance sequences. When the dramatic tension fell the boards were lowered. They were most often employed in performances featuring the mythic characters associated with the *hamatsa* and *toogwid*. *Toogwid* performances were shamanistic-inspired rituals in which an individual performer demonstrated his or her magical powers derived from supernatural benefactors. Painted *mawitl* designs were also used to represent the shaman's spirits protecting the *toogwid* dancer (Curtis 1915:210). These boards served other functions as well as they were occasionally used to hide the action of the dancers when costume changes were required.

The other type of painted board, the temporary totem, is similar to *mawitl* but was used in a different capacity. The few photographs that capture their presence were made by none other than the nemesis of native ceremonial activities, William Halliday, former agent of the provincial government for Indian affairs stationed at Alert Bay. The few pieces that were collected remain a mystery as to purpose and function.

One of the most intriguing examples is illustrated in Figure 46. In its original setting it played a part in a potlatch proceeding that Halliday captured on film (Plate 42). It stands in the center of the photograph in front of the porch. Clearly scores of Kwakiutl guests were present to witness the drama-filled moment when the man, a host or his orator, holds a copper aloft. What challenge was

being thrown down to shame the guests? Or is he merely reciting the history of the copper, or its name, its former ownership, or its present monetary value?

Bill Holm wrote eloquently and at great length that no other object or image so graphically represented the notions of rank, privilege, tradition, wealth, and pride in northwest tribal life as did the copper (1983:67). Coppers symbolized the honor due deceased ancestors and leaders. They were portrayed on house fronts (Figure 36; Plates 39 and 40), and pegged on totem poles especially among the Haida and Southern Kwakiutl. They were worn with ceremonial paraphernalia, even dress garments, as symbols associated with the highest levels of class and rank.

The dominant painted figure in Plate 42 and Figure 46, is a fierce-looking creature whose head occupies the entire width of the board. Its lips are spread apart revealing two rows of teeth. Its ears are placed directly over the head, suggesting an animal. Its torso is suggested and both arms are raised. Five digits are on each hand. A variety of eye designs represent the palms, the shoulders, and the elbow joints. Its legs are spread apart, the knees raised to join the elbows in the hocker position. The lower torso is represented by a frontal face that suggests a frog or toad. Directly below the large figure is a representation of a copper with an animal face in frontal position. Its two forepaws are positioned below the face.

At the top part of the board a depression in the carving provides a space for a three-dimensional, birdlike creature, perhaps an eagle, to perch directly above the dominant image. The entire board appears to be between 14 and 16 feet (4.3 and 4.9 m) high and was probably supported in the rear by a vertical pole. Probably red, black, and some green colors were used in the painting.

Mortuary paintings were a late but important form of Southern Kwakiutl flat painting. Found in Kwakiutl cemeteries, these paintings used often huge representations of traditional symbols and images as memorials to departed relatives and persons of high rank. Exactly when this graveyard art came into being is not clear but it would seem that the practice antedates the Western incursions of the late 19th century. It was a widespread practice along the Northwest Coast, for the custom was found from Tlingit villages in the north to the southernmost parts of the British Columbia coast. Examples have been recorded among the Bella Coola, Southern Kwakiutl, and Nuu chaa nulth tribes, as well as among the Coast Tsimshian people. The photographs taken of the grave sites in Alert Bay during the 1910–12 period provide especially meaningful documentation. Plates 44 and 45 were photographed in Alert Bay, for example. This art form continues in some villages to the present.

Mortuary art included both sculptural and flat-painting media. The carved mortuary figure and screen from Fort Rupert in Plate 43 was seen in 1947 when I was doing research there. Informants disclosed that it had been raised in the 1920s; when I saw it the painting had already withstood a long period of wind and storm and the original colors and painted details had faded. A white picket fence surrounded this particular memorial. Some of the original boards of the painting had fallen. Marius Barbeau thoroughly documented this piece in his study of totem poles (1950:663). The entire piece was dominated by a sculpted figure at the top of the memorial, which represented the sun in human form. This symbol was the deceased woman's family crest. Below the sculpted figure was a flat screen about 6 feet (1.8 m) wide on which was painted a humanlike face that actually represents a bullhead, a type of rock-bottom fish similar to a sculpin. This memorial was raised by the deceased woman's father, a man named Kwasistal of the Tenaxto tribe from Knight Inlet. The woman was of very high rank and was known as Kwakwabalis, or Her Setting Down Place.

A fine mortuary painting was seen by Harlan Smith in the 1920s in the village of Kimsquit in Bella Coola country. It depicted a thunderbird with great outstretched wings. A human face was on its breast and a large wood appendage representing the bird's head and beak was attached on the board at the neck. Other memorials recorded in the Bella Coola region include depictions of dugout canoes, coppers, and numerous crest symbols.

Many examples of mortuary painting have been observed in villages scattered throughout the Northwest Coast. The most common memorials were plywood boards representing coppers, killer whales, thunderbirds, and ko-loos, the mythical thunderbird's younger brother. All such crests were associated with the deceased person's family prerogatives. Notice the proliferation of paintings of coppers placed on standing poles in Plates 44 and 45. The designs painted on them may reproduce those on the real coppers kept in the family treasure chests or they may simply be decorative. Notice the whales at the extreme left corner, the ko-loos or thunderbird above the whale in the left center of Plate 44, as well as the large wolf figure that was on one of Chief Tlah go glas's monuments at the right side of the same photograph. Plate 45 is a close-up of the central section of the mortuary memorials shown in Plate 44. It is included because the human figures standing at the left side of the photograph will give the reader a keen sense of the enormous extent of this display of wealth and position.

Nuu chaa nulth Painting

The tradition of house front and interior screen painting never played as prominent a role in the life ways of the Nuu chaa nulth tribes as it did among the more northern peoples. Nevertheless, flat paintings were occasionally commissioned by a leader. Though house front paintings were rare, interior screens were more commonly utilized for public ceremonies and some fine examples exist. Philip Drucker wrote a definitive work on these tribes, *The Northern and Central Nootkan Tribes* (1951), but he does not mention house front painting as one of the tribal practices. He does mention their occasional appearance in another publication, *Culture Elements Distributions: The Northwest Coast* (1950:180). Unfortunately, his reports and comments on the uses of interior painted screens are, in most cases, too brief to be fully helpful.

The Nuu chaa nulth painting tradition derived from the Southern Kwakiutl style, and so is even further removed from the northern Northwest Coast style. This was in part the consequence of the radical changes in Southern Kwakiutl style in the mid-19th century. Nuu chaa nulth painting stands on its own merit, however, and is easily recognizable. Nuu chaa nulth painting was more naturalistic and representational in style than that seen among the more northern groups (Holm 1990:611). Yet the subjects dealt with were generally creatures derived from myths, the crests associated with family histories. A limited number of mythic creatures and themes were the stock in trade of the Nuu chaa nulth artists —thunderbirds, whales, lightning serpents, the servants of the thunderbirds, and wolves—all playing a larger-than-life role in the stories and rituals associated with the possession of such prerogatives.

The photographic records of Nuu chaa nulth house front paintings are sparse indeed. A photograph taken in the 1860s at Friendly Cove on Nootka Sound reveals no house front paintings whatever in this village. Nor does another photograph made sometime in the 1860s or 1870s in the village of Ahousat on Clayoquot Sound. A lone exception is found in an 1896 photograph of Chief Maquinna's house at Friendly Cove. Constructed with vertical plank siding, it bears a dim outline of a painting. The design cannot be distinguished save in its general configuration— it was circular and surrounded the entrance to the long house. It seems a pale shadow of the house fronts seen farther north.

Another house front painting was brought to light through some ingenious research at the Canadian Museum of Civilization in Hull, Quebec, in connection with the curatorial work for an exhibit of Northwest Coast Indian architecture located in the Grand Hall of the museum in 1990. A long house was reconstructed to illustrate the Nuu chaa nulth tradition based on an actual dwelling known to have belonged to a chief of the Tseshe'ath people who lived near the town of Port Alberni. The original house dated back to the mid-19th century or earlier. The house and its painting were described in field notes written by the scholar Edward Sapir who was doing linguistic research in that part of the coast in the early years of the 20th century. Sapir recorded the remains of a complex painting containing numerous figures on the front wall. With his description in hand, the museum staff and artists proceeded to recreate the Nuu chaa nulth stylistic features thought to have been painted on the house front (Figure 47). Notice in my drawing the vertical struts supporting the horizontal planks on which two thunderbirds, two lightning serpents, and two codfish are depicted. All these creatures were painted in black and red colors. This painting is a remarkable reconstruction of a flat painting long considered lost.

Though similar evidence for earlier paintings is not easy to find, a number of examples of interior painted screens have survived, in particular the two screens that were described in Chapter II (Figures 8.1 and 8.2; Plates 11A and 11B) along with the myths associated with them. These screens are steeped in mythological associations, forming a part of the heritage of the prominent families. But in fact there were more boards collected than there were the myths intimately intertwined with them.

As with examples from the north, the Nuu chaa nulth screens were raised as backdrops for potlatching occasions. Several were painted on cloth materials following Southern Kwakiutl innovation. There was a significant functional difference between Kwakiutl and Nuu chaa nulth screens, however. The most honorable of the Nuu chaa nulth wood board paintings were often associated with a young woman's coming-of-age ceremonies, although they were not confined to such uses. A man honored his eldest daughter as she assumed a woman's role within the tribe. At this time a new name was publicly bestowed upon her while she sat before the heirloom screen. Her father invoked the special privileges she was to receive and hold in trust for her future children. The public at large was present to witness these proceedings, thus validating her changing role and status (Drucker 1951:141). I suspect there were a good many of these screens around some of the villages, but they did not draw the interest of collectors when other items of a more spectacular nature were being sought.

The paintings on these interior screens were bold in concept. Mythic figures were outlined in solid black paint so they stood out from the rest of the board. The employment of northern formline art surfaced only occasionally. Nuu chaa nulth art has a far freer form than that of the tribes to the north. The confining rules that applied in the northern-style painting, the formlines, the eye design constructions, and the use of color, were far less rigidly employed among Nuu chaa nulth artists and consumers.

One theme stands out above all others in Nuu chaa nulth art: thunderbirds holding whales in their talons. An example from the

Royal British Columbia Museum in Victoria was at one time on display in Thunderbird Park (Figure 48). It reveals a whale with its mouth open, devouring a human head. At the rear of the whale is a humanlike face with bared teeth. The whale is in the clutches of the thunderbird. In mythology whales were the food of thunderbirds. Directly above the thunderbird's head are twin serpents facing each other. Additional human figures fill the upper corners of this painting. There is no extant information as to what all these creatures are doing or what action is taking place. Philip Drucker has pointed out that thunderbirds were often conceived as huge men who put on birdlike garments to hunt whales (1951:153).

Two wood screens come from the Port Alberni area on Southern Vancouver Island. Both show similar thunderbird and whale motifs and were used in association with the ceremonies connected with a girl's puberty rite. The photographs recording the presence of the screens were taken by Fred Brand in 1910 and around the turn of the century.

At the other extreme is the masterpiece illustrated in Figure 49. It is painted on a large piece of fabric, 7 feet (2.1 m) high and 21 feet (6.4 m) wide (Holm and Reid 1975:250). A man named Chulatus is reported to be the artist. It is a pity that more of his work has not surfaced. Once more the theme is the thunderbird and whale, but this is an elegant handling of the space by this artist. The bird is massive in size, its wings stretching across the upper portion of the painting. Its red and black wing feathers are repeated in alternate horizontal rows from its breast to the fabric's borders. The breast is painted as a face design. A humanlike hand

extends to the right of the bird's body where a leg and talons might normally be positioned.

The whale is outlined in bold undulating black lines. Its mouth is open and a small figure painted in red is contained within. The whale's flukes are deceptively small relative to the enormous expanse of its body; its dorsal fin is disproportionately tiny as well. Within the whale's body are two wolflike creatures presented in profile, facing to the right of the screen. Their eyes are similar stylistically to those seen in Southern Kwakiutl paintings. The wolves' lips are parted revealing rows of teeth. A mere suggestion of the presence of their bodies shows in the thick black lines extending from the heads. Two lightning serpents are positioned along the top border, facing outward. They are rendered in black and red and suggest some northern influences in the eye designs. Some blue was said to be used, but where is not easily discernible. This curtain was probably used like an interior screen in potlatching occasions in ways similar to adjacent regional practices.

Another painted cloth screen of large dimensions was collected from among the Hopachisat people around Port Alberni in the 1920s. It portrays a great bird painted inside a large circle. Lightning serpents are positioned within the circle on each side of the bird. The serpents' mouths have extended tongues. Two birds, ravens perhaps, appear with their wings positioned as in flight facing the outer parts of the screen. Another head of a serpent with tongue extending outwards protrudes from the right side of the thunderbird's neck. This is a rather extensive cloth painting somewhat like the screen from the Nakwoktak tribe pictured in Figure 43. However, it has its own Nuu chaa nulth stamp. Several more painting examples were found in Nuu chaa nulth territory, but the subject matter and their ancient ties with a mysterious past now appear lost to our understanding.

Coast Salish Painting

The Coast Salish tribes were the southernmost representatives of the native Northwest Coast tribal ambit, but the flat painting of the kind described in the foregoing pages seems on the basis of the tangible physical evidence to have never established a foothold in the Salish region. But this is not to say that no paintings were done by these groups. The limited evidence of the painting arts among the Coast Salish indicates that their paintings differed markedly from those found northward in content and style. Salish tradition also differed in the intensity of use of paintings and the material incentives for commissioning them.

The individual Coast Salish tribes occupied the regions south of the Kwakiutl and east of the Nuu chaa nulth Vancouver Island tribes. Considerable variation in folkways, material possessions, architecture, art, and ceremonial activities separated these 14 tribes both from their northern neighbors and from each other.

In the southeast corner of Vancouver Island many villages occupied the numerous bays and inlets marking the coastline; some abutted Southern Kwakiutl groups. The reports prepared by explorers and visitors early in the 19th century tell of carved and painted ritual paraphernalia used by the natives. These items included house post carvings and an occasional house front painting as well as painted mortuary figures.

Early European observers reported seeing decorated house fronts on the lower Fraser River, but they do not seem to resemble in complexity or scale those known in the north. In 1808 Simon Fraser, the famed explorer, discovered on the Stalo River a Coast Salish village containing carved figures of birds and animals. Though such observations lend credence to the idea of some publicly displayed art among the Coast Salish in the early 19th century, long before significant European infiltration and settlement, it is something else again to point to specific examples. I have found none that could be used to illustrate this volume. What once was has disappeared.

Direct observations recorded by outsiders prove that an occasional flat painting was prepared, but these limited sightings inescapably imply limited usage in the life ways of the Coast Salish tribes. It is quite possible that some form of painted art was practiced relatively early in the tribal past and that it did not prosper in the changing cultural circumstances in which the people found themselves in the latter half of the 19th century. On the other hand, it is possible that no such tradition could develop or be stimulated by northern practices because the Coast Salish did not have the resources or opportunities to foster it. Additionally, it is well known that these tribes were the most thoroughly immersed in the new customs, new economic pressures, new religious ideas, and new ways of living associated with the arrival of Western culture. In such an environment the traditional arts could be expected to not only fail to flower but to wither and die.

What seems a more plausible explanation for the absence of the painting arts was advanced by Professor Wayne Suttles, a Salish expert. He suggests, in a paper entitled "Productivity and its Constraints" (1976), that the dearth of house front and screen paintings as well as other arts found in the villages of the northern tribes was due to social constraints at work among these people inhibiting such usage. There were distinct social limits on what a person or family could show in public of their wealth or mythological background. To engage in such displays would lead to censure and ridicule.

However, early 19th-century photographers do tell of some painting among the Coast Salish. An 1860 photograph of a native house near Nanaimo shows several scattered paintings depicting thunderbird and serpent designs. But they were done with very basic aesthetic skill. A house painting and a grave marker were seen in the Musquian village north of the Fraser River in southern British Columbia (Barbeau 1950:747). Franz Boas reports paintings on some houses that included killer whales, moon, eagle, swan, and heron designs. Marius Barbeau also mentions paintings in his documents, but in neither explorer's case can the sightings be verified as to date, place, or other pertinent data. In short, though there may have been a few Coast Salish paintings made in the early to mid-19th century, none survived long and none were recorded by photographers.

The dearth of evidence from this region suggests the climax of flat painting occurred in the north and central regions of the Northwest coast, culminating in the creative outbursts of the Tlingit, Tsimshian, and Kwakiutl tribes. Barring the rare exception, the painting arts faded and disappeared among the Salish groups.

"Art, like so much else in Tlingit life, was often
used for power. It was even used as a weapon."

Edmund Carpenter
Introduction to *Form and Freedom:
A Dialogue on Northwest Coast Art*

CHARACTERISTICS OF NORTHWEST COAST NATIVE FLAT PAINTING

WITH THE sample house front and screen paintings that
have been depicted and described in the foregoing
chapters, the background is now available to proceed
with an analysis of the similarities and differences in style and presentation between the tribes. This chapter examines the characteristics of the flat painting of the Pacific Northwest Coast tribes
to distinguish those features that were distinctive to certain groups
and those that were shared.

I have already discussed the fact that house front paintings and
some types of interior screen paintings served thoroughly transitory purposes; they were created by artists and craftsmen for powerful leaders to fulfill a specific purpose or to represent or com-
ment on some social or political event. Though clan and lineage
heads commissioned such works and paid dearly for them, they
were almost thoroughly indifferent to the long-term preservation

or survival of the pieces. Neither interest nor wealth was expended in maintaining or sprucing up the vast bulk of these symbolic artifacts. Maintenance or repair yielded their owners little esteem or merit in the eyes of either their competitors or the members of their tribe.

With the exception of Johnny Scow's Sea Monster House painting at Gwayasdums, which was refurbished before 1914 (Plate 38), and one or two other scattered cases, no house fronts were repainted or in any way protected in an effort to preserve them. Indeed, the Scow house may have been refurbished largely at the instigation of Edward Curtis who invested years in romanticizing the Kwakiutl villages via the medium of photography. The natives' nearly universal lack of interest in preserving house front paintings extended to other monumental art of the Northwest Coast, such as totem poles. Once they had been raised and dedicated formally at potlatches, there was little recognition obtained from efforts to preserve them. Most eventually toppled and disintegrated in the moist climate (Malin 1986:30).

The tribes residing along the northern stretches of the Northwest Coast, particularly the Tlingit groups, clearly viewed interior screens in a different light. Clan members considered such property as an integral part of the bundle of household possessions closely bound up with ancestral pride. The screens of some northern clans were guarded and preserved against all onslaughts, both natural and human inspired. According to Tlingit informants some tribes that relocated from one winter residence to another at a different site carefully dismantled and transported the screens to the new dwellings. Many interior screens from these groups have sur-

vived largely in their original state. Far more of these old interior screens are known to have survived than house front paintings.

Further evidence compels the conclusion that house front painting preceded the carving and erecting of monumental totem poles along most of the Northwest Coast. Pole carving flowered in the early to mid-19th century in numerous settlements, and house front painting flourished from the late 18th to late 19th centuries. In most cases, poles supplanted house front paintings, rather than the reverse, particularly among the central tribes. Among the Haida of the Queen Charlotte Islands and those Tsimshian residing along the Nass and Skeena river valleys, totem poles dominated the village landscapes; painted house fronts were rarely recorded. Contrariwise, exterior totem poles were not commonly raised by the Tlingit tribes in Alaska, save in those few villages geographically contiguous to Tsimshian and Haida neighbors, and totem poles never achieved the prominence in the southern part of the Northwest Coast as they did in the central region. As with house front paintings, totem poles were allowed to simply waste away after serving a one-time purpose. They might be cut up for fuel after they collapsed, allowed to disintegrate in total indifference, or simply sold to collectors when the opportunity presented itself.

Interior screens and smaller interior house post totem poles were widely pursued forms of display among most of the tribes of the Pacific Northwest Coast. This expansive geographic distribution of such artifacts suggests that the tradition of interior screen painting and use holds considerable antiquity, dating from long before the period of their flowering in the 18th and 19th centuries. Many more Tsimshian screens were likely produced than the present inventory of known examples suggests. The Tsimshian may have purposefully destroyed many during or following the performances of various ceremonial and ritual functions, a practice that was repeatedly observed. The same practice was also followed by the Southern Kwakiutl and Bella Coola peoples.

Though interior screen painting was an ancient form of social art, only the more northerly tribes saw them as permanent tribal possessions. But even in the north some communal practices required their destruction. The symbolism of destroying the paintings was probably akin to sending the crest symbols back to the spirit world whence they had originally been derived. The social function of publicly destroying objects of great value was meant to impress the gathered notables of other tribes, to show that even this possession of wealth so great could be destroyed without compunction. By so doing the social position of the host group was elevated in the eyes of the guests.

Beyond the intentional destruction of interior screens and other tribal possessions as an integral element of various ceremonial rites, further destruction resulted from the conversion of many tribal members from shamanistic religious practices to Christianity. Marius Barbeau, the Tsimshian expert, reported that house front paintings depicting the clan myths were once far more commonly seen than records indicate (1950:777). The preponderance of the evidence suggests that massive destruction of native ritual possessions was commonplace in the latter half of the 19th century, just when Christian influences were making considerable inroads into the native way of life.

Content of the Paintings

The entire purpose and role of the flat-painting tradition among the Northwest Coast tribes centered around the fundamental meaning embodied in each of the paintings. The declaration of these meanings through symbolic and stylistic means was the sole driving force behind this form of social display. However, getting some sense of the content of the painting requires penetrating to the very core of the people's social and emotional construct of the world. Unhappily, meanings implicit in each of the paintings present daunting challenges and are at best elusive to most modern researchers. The recorded observations of explorers, travelers, and later trained anthropologists are helpful resources, of course. But since these tribes did not have written languages, present-day scholarship largely depends upon piecemeal oral accounts from native informants, many of whom are reluctant to discuss such content with strangers for fear of ridicule and derision or because they lack the rights to do so according to strongly entrenched attitudes associated with family rights of possession and ownership.

For similar reasons, the matriarch presiding over the Killer Whale House in Klukwan laid down strict conditions for our visit during the research expedition led by Frederica de Laguna that I described in the Introduction; no questions about the clan's heirlooms would be tolerated. In this conservative village her response to my questions was probably a norm. On the other hand, among the more liberal Tlingit in Yakutat, clan members responded in another manner. They spontaneously narrated parts of the myths with a sense of great pride, telling the narratives underlying the

Wolf Bath House and Thunderbird House screens (Figures 6 and 7). These two examples of quite different responses to outsiders reflect the different acculturation situations in Alaska in 1949.

De Laguna and I were fortunate to record parts of the myths associated with the Yakutat screens. Cursory data provides limited grounds for interpreting some paintings, offering for the most part only fragments of larger, richer stories. The myths associated with the illustrated examples in this book are but simple abbreviated narratives—none portray the breadth and depth of the original meanings. Virtually no information is available about the content of the thunderbird and whale crests illustrated in the Kwakiutl and Nuu chaa nulth paintings (Figures 8.1, 8.2, 33, 34, 37, 39, 47, 48, and 49). The same is true of the Tsimshian examples (Figures 22, 24, 25, and 26). The Tlingit masterpiece in the Killer Whale House in Klukwan (Figure 1.1; Plate 1) must mirror a dramatic narrative, but its content is completely unrecorded. Another example that eludes explanation is the house front painting depicting the killer whale chasing the seal (Figure 51; Plate 21). Both examples could provide valuable insights into clan politics as well as the emotions and feelings they engendered. It is a sad fact that the richness of the mythical narratives displayed in flat paintings was virtually inaccessible to outsiders and has been largely forgotten by modern native descendants, leaving it in danger of being irretrievably lost. Facing such an enormous gap in the data, scholars are left to piece together the underlying symbolism and meaning of these artifacts as best they can. These fragments of interpretive data range from fairly extensive to nonexistent.

The Question of Provenance

When a particular painting is designated as Tsimshian, Kwakiutl, or Tlingit, reference is simply being made to where it was originally displayed and dedicated. The location of a painting, though, provides no necessary evidence that it was conceived and built by artists from within that community. An artist residing in another village, or perhaps a member of a distant tribe, may as likely have been hired to create the painting. The skill and fame of the artist, given the competitive social purposes that such paintings were meant to serve, were the paramount concerns of the leader bent on mounting such a display. Though there were local craftsmen residing in each community who were employed in the making of objects of lesser social import, only a person placed on the highest rungs of artistic status and prestige would be considered qualified to undertake the momentous task of painting a house front or interior screen. Indeed, a tiny handful of craftsmen acquired regional reputations for their skill and imaginative, powerful presentations. It was to these individuals that the leaders routinely turned to execute works making major ceremonial and social statements. Virtually all such paintings were done by way of a contractual arrangement between a house leader and an artist who might reside in a neighboring village or a more distant settlement of a different tribe. What mattered was not simply his skill but more importantly his social position, his prestige, expertise, and reputation.

The intervillage or intertribal movements of artists helps explain how tribal leaders became aware of the intentions of rival chieftains. Every tribal leader was willing, indeed eager, to borrow any new ideas or motifs that might support his social and political pretensions. The movements of reputable artists along the coast also helps explain the similarity in design motifs in quite distant villages. This continual exchange greatly stimulated the development and elaboration of ideas, designs, and artistic productions.

Tsimshian artists were held in highest esteem by Tlingit people generally, suggesting that the former were the acknowledged masters of monumental two-dimensional painting. Tsimshian painters were probably commissioned to make at least a significant amount of the finest and most elaborate paintings found on northern clan house screens. But masterful Tlingit painters are also known; some of the finest existing flat paintings were done by artists belonging to these tribes. It must be noted here again, however, that southern Tlingit and Haida tribes were less devoted to mounting monumental house front paintings than totem poles, great maritime dugout canoes, and works of a more modest scale such as painted carved boxes and storage chests, ceremonial settees, ceremonial canoe paddles, and chiefly ritual possessions such as painted hide robes and tunics.

Tsimshian influences also spread southward. I pointed out earlier the northern stylistic features found among the Heiltsuq groups at Bella Bella as well as neighboring peoples in the Bella Coola valley. Intrigued by the visual displays they observed during various pan-tribal ceremonial exchanges and periodic trading forays, artists and painters sought to emulate or surpass those Tsimshian examples that made great impressions and aroused envy. On occasion these more southerly imitators succeeded in their efforts, resulting in truly dynamic insights and productions; more commonly the results were but poor imitations, and in general both the symbolic and pictorial quality of house front paintings declined among the southerly tribes. And, indeed, the few house fronts known among the southern tribes can be likened to a trailing off of the entire flat-painting impulse and its traditions.

Color

One of the primary tools employed in my analysis of the flat-painting tradition was the examination of the selective uses of color in the paintings. Two colors were employed exclusively for house fronts, black as the dominant and red as the secondary. Interior screen painting also depended upon black and a few shades of muted red. Besides these two primary colors, the northern tribes incorporated a variety of shades of blue or blue-green. I am not aware of a single house front painting that used the tertiary color blue. Blue, however, fades rapidly when exposed to weather and would, if in fact used, be very difficult to detect in the late 19th-century photographs. The examples preserved in museum collections bear no painted blue parts. However, a few specimen house fronts of later vintage along the central Northwest Coast utilized other colors, particularly dark green, yellow, white, and orange (Figures 17, 29, 39; Plate 21). The later house screen paintings associated with the Tlingit also used nontraditional colors, as in Figures 6, 7, 17, 18, and 19. Such colors were employed only in the late 19th century after such paints were made available through commercial sources.

The traditional colors used in the paintings were derived by native artists from material sources naturally occurring in the coastal environment. The Canadian Conservation Institute in Ottawa conducted a study of native materials that analyzed the paint content of almost 600 artifacts dating back to the early 1850s (Miller, Moffatt, and Sirois 1990). The pieces were scanned with electron microscopes equipped with X-ray energy spectrometers in order to determine the chemical elements present in the paints. Red vermilion or hematite vermilion mixed with red lead was found in the overwhelming majority of these artifacts. This form of vermilion is produced naturally in mineral cinnabar formations. It was packaged by the Hudson's Bay Company as China Red and was probably the first trade pigment available to the artists (Miller, Moffatt, and Sirois 1990:20). As Western traders, especially the Hudson's Bay Company, brought packaged pigments to the area, native artists adopted these more ready sources of color. A Southern Kwakiutl artist and informant named Mungo Martin maintained that China Red was available to the native peoples in paper packages (Holm 1965:26). An original dull red hue was often used in Tlingit paintings and was derived from various native earth ochres. George Emmons, the Tlingit scholar, contends that the Tlingit from early on acquired red pigment from hematite, cinnabar, or iron oxide deposits that are widely available along coastal Alaska (1990:196). Before contact with white men there was in all probability also some trading in mineral sources between tribes.

Black was also a mineral-derived color. The Canadian Conservation Institute study cited magnetite and bone black (burned bones) as the two sources most often utilized. These might also be mixed together to form a base black. Other sources of black pigment were coal and charcoal, the former found in a number of seams along the coast. One of the reasons the Hudson's Bay Company established a trading post at Fort Rupert on the north coast of Vancouver Island was to more effectively exploit for commercial purposes the coal veins that were discovered there.

The blue or blue-green was acquired from the Hudson's Bay Company product called Russian Blue, composed of ferric ferrocyanide. And the pigment Green Earth was derived from two minerals called celanite and glauconite, both silicates of iron and potassium. As mentioned earlier, these colors had almost no use for house front paintings but were essential in northern interior screen painting.

These paint pigments were ground in shallow stone dishes or on flat stones by the artists or their apprentices. The ground pigment was then mixed with salmon roe and either water or saliva, all natural fixatives. Often the roe was chewed until it formed a pasty mass and then spit out into the pigment. The paints were remarkably long lasting in the moist climates of the Northwest Coast, withstanding the elements for some years. Fragments of paint were still to be seen on totem poles that had been exposed continuously to the elements for 50 and more years, something modern commercial paints can hardly succeed in boasting.

Some writers have contended that color selection and use reflected tribal emotional sentiments: black represented anger, death, or sorrow, and red was symbolic of life and peace (Kan 1989:68). I tend towards greater caution in making such an assessment. Rather, I think traditional preferences and usages of color were based on the more mundane considerations of the ready availability of pigments from the natural environment and the visual impact made by these powerful hues.

Wood

House front and interior screen planks were constructed almost exclusively from the primary material resource of the Northwest Coast, the ubiquitous Pacific red cedar tree (*Thuja plicata*). This tree filled countless needs and enhanced and enriched the material well-being of the people. All the tribes on the coast utilized this resource in hundreds of imaginative, aesthetically pleasing, and utilitarian ways, including making planks for paintings. The northernmost Tlingit groups were the exception to this rule as the red cedar tree does not thrive in the more northern latitudes. Though some red cedar was traded to be used in very specific ways, the wood of local tree species, primarily spruce, hemlock, and yellow cedar, were commonly used.

Red cedar is a delightfully easy wood to work and is highly praised by the carvers I have known. Their attitudes border on reverence for its pliable characteristics. They treat it with an almost mystical sense of awe. In traditional Pacific Northwest Coast Native American spiritual beliefs, a tree is considered to have a spirit of its own. Supplication and prayers might be directed to a particular tree before it is downed. Before craftsmen fell a cedar they first test it for its soundness and lack of dry rot. Specific trees were selected for particular uses, some provided good house beams, others formed seagoing canoes, still others made planks to adorn the outer layer of the house walls.

Not infrequently, planks were hewn from living cedar trees. This might be done to spare the tree from complete destruction. Hilary Stewart, who has written at length about the cedar tree, has pointed out two different procedures used to fell trees in traditional times: one was to burn the tree's base until its weight gradually forced it to topple over—a long and drawn-out process—or the tree could be gradually chipped away at its base with adze tools until collapsing of its own weight (1984:43). Such tasks were difficult at best, requiring long hours of labor-intensive efforts involving a number of men.

When the tree was downed, or if boards were taken from a living tree, workmen proceeded with elk antler and bone wedges to split away the necessary raw planks. Cedar splits naturally along predictable lines and as a consequence separates from the trunk in roughly uniform boards. The rough planks were subsequently squared using stone and later iron-bladed tools acquired through trade with Westerners. If some warpage was observed in the plank it would first be leveled with adzes then weighted down with large rocks until the plank dried and the warpage disappeared. Planks had to be further adzed to smooth the surfaces and then fitted closely together for the dimensions of the proposed house front or screen surface that would contain the flat painting. In finishing the planks the cedar would be squared then adzed to either a pleasing smooth surface or the attractive stippled surface frequently seen in facade constructions as well as in the screens within the houses (Plates 7, 15, and 41).

The craftsmen working with such wood were painstaking in their demands as to its quality and desirable working characteristics. The artists moved slowly, methodically, efficiently. The end results effectively revealed their attention to all the details that made them highly esteemed professionals.

The number of planks necessary to cover a house facade presented a considerable undertaking. Take, for example, the planks required for Chief Sqagwet's Tsimshian house in Plate 2. And consider those in Plate 31, which were not only of considerable length and width but also of great thickness and weight. Stewart has pointed out that some early writers observed planks that were as wide as 2½ feet (0.8 m) and as long as 40 feet (12.2 m). The preparation of such planks, their move to the house site, which might have been some distance, their raising and securing to the house front, plus other required procedures suggest a staggering effort demanding the energy and engineering skills of many men, many months of intensive labor, and an expense that must have been staggering in terms of the tribal economies of the participants. A potlatch celebrating such an event simply added further expense.

The cedar planks were placed either horizontally or vertically on the house fronts. Facade construction dominated among the Tsimshian, Bella Coola, and Southern Kwakiutl. A tripartite facade construction was used by the Bella Coola and nowhere else along the Northwest Coast. The house front planks of Haida, Tsimshian, and Tlingit tribes were vertically arranged as were the early Kwakiutl examples. Those from the late 19th century and later used sawed lumber from commercial mills and tended to-

ward horizontal arrangements of the narrower planks (Figures 33, 35, 39 and 40; Plates 6, 8, 13, 20, 31, and 37). A few combined horizontal with vertical combinations, as in Plate 24. For interior screens, the planks of some of the oldest screens were arranged vertically but others were positioned horizontally.

The Arrangement of Figures

The paintings reproduced in this book depend upon certain formal characteristics that provide some clues as to the types and variations of the figures portrayed. The first outstanding feature that captures immediate attention is the frontal presentation of the dominant painted figures. These frontal figures are usually placed centrally and seem to lean forward. They meet the viewers gaze head-on, looming upright with fore- and hind limbs or wings and talons encircling the entrance, an opening either round or rectangular in shape. The most commonly employed figures within the central frontal space are thunderbirds, ravens, whales, bears, humans, or sun symbols.

The central figure typically dominates the other figures by the very nature of its size but occasionally the central figure is roughly equal in size to those of the side figures. The positioning of the large central figure suggests a hierarchical arrangement to some researchers, but I do not believe this message is intended, because the creatures on each side of the centrally positioned figure are frequently of equal symbolic importance. It was mainly the sloping of the roof lines that imposed a hierarchical relationship (Figures 5.1, 30, and 31).

The peripherally placed figures are considerably smaller in scale than the central figure (Figures 8.1, 8.2, 17, 22, 24, 25, and 26, to name but a few). They may be presented either frontally or in a profile view (see also Plates 30, 33, and 34). The side or peripheral figures often provide a sense of balance with the central dominating character for they are often mirror images. However, closer scrutiny often reveals subtle shades of difference in shape, color arrangement, and details of anatomy. Whether these variations were intentional or not is unknown. Occasionally, there is considerable variation between the two sides of the house front, as in the Fort Simpson example illustrating the two killer whales in Plate 10 (see also Figures 22, 26, 28, 31, and 48).

Some paintings are composed of but a single face possessing no appendages or body parts. Two such examples are the sea monster paintings shown in Figure 33 and Plate 40. No attempt was made by the artist to portray other bodily characteristics such as flukes, fins, or limbs, elements that could otherwise assist in identifying the kind of creature and hence possibly its meaning.

The overwhelming character of the flat painted house fronts and screens depict the creatures of the mythic past in static poses. Little movement or action is suggested or implied as the figures seem frozen into the positions the artists assigned them. As mnemonic symbols of events that stirred memories of past greatness, the connection would become instantaneous for those belonging within the house. But not all paintings conform to the traditional structure or format. There are a relatively few paintings that possess action-laden qualities, depicting not only the primary crest of the house but one in the act of doing something. One example

of this action-oriented quality is in Plate 21 (Figure 51), the Kit Hit House in Angoon village in Tlingit country where a profile configuration is the primary composition. It graphically illustrates a killer whale pursuing a hair seal whose demise appears imminent. This is not a traditional house front painting but the theme does parallel the tradition-steeped screens seen in the Killer Whale House in Klukwan.

The Kit Hit House painting was eventually whitewashed out of existence. Some years later, however, the leader of the house, in an attempt to resurrect some of the clan's symbolism, had a much smaller copy painted and cut out of plywood lumber. About 2½ to 3 feet (0.8 to 0.9 m) in length, it was installed on an inside wall of a modest frame house. I sketched the replica screen in 1949 (Figure 52). Though the later reproduction retains the theme of the original house painting, the work is second rate. The matriarch residing in the house was unable or unwilling to explain what the free-floating figures represented.

A few other action-type screens are known. One is shown in Figure 7 where the hero armed with a bow and arrow pursues a muskrat across the Milky Way. Other aberrations, though not implying action qualities, are seen in Figure 36 and Plate 40. The former is the Alert Bay house festooned with dugout canoes and copper silhouettes. In Plate 40 is the house front from Tsatsichnukwomi where a human figure is portrayed surrounded by copper wealth symbols. Both types of deviations from the traditional static crest poses suggest evidence of a continuing artistic effort to experiment with new forms and to break out of the rigid mold that encased the northern style of painting. They may also suggest efforts to reflect the loss of traditional values and the partial replacement of them by Western values during the late 19th century. This period was one of convulsive change for the native peoples of the Northwest Coast. The demise of a corps of traditionally trained and disciplined artists left a vacuum within the changing culture that was not filled again until the last decades of the 20th century. Eventually, a revival of an attenuated form of painting grew in part out of a renewed interest from turn-of-the-century artists, but it represented a feeble attempt to revive customary aesthetic practices and values that had been displaced or lost.

Bilateral Symmetry

Though a common characteristic of Northwest Coast art, bilateral symmetry clearly bears no relationship to the proportioning of the figures in the space available. But this means of rendering real or imagined creatures represents an important, deeply rooted dimension in Northwest Coast artistic style. Bilateral symmetry is the technique Northwest Coast artists resorted to in an attempt to represent three-dimensional creatures on a two-dimensional painted surface. The technique involves figuratively splitting the creature down the backbone from neck to tail and spreading the two sections 180 degrees apart. In this way the artist was able to present views of both sides of the body, all four limbs, as well as a full frontal view of the head. An example is the raven figure centrally placed in Plate 22 (Figure 19).

In another case, the technique was effectively employed in an exhibition house screen raised in the mid-1970s at the Tsimshian model village of Ksan, near Hazelton, British Columbia. The figure represents a wolf crest and is painted on a vertically oriented series of cedar planks (Figure 50). Though this technique of showing multidimensional figures on a flat surface led to some distortion of the design, it had the advantage of being useful in filling any required space. The technique was more commonly employed among the northern Northwest Coast tribes where it was used in not only house screen surfaces but other ceremonial accoutrements. The house front example that best demonstrates bilateral symmetry is the Tlingit dwelling in Gash village at Cape Fox, Alaska (Plate 25). The grizzly bear's body in this photograph is split at the neck, the two sides filling the left and right sections of the house front. Its head dominates the central part of the space.

Though bilateral symmetry is a definitive characteristic in a number of examples of Northwest Coast flat painting, some asymmetrical departures can be documented. In the Beaver Screen in Figure 7 the hero, an ancestor, is portrayed on the left side of the screen and a sky-dwelling muskrat is painted on the right. The remainder of the screen, comprising the lower half, features the centrally positioned beaver crest, its beaver dam home, and the wolf crest symbols, all conforming to the traditional symmetrical characteristics. The Nuu chaa nulth paintings from Vancouver Island reproduced in Figures 8.1, 8.2, and 48 are also asymmetrical. A Tlingit screen in Figure 18 depicts a mother eagle in a semi-profile position, its tail and beak turned to the right side of the screen. The branches upon which the bird's nest rests appear to be in balance but closer scrutiny reveals this is not so. A single diminutive eaglet is nested at the lower left side of its protective mother.

Bilateral symmetry is a leading characteristic of Northwest Coast native flat painting, but it was by no means rigidly required. The large majority of the paintings I have studied present more frontal or profile views of animals and bird creatures. Artists, particularly late in the history of this form, took considerable liberty with this traditional element.

Horror Vacui

The term "horror vacui" is used to describe an artist's compulsion to fill the corners and all other available spaces of a painted surface with various designs that may or may not relate symbolically to the rest of the painting. It is a characteristic associated with painting and other art forms found in the region. Occasionally, these space-filling designs may relate in a meaningful way to the overall configuration, but in most examples the artist's objective seems merely to be able to fill the leftover spaces, their function being truly decorative rather than symbolic.

The profusion of designs resulting from this traditional imperative lead to difficulties in recognizing what is being represented or intended. The configuration becomes so infused with multiple elements—eyes, faces, ovoids, U-forms, curves—that the viewer is frequently unable to distinguish the significant parts of the presentation from the purely ornamental. A case in point is reproduced in Plate 22 (Figure 19). After the raven and stone, all the other elements seem to be simply filler to occupy the remaining empty space.

Further, anatomical parts belonging to the primary creatures may be placed in positions or relationships having little connection with physical reality; or anatomical parts are attenuated, turned, enlarged, or made to impinge on unrelated parts of the creature's body. In short, a creature's assemblage of physical components is often not accurately reflected in a painting. Much of this manipulation is done for no symbolic or ritual purpose but is rather distortion for the sake of aesthetically filling the space. Artists often felt compelled to represent an animal or bird by depicting not only its external body configuration but also, in a variety of designs, internal organs and skeleton that otherwise could not be seen with the naked eye. Body parts become unrecognizable as they are transformed into highly stylized representations.

To further illustrate, turn again to the Killer Whale Screen from Klukwan (Figures 1.1 to 1.8). Within the body cavity of this creature each of four ribs are depicted with a face shown in profile, facing to the right side of the screen (Figure 1.3). Directly below these faces is a representation of the whale's visceral organs. These are rendered in red paint and decorated with eye designs from which four sets of arms and legs emerge, each limb possessing protruding fingers and toes. At the base of the screen, the whale's large ventral fin is portrayed as a series of smaller designs that include a face similar to those decorating the whale's ribs. The whale's penis is located to the left of the ventral fin and is a stylized design with a large U-form outlined in black and duplicated in red, together with an inverted eye pattern (Figure 1.1). These representations provide a virtually complete inventory of the whale's anatomy.

Beyond those elements, the artist added a prominent eye design and a sweeping U-form that extends to the nose area, within which there is a salmon-trout eye design outlined in red in the whale's head on the right side of the screen. Below this is a profile face with mouth wide open and an extended tongue painted red, terminating in a large black eye design. Further compelled by horror vacui, the artist added more design elements outside of the black form of the whale. Of the several figures painted in red surrounding the whale, one flows out of the whale's blow hole and spreads across the top of the screen. It is given a head and limbs and suggests the whale's spray. Another creature with a head and limbs is positioned directly above the whale's nose at the extreme right side of the screen. Still another form is riding on the whale's back behind the prominent dorsal fin. Its head thrusts downward, its mouth accented by rows of teeth. The face almost touches the whale's flukes, which are positioned in the lower left corner of the screen. Given the additional designs that compose the lower border and right-hand corners, there is no empty space remaining on the boards. This painting is but a single example reflecting the principle of horror of empty space in Northwest Coast art.

In a similar vein the Raven Screen in the Beaver House from Angoon (Figure 2) shows a more confusing example of the application of the aesthetic horror vacui. Though the central raven is identifiable, the remainder of the designs cannot be interpreted. More examples of horror vacuum are in Plate 10 and Figures 5.1, 6, 10, 12, and 28, to name a few. My impression, after examining hundreds of examples of such paintings, is that the horror of the vacuum is primarily centered in the northern tribal region rather than being typical of Northwest Coast flat painting as a whole.

The X-Ray Motif

The X-ray type of representation is a common feature of the art of indigenous people. It is to be found in widely diverse settings ranging throughout the far-flung corners of the world, from the western Pacific eastward to the American continents, from Australia to the Melanesian archipelagos, and into the vast ocean areas to touch upon the Northwest Coast and beyond. The X-ray form of pictorial presentation reached the American Plains Indians as well as those residing in the American Southwest. This distinctive mode of portrayal was particularly prominent in the paintings made along the northern and central reaches of the Northwest Coast. Virtually all the creatures depicted in the paintings—whether human, animal, natural or supernatural—depended more or less extensively upon X-ray representations of anatomical features.

In this form of pictorial presentation the artist visualized the elements meant to represent the bony structure as well as other internal parts of the creatures depicted. X-ray features were commonly positioned within the outline of the creature, thus showing the anatomy under the hide or layers of protective feathers. These X-ray parts were drawn as fairly naturalistic representations or as symbolic forms, but usually little or no attempt was made to accurately replicate a skeleton; a mere suggestion was sufficient. And there was no requirement that the internal parts portrayed should be within the bodies in an anatomically correct place. Frequently such renderings include a cursory portrayal of only the vertebrae and rib cage of the animal or bird being depicted. In addition other visceral organs could also be included (Jonaitis 1986:

130). None of these features are represented by standardized patterns that follow a traditional form or structure. Each artist employed his own sense as to what such parts looked like.

Figure 24 is an excellent example of the X-ray form of presentation. Considerable emphasis was placed on the inner anatomy of the two bear cubs and the centrally positioned grizzly bear that compose the house front painting. Parts contained within the abdomens of these creatures are shown in a variety of different shapes and forms, some having faces that are shown in either frontal or profile perspectives. None conform to the actual shapes or relationships of the organs depicted. Some parts are merely suggested by the rendering of eye design patterns, simple or complex, such as the salmon-trout or double-eye designs.

Yet another example, a superb brush painting on paper by an unknown artist, represents a human form in full stature. (I have drawn this painting for Figure 53.) It probably symbolizes a bird, judging from the featherlike projections above the eyebrows. The X-ray technique is superbly employed. The body contains a detailed display of internal characteristics including spinal column, rib cage, and some visceral organs, a portrayal of the classic best in Northwest Coast art.

The X-ray motif was used in countless different situations. Natural phenomena such as the oval sun or moon symbols not unusually bore within the external outline humanlike figures with rib cages (Figure 41). Figure 17 depicts a mother wolf whose body contains both eye designs and a front-peering face. Figures 23.17 and 23.18 are birds with internal body designs meant to illustrate rib cages and spinal columns. Notice also the stark upright figure centrally positioned in the Kaigani Haida screen in Figure 28. One of the finest examples of X-ray imaging in Northwest Coast painting is the great whale portrayed in Figure 34. Its vertebrae extend over the entire length of the house front from the flukes positioned on the left to the head on the extreme right. Such images are repeated in Figure 37 located in another village. Figure 47 shows two thunderbirds with distinctive portrayals of the body anatomy.

The epitome of X-ray painting is found in Tsimshian and Tlingit examples. They most graphically reveal the artists' efforts to incorporate body parts that are not readily seen. The X-ray technique in conjunction with the several other defining characteristics outlined above work together to define an array of stylistic features employed in Northwest Coast art, features that are instantly recognizable, assuring the art's unique place within the annals of human aesthetic expression.

The Anatomy of the Face

The preceding chapters point out the prominence, indeed, overriding importance bestowed upon the depiction of faces in their great variety in flat painting. Faces appear everywhere in the examples reproduced in this book, from those seen as primary crest symbols to others in seemingly unrelated or inconsequential positions. In addition to the heads that represent various beings, faces are shown with recognizable features in different parts of a being's body and appendages, such as faces that peer out of parted lips or open mouths. There are faces in both frontal and profile representations positioned on dorsal fins, flukes, wings, and tail feathers. Faces are most frequently shown in flat-painted surfaces but occasionally are depicted in detailed sculptured surfaces presented in low relief (Plate 15).

Faces peer out of both animate creatures and inanimate objects, such as clouds, raindrops, rocks, or mountains, to name but a few examples. Two cases in point are the nest in the Eagle's Nest Screen in Figure 18 and the beaver dam in the Beaver Screen of the Wolf Bath House in Figure 7. Another worthy example is the many faces rendered in the crown of Nagunaks shown in Figure 5.1. All the faces have many features in common regardless of what they were purported to symbolize. They had eyes, eyebrows, noses and nostrils, mouths, prominent teeth presented in a variety of shapes, and either naturalistic or greatly embellished tongues.

Eyes might be shown as ovoids enclosed within narrow or wide formlines. Eyebrows were stylized but easily recognizable by the positions assigned to them over the eyes. The eyeball itself could be illustrated containing miniature posturing humanlike figures (Figure 22). Mouths were often shown wide open (Figure 5.1; Plate 32), containing jagged, pointed, squared, rounded, or even scimitar-shaped teeth, fearsome to say the least. Lips might be rendered as two thin bands spread wide apart, or they might be portrayed as thick bands. Occasionally the corners of the mouth were turned downward.

Mouths are particularly significant features: expressive, active, revealing a great range of emotions through their shape, prominence, and teeth. Occasionally the depictions are benign but more usually they are fearsome-looking. Mouths are depicted in simple realism or, alternatively, with immense elaborations including complicated and expansive tongue compositions. They may be included in a variety of design contexts: frontally positioned human faces, eye designs, hands and arms, talons, claws. Figures 1.1, 10, 12, 15, 22, 24, 26, 29, and 31 are good examples. Northern paintings relied on more elaborate tongues in the house front and screen paintings relative to those found further southward.

The manner in which the artists depicted such anatomical features assumed a great latitude and freedom to experiment and to express individual stylistic interests. Yet they remained bound by tradition and stayed close to those tenets laid down by their teachers and by society at large. They also accepted the ancestral vision of the two-fold nature of the universe: the supernatural realm and the world of humankind which extensively impinged and acted upon one another, remaining separate yet inextricably bound together. This supernatural intimacy provided people with the means to explain the interaction of all living creatures. Every physical and organismal element of this Northwest Coast universe could be visualized in some tangible form. It was the artists' challenge and responsibility to give these ideas a visual reality.

A face was portrayed with attributes of a human being even when a human representation might not be intended. Subtle shades of differences prevailed and such clues helped reveal the identity of the spirit or force. For example, a humanlike face was a recognizable feature but it contained within its image the suggestion of feather tips that revealed the true intent of the artist. By the same token, a bird could be shown in human form but a mere suggestion of wing feathers behind its arms told its underlying meaning.

The world of the Northwest Coast artists depended upon these subtle distinctions in order to give visual form to the dual nature of all beings, in order to recognize true identities.

This perceived dual universe with its associated mundane and magical properties was the very essence of the world artists sought to portray. It is a given that such mythological creatures that inhabited the spirit world were not located in the lowest rung of the primordial ladder, but rather occupied the very pinnacle of it by virtue of both the inherent nature of their knowledge and their powers of transformation. They possessed the knowledge of the forces required to make things happen, including moving about from human being to bird or animal or other supernatural creature and back to human form again.

Secondary portrayals of faces therefore emerge as critical features in all the representations in Northwest Coast paintings. Hardly a house front or interior screen exists that does not portray in one form or another a considerable number of facial renderings. Faces are of such fundamental importance that they follow eye designs as the single most frequently utilized design in the art. These facial depictions constitute, in my judgment, the numerically most significant symbols in Northern Northwest Coast paintings.

Eye and Face Designs

The most consistently conspicuous single element in the flat painting compositions, especially in those of the northern coastal tribes, is the eye patterns. This design element was central in the artists' perceptions due to the predominant role the convention played in the art of flat painting. Indeed, if a painting that lacked eye pattern decorations was assigned to the tradition of the Pacific Northwest Coast, it would rightly be deemed inauthentic by a critical native audience.

Any surface decoration—whether a few inches in size or stretching across scores of feet—contained eye patterns as varied and as complex in form as can be imagined. Further, eye designs are included in the most unnatural places—across the anatomy of the creatures depicted as well as in spaces where no figural representations are delineated. Given the universality of this convention, artists sought myriad innovative ways to include them in their compositions. The widespread imposition of eye patterns was particularly important in the Tsimshian tradition. Tsimshian artists continually surpassed themselves in producing the numerous eye designs found in one monumental painting after another.

The Tlingit also were committed to the extensive use of eye designs, as seen in Figures 1.1, 10, 14, 15, and 16.4, for example. But the Tsimshian outdid them. Eye designs appear in the Tsimshian tradition with such frequency and consistency as to dominate the paintings. Such extensive and varied use of this convention is not duplicated among the other tribal groups, particularly those residing southward. To illustrate the extent and ingenuity of this design I have recapitulated the core eye patterns used in the screens known to us. All are northern-style designs, but many of them are replicated among the tribes living to the south. These eye forms were incorporated in differing ways into the local tribal stylistic conventions.

The simplest and most commonly encountered eye pattern is

a solid black sphere or ovoid (Figure 23.1). It can then be slightly elaborated to include an eyelid that encloses the sphere (Figure 23.2). The variations on these two simple patterns are many, for example, the internal extensions of the ovoid form as seen in Figures 23.3 and 23.4. An eye design with a solid black ovoid surrounding the eye seems to have evolved into a form that includes line decorations called light formlines (Figure 23.5). The light formlines may surround the solid black ovoid as well as the central eye itself. From such elementary eye patterns a growing inventory developed, progressively more varied and complex.

Figure 23.6 represents a significant departure from the earlier and simpler patterns to a far more complicated eye design. It was once commonly referred to as the head of a salmon-trout design. This distinctive design is seen in innumerable variations but it does not in any way represent a fish. It is an elaborate ovoid that encloses an eye design that in turn includes a smaller black sphere surrounded by an eyelid. This design is characterized by a very subtle flow of narrowing and expanding lines within this inner eye pattern. Notice the light formline enclosing the salmon-trout eye.

Both single eye structures of this type as well as those with double eye structures were employed along the Northwest Coast. Figures 23.7, 23.8, and 23.9 are examples of double eye designs. In 23.7 the two ovoids are connected and each contains a smaller ovoid surrounded by eyelids. Figure 23.9 exemplifies the gradual proliferation of surface details of double eyes. Figure 23.8 is intended to illustrate the roles various colors play in more sharply defining the respective anatomical regions of the eye designs. I encourage readers to translate these figures to the photographs

and drawings in order to both fully recognize and appreciate the many eye pattern designs contained in painted house fronts and interior screens. For additional details relating to this complex scheme of figuration I recommend a classic study of painted forms by Bill Holm entitled *Northwest Coast Indian Art: An Analysis of Form* (1965).

The above examples represent the common core of the eye designs employed in known paintings. Every artist working in this medium was free to innovate and create new forms, but to be acceptable the work had to fall recognizably and understandably within the tradition. Acceptability was determined by the public-at-large, not by the artist or his coterie. Innovation was good and it was possible, even recognized and rewarded as well as applauded by the people, but any marked deviation from the accepted mainstream conventions was rejected. Public disapproval assured the historic continuity of the tradition. The public was the final judge of an artist's place in the society.

In another widely accepted convention, face patterns were second only to eye patterns in their symbolic significance in Northwest Coast tradition. Both profile and frontal face patterns were employed in house front and interior screen paintings. They were used to emphasize the figures represented by virtue of the space they occupied. As eye designs were utilized to connect arms to shoulders, legs to hips, and to show other joints within the bodies, so face patterns were used to serve similar ends. Faces were not only important decorative devices however, they also served to signify symbolic power beyond the ordinary.

Frontal faces have eyebrows as well as eyelids enclosing simple eye designs. Noses are clearly delineated as are the nostrils and mouths. Mouths have different expressions, from smiling countenances to those baring teeth (Figures 23.10 and 23.11). Profile faces, in contrast, are generally enclosed within a solid black formline as in Figure 23.13. Once again the mouth and nostril are clearly articulated and easily identified as are the stylized eyebrows which cover the width of the ovoid space. Teeth are usually depicted (Figures 23.12 and 23.13) but sometimes are absent (Figure 23.14). Teeth are only occasionally suggested as they are in Figure 23.15. Cross-hatching patterns in red or black may be used to highlight cheek and eye areas, or their anatomical features may only be presented as broken lines breaking up these spaces into smaller units (Figure 23.15). The variables upon these several alternatives run into scores of options providing the artist with wide areas for introducing alternative touches into his work.

Looking beyond these examples of commonly employed conventions to the depiction of birds in the paintings, it becomes obvious how strongly artists relied upon eye patterns to add both symbolic meaning and decoration to otherwise empty spaces. Eye patterns were often inverted, that is, the eye was drawn upside down relative to other figures. Observe the raven tail feathers in Figure 23.16, the eagle in Figure 23.17, and another eagle in Figure 23.18. All were painted with inverted eye designs in both profile and frontal face figures. Notice additionally, the eye patterns enclosed within the talons of the birds in Figures 23.16 and 23.18. Look again at the Tsimshian Sea Monster House Front of the Nagunaks myth (Figure 5.1; Plate 10). Though an initial survey of this immense work might lead the viewer to conclude that the two halves of the painting are mirror images, careful comparison will reveal that they are, in fact, very dissimilar in a number of their secondary design features. Take note of the large number of different eye designs. Many are utilized as space fillers, others as symbols of extraordinary power—palms of hands, foot or knee joints, and flukes and fins as well.

The Extraordinary Place of the Tongue

The portrayal of the tongue is surprisingly common in Northwest Coast painting. This repeated depiction of such an obscure anatomical part forces the sense that the tongue was of considerable symbolic significance to all the Northwest Coast native tribes from north to south. Tongues are to be found in both profile and frontal faces in the paintings. Most are associated with the predominant figures, or occasionally they are portrayed simply as decorative elements in the painting. By contrast a very elaborate tongue is given a central importance in a number of configurations.

Tongues appear more frequently on interior screen paintings than on house front paintings, except among the Tsimshian. The wolves positioned at the base of the Wolf Bath House screen in Figure 7, for example, possess long, slender, realistically drawn tongues. Extremely ornate tongue configurations are in the killer whales' mouths in Figures 1.1 and 5.1. The central dominating figure in the Rain Wall Screen, the ocean-dwelling monster (Figure 10), was also provided with an elaborate tongue. The marvelous rendering of the four ravens in the Raven Screen (Figure 15; Plates 18A and 18B) is enhanced by the inclusion of the symbolic tongues. Figures

30 and 31 depict ravens and thunderbirds, respectively, all bearing ornate tongue configurations. The figure in the Southern Kwakiutl example in Plate 34 likewise displays an intricate tongue.

There has been a good deal of speculation as to what all these elaborate tongues portray, whether in secondary or primary figures, or symbolize. To Aldona Jonaitis, writing about the Tlingit, the protruding tongue generally represents the immense power associated with the utterance of words that originate from supernatural mythological creatures (1986:135). Tongues symbolize special kinds of communication as, for example, between a shaman and the beings in the spirit realm with whom the shaman associates. The imparting of special knowledge through mystic visions may be associated with tongue symbolism. Certainly the numerous ritual paraphernalia associated with chiefly rank and shamanism reveal countless examples of tongue connections between animal, bird, and other creatures of the supernatural realm; however, these renderings are seen on carvings rather than on flat paintings.

When these treasures are advanced to explain the symbolism of tongues in house front and screen paintings they fail, because the raising of flat paintings has never been shown to have anything to do with the workings of shamanism. The crests employed in flat painting may have indeed in the first instance been derived from ancestor exploits or at some point in the past been received as gifts in a spiritual quest. However, so many crests were, in contrast, derived not from such mythic undertakings but rather from the transfer of crest prerogatives amassed out of negotiated marriage dowries between the powerful and influential lineages and clans.

Stanley Walens, writing on the Southern Kwakiutl, advanced the alternative hypothesis that tongues symbolize the priorities the people gave to eating and feasting (1981:12). The central role of these activities in the lives of the natives, particularly of feasting, seems to me to offer the most compelling explanation for the common portrayal of tongues. My own impression, garnered from periodic field work in the region, confirms this association of tongues with the act of eating with supernatural beings and with the concomitant ceremonialism such ritual feasts implied. The ostentatious display of food in quantities far beyond the amount that could be consumed by those attending a feast or potlatch and the subsequent abandonment of that food was a display of great wealth designed to impress and humble the guests. Such feast displays were in line with the principle values driving Northwest Coast Indian culture. Representing this practice in their art, native painters showed mythical creatures with large extended tongues and gaping maws to dramatize a gluttonous appetite, which in turn represented inordinate power and wealth.

Depictions of whales with mouths slightly open are commonplace in house front art but do not relate to tongue symbolism. They display teeth, not tongues, and appear to be hungry or poised to ravenously swallow victims. These designs were more likely intended to intimidate rivals.

I do not subscribe to the hypotheses of many writers who envision hidden or esoteric meanings behind the wide variety of faces with prominent tongues. Some presume sexual meanings, for example. Nor do I view the various orifices as symbols of birth canals, vaginas, or the act of ingesting special powers. Far too many writers find all manner of hidden meanings in these surface decorations and assume the symbolism reveals all kinds of hidden psychological feelings, deeply submerged within the imagery of the art. It is far more likely that artists devoted such attention to facial details in an honest attempt to capture a sense of the creature's vital forces—and hence of the owner's power and wealth—and to provide others with the opportunity of seeing that force, power, and wealth for themselves.

Appendages

Sculptural wood additions were often associated with house front paintings to accentuate prominent features dramatizing primary crest symbols. Such usage extended from the Coast Tsimshian tribes in the north to the tribes in the central coastal areas. These sculptural additions are crude, if imaginative, features that could not have gone unnoticed by visitors to the villages. Some appendages are of enormous size, clearly aimed at generating a sense of awe and power toward the beings represented on the house fronts. In some cases, if one lineage added an impressive appendage to a house front, another lineage followed suit shortly thereafter. Such behavior was a blatant form of one-upmanship on the part of some of the more competitively minded tribal leaders. Appendages are even more ephemeral than the paintings they were meant to enhance, for commonly they lasted but a few years before wind and storm buffeted them to the ground.

In a few cases appendages appear to have been added some time after the completion of the house front paintings they adorned. Whether such additions required additional expenditures by the patron is uncertain, but it would seem likely that they did. The patron would derive little social recognition from this effort without the associated public knowledge of the expenditure of his wealth.

It seems likely that the practice of adding a sculptured appendage to house front imagery was a relatively late custom along the Northwest Coast. Beaks of great birds or dorsal fins of mythical ocean creatures may once have been generically related to carved interior house posts. Or possibly the later custom of totem-pole carving provided the inspiration for adding extensions to crests on house front and screen paintings.

Appendages on interior screens were few in number but are of considerable interest nevertheless. Such appendages remained permanently attached to house screens for they were not exposed to the rigors of the northern Pacific climate. Wherever they appear they add another dimension to the total symbolic effect of the art.

The geographical distribution of house front painting appendages shows that the Tlingit occasionally added appendages to screens and in rare instances to house front paintings. These were minor features, however. One single example is the ears attached to the head of the grizzly bear in the house front painting from Gash village at Cape Fox, Alaska (Plate 25). Two Tlingit interior screens are known to have had added appendages serving as integral parts of their composition. One is Chief Shakes's house screen which had a set of ears attached to the brown bear (Figure 14; Plate 17). The other is the Killer Whale Screen in Klukwan, which had an erect dorsal fin appendage fitted to the topmost plank (Figure 1.1; Plate 1). Tufts of hair were attached to one side of the fin in a final effort toward verisimilitude.

In the Haida region, Chief Gold's house was embellished by a humanlike face representing the moon sculptured from cedar wood. It was attached to the apex of the house front (Figure 29). This sculpture was salvaged from the toppled remnants of the house and is now in a Canadian museum collection.

Among the Coast Tsimshian and their brethren along the Skeena and Nass rivers, house front appendages seem to have been added more frequently, but they were not common. In this case appendages can be construed as a highly imaginative experiment. The most remarkable appendage of all was erected on Chief Sqagwet's Thunderbird House at Fort Simpson (Figure 22; Plate 2). This magnificent Tsimshian painting once sustained an enormous carved beak that required propping and the further support of being attached to a nearby totem pole. It had fallen by the late 1880s and was not replaced. Another pretentious example was mounted at Chief Minesqu's house which once stood along the upper Nass River at Gitlahdamsk village. Its narrow, arrow-straight beak appendage extended far beyond the creature's face (Plate 28). Though it was secured in several places—on the pole directly in front of the house as well as to the two separately erected scaffolds —it did not survive for long. The beak collapsed a few years after the photograph was taken in 1903. The two smaller figures painted on each side of the large central figure also held beak appendages but of a much reduced size. The Tsimshian screen in Figure 25 also had a short, straight beak attached and fitted to the raven's face. Red cedar bark strips were attached to the raven's lower jaw. But these appendages, too, collapsed, deteriorated, and eventually disappeared shortly after a photograph was taken in the early 20th century.

It is among the Southern Kwakiutl tribes that appendages were most extensively used on house fronts, all dating from the 1870s to 1900s. Most notable is the large beak extension fitted to the thunderbird illustrated in Figure 34 and Plate 36. A few years later a nearby house front painting was installed with an enormous beak and maw attached to and supported by the raven totem in front of Chief Wakias's house (Figure 35; Plate 37). A third example is the raven beak fitted to the house front at Gwayasdums village (Figure 38). And for sheer visual intimidation the whale's face with an open mouth revealing a row of formidable-looking teeth installed over the doorway on the house front at Humdaspi is hard to surpass (Figure 33).

Though these appendages added tremendous dramatic impact to the crest symbolism contained in the paintings—a quality the tribal leaders certainly relished—they added no aesthetic value to house front and interior screen paintings. The only artistic value they may possess arises out of the joining of the craft skills of the painter with those of the carver. Whether these distinct skills were possessed by a single person or whether two craftsmen were retained is not known. I incline to the view that both skills were among those every artisan was expected to possess. Evidence suggests that native artists mastered a wide range of artistic skills and were perceptive, curious, cosmopolitan, and prolific in their work.

Having identified and explicated those elements of flat painting that were widely shared among the Northwest Coast tribes, as well as those qualities unique to particular groups of tribes, I turn next to the consideration of the men who created such monumental works of art. Who were the Northwest Coast artists?

"History is no more than memories refined and because memories fade they must be refreshed."

Peter Newman
Caesars of the Wilderness

THE NATIVE ARTIST AND HIS WORLD

THROUGHOUT the previous chapters I have referred briefly to the artists' role in the creation of house front and interior screen paintings. In this chapter the artists become the primary subject. I examine their training, details related to their work and productions, and the pivotal position they occupied within Northwest Coast society.

It is difficult for me to believe that the many examples of flat painting that have survived or were recorded in photographic records are the fruits of only a handful of artists. The few whose work has been preserved and documented must simply be representative of a far larger number of artists. The actual volume of production, suggested by the carvings and paintings presently extant in museum and private collections worldwide, must have been simply staggering. There must have been a force operating in the culture that, encouraged, not only led to the training and supporting of a substantial cadre of craftsmen but also induced the momentum to uphold the values that were intrinsic to the Northwest Coast society. There must have been a system that encouraged, rewarded, and helped to perpetuate the design characteristics, symbolism, and high standards of the craft of painting. Indeed, here was a body of master painters and artists who conceived and executed countless numbers of paintings and carvings —monumental and minuscule in size, on wood, stone, bone, hide, copper, and trade cloth—to nourish the aesthetic and emotional needs of the people, a people dedicated to the repeated explication of the stories that tied them to their past origin and future destiny.

Northwest Coast Indian painting and its symbolic underpinnings were in a continuous state of change, accompanied as they were by discoveries and transformations, adjustments and modifications. A static art it was not. But while visual expressions were changing, the content remained rooted in tradition. In introducing new themes and innovative images, craftsman merely reflected the changing perceptions of their times, encouraged and supported by clan and tribal leaders. New materials were grafted onto older techniques. Entirely new techniques were explored, experimented with, and sometimes accepted and further refined. Those proving useful were more or less quickly incorporated into the canon of aesthetic standards. New tools, new methods, new paints, and new sources of raw materials—even changing demands of production—were combined to enrich and enliven the artists' repertoire and the native world view. Such changes simply reflect the mercurial character of a vital culture and tradition. Scholars

have been able to trace many of these changes through the past to 1700 and earlier.

The native artists were neither the product of a common mold nor doomed repeaters of traditional models. Rather, they were innovators who sought out new and challenging alternatives. At times some were pacesetters of change, introducing new ways, new approaches, and new materials into their work. Others meanwhile codified and legitimized those new elements that seemed in harmony with the tradition.

It has taken a considerable period for Northwest Coast art to receive the recognition and approbation it deserves from the world of museum art. Until the 1950s and 1960s, Northwest Coast Indian art was relegated to the domain of natural history studies, a branch of ethnographic research, rather than being appreciated as a major human aesthetic achievement. Few art museums were interested in the painted and sculptured productions of the North American continent's native population. But akin to the continuous change of the native art forms, attitudes within art museum circles also changed. Finally, Northwest Coast Indian painting is being recognized as a unique and vital creative accomplishment, and the work of contemporary native craftsmen is beginning to be understood to rival that produced by their predecessors of the 18th and 19th centuries.

Facts about the Indian artists themselves, their techniques and means of production, and their training and rewards mostly remain a mystery. Having to rely on oral tradition in the absence of a written history, Western scholars and collectors were little concerned with recording the details of the personal life experiences and technical mastery of the native artists. Unlike the great names associated with the Western art traditions—or, for that matter, those from the magnificently endowed East Asian traditions—little is known of the artists involved in the brief florescence of native art.

Historians have endlessly pursued the most minute aspects of the lives and practices of the great artists from the Western world. They have been analyzed from their childhood forward—family ties, schooling, the masters who taught them, the privations they endured, the ecstasies of their discoveries. Volume after volume has been written about the most intimate aspects and incidents of their lives. Their practices and interests have been repeatedly scrutinized. Finally such details have begun to emerge with respect to a few Northwest Coast artists who lived and worked during the period of cultural transformation of the late 19th century to the mid-20th. The published work provides, unhappily, only a fragile framework encapsulating but limited insights into the lives and works of a handful of late artists. All is lost regarding those artists who worked during the beginning and middle parts of the 19th century—a period when the arts not only flowered but exploded in one village after another up and down the Northwest Coast. The men who created most of the paintings illustrated in this volume may never be fully identified.

A Few Known Artists

One of the most highly regarded interior screens is that known as the Sukheen or Rain Wall Screen, also *Su Cou Nutchi*, or Raindrops Splash Up (Figure 10; Plates 14 and 15). George Emmons nominated this work as the finest painting of its kind in existence (1916:24). Even the name of the painter who made it in the early 19th century is lost. It has been suggested that a Tsimshian artist created it, but its symbolism is that of Tlingit mythology. This screen was possibly produced by a Tsimshian artist who was one of the most prolific painters. Marius Barbeau mentions a man named Kalksek who was an acknowledged master. He is known to have painted six Tsimshian house fronts in the lower Skeena River village of the Gitsees tribe. He likely painted others elsewhere. Barbeau further reported that every one of these house front paintings, as well as other works by this artist, were swept away by a devastating flood in mid-century. Aside from his name, which was provided by Tsimshian informants, nothing is known about Kalksek. Yet informants were specific as to what crests these houses possessed prior to their destruction: Where Stands the Bear House, the Eagle House, the Supernatural Halibut House, Blackfish House (1950:774). To my knowledge, no photographs have survived recording these houses.

Ronald Olson, who did much illuminating research on both Tlingit and Kwakiutl tribes during the early and middle 20th century, writes of what appears to have inspired an unidentified house front artist. Olson tells of Chief Shakes, who resided in Wrangell, and a sea journey that left a deep impression upon him. The chief was made very wealthy thanks to the discovery of gold on the Stikine River. He eventually used some of his riches to built eight lineage houses. The last and the biggest of them was inspired by the sea journey and was named Gonakadet House, the Sea Monster House. Its house front painting depicted a monster who inhabited the vast ocean depths, as in the Nagunaks myth. The monster was positioned on the right side of the house front, and the monster's wife was on the left. Below both figures were representations of their five monster children (1967:105–106). Absent knowledge of Shakes's mythical journey, any interpretation of the figures depicted on this particular house front would have been entirely conjectural and of no genuine substance. This example clearly delineates the grave difficulties incident to interpreting the subject matter within Northwest Coast paintings.

A few more names can be associated with some Tlingit house screens. Though I have assigned artists' names to some screens illustrated in this volume, my basis for so doing is imperiled by certain discrepancies relating to sources and attributes. It is only after cross-checking names from a variety of recorded accounts and in full recognition of often conflicting evidence that I have suggested the names of some Tlingit artists.

One painter is identified as Daniel Benson. He created the Beaver Screen in the Wolf Bath House in Yakutat in 1905 (Figure 7). Benson also painted the screen in the Moon House in the same village and possibly a third screen, the Raven and King Salmon Screen (Plate 22), now in the Sheldon Jackson Museum in Sitka (de Laguna 1972:323). Benson was born in 1869 into the Teqwedi clan on the wolf side of the Tlingit tribe in Yakutat. He was a hunchback. At the elementary levels he was educated in Sitka. As a young adult in the years following 1886 he found employment as a law court translator and interpreter. He was also known as a capable totem pole carver and carver of ceremonial paraphernalia. In his mature years he served as an interpreter for missionaries stationed in Yakutat (de Laguna 1972:322–323). That he worked for missionaries yet painted the traditional crest screens for the clan houses raises intriguing questions. All but this meager information about him is lost.

Another artist's name kept cropping up in my research, a Tlingit man named Yehlh Nawu, or Dead Raven. He belonged to the Tluknaxadi ravens in Sitka. In the later years of the 19th and the early years of the 20th centuries he painted several screens, including the Golden Eagle or Kadjuk Screen (Plate 23). He was also identified as the artist who created the painting on the Killer Whale Dorsal Fin House in Angoon (Plate 20). While in Sitka in 1990, I inquired of several Tlingit whether they had heard his name. One man volunteered that he believed a gravestone bearing that name was located in the Sitka cemetery. Not wanting to offend the tribe's desire for privacy, I asked whether he would inquire and provide me with information as to any dates inscribed on the headstone. He agreed to do so, but to my chagrin I never heard from him despite several appeals. Such frustrating dead ends marked most of my efforts.

A Tlingit man named In Everybody's Arms Father, a Tluknaxadi raven, may have been a clan brother of Dead Raven. For a time he resided in Douglas, Alaska. He was known as the artist who painted the Thunderbird Screen in Yakutat (Figure 6). It was standing in the clan house when I drew it in 1949. Now it is housed in the Alaska State Museum in Juneau, but its former owner was Frank Italio who inherited rights to it from a maternal uncle. Italio provided the story associated with this former clan property, the story of Qwachna and the thunderbird. This screen of the late

19th century is an accomplished work. It is difficult to believe it was this man's only effort, but no other screens have been attributed to him to date.

Other Tlingit artists of this period were Rudolph Walton and Tom Coxe. The former was from Hoonah village and was another possible creator of the Raven and King Salmon Screen (Plate 22). Coxe painted a golden eagle screen that was once the property of the Drum House people in Yakutat. Through my investigations I came across a number of men who were known as Sitka Jack, Sitka Jim, and Sitka Charley, all identified as artists, but the nature and locations of their works are unknown.

Among the Haida, carvers were considered the supreme masters of Northwest Coast art. Some also painted, but the house screens and house fronts were not among their acknowledged interests or accomplishments. A famed carver named Charles Edenshaw is considered by many to represent the epitome of the artists' achievements. His mother's oldest brother was a leading chief of the eagle division of the Kiusta village, which was located on the northern tip of Graham Island in the Queen Charlottes. The chief was also a noted artist who carved and painted totem poles. Edenshaw eventually succeeded his uncle as chief. He was considered a man of great integrity and modesty; many scientists visiting the islands sought him out as a source of information about his people. Edenshaw carved in a great range of materials: giant cedar, for canoes and totem poles, ivory, and carbonaceous shale, also called argillite stone. He was a skilled silversmith, and he made drawings in pencil and paper of beings from Haida mythology. These were often employed as illustrations in various scientific and ethnographic publications at the turn of the century. A man of such high status and creative talent appears but rarely in any society.

Another Haida artist, Geneskeles, is known as the painter of a masterful set of designs that graced an enormous dugout canoe now stored in a warehouse in the National Museum of Natural History in Washington, D.C. He died of smallpox in 1876. There is no question that other painters worthy of note were living at about the same time, but their names have escaped researchers. As my research efforts turned to the Southern Kwakiutl territory the names of artists became even more difficult to document. All significant details continue to elude detection.

But the painting tradition has not entirely spent itself. Among several of the tribes, a number of painters as well as wood carvers have become active participants in the effort to slow and reverse the steep decline in traditional cultural practices, to preserve some semblance of the noble late 19th-century past. Modern carvers and painters are at work reclaiming the elements of their crafts to become accomplished masters within the native tradition.

Apprenticeship of Young Artists

It is a nearly impossible task to separate the social role of the artist from that of Northwest Coast native life as a whole. Artists and their work were part of the very marrow of the culture. The artists provided the visual images required to give sensory substance to the range of entrenched social beliefs and privileges that made up the fabric of the society. Artists brought important elements of the spectrum of traditional beliefs and visions into appropriate focus and illustrated again and again the people's perceptions of their environment, their universe, and themselves. They transformed much of this vast invisible world into a visually recognizable reality through their paintings and sculptures. Despite the role such men played in Northwest Coast life, little information has survived on the details of their education, artistic development, and lifestyle. Notwithstanding the major gaps in late 20th-century knowledge about their world, a few generalizations may cast some light on certain aspects of their development.

Northwest Coast native society developed a highly stratified class system within each tribe. People were not equal and seem never to have sought to be. Each person was recognized as holding a particular graded position involving rank and power. Each person occupied one or another of a series of rungs in the social order based on membership in his or her particular tribe, lineage, or clan. These gradations depended decisively upon the rank of the family into which one was born and on the birth order within that family. People were measured and judged according to these numerous subtle levels of rank, which revealed themselves through the wealth and power that a person commanded, the names one inherited from ancient and venerable ancestors, and other forms of socially recognized power.

This social class system was divided into two basic groups supplemented by a nonclass group. Forming the apex and the leading group in the power structure were the aristocratic families who occupied, on the basis of being first born, the highest social ranks. They held the positions of power, controlling the economic resources of the tribe, the ceremonial life, and the public displays of wealth and power that perpetuated family prestige and position. The second group included the vast mass of common tribal members. These were the lower-ranked members of tribe, lineage, or clan. They possessed fewer inherited marks of rank and status, fewer honorary names. They were regarded as the poorer relatives of those who dominated the power structure.

The dregs of this social system were the nonclass, the slaves. Never overly numerous, rarely representing any value in purely economic terms, they nevertheless were important in the social structure as a portion of the wealth of aristocratic families. Slaves were never an integral part of any tribe. They were acquired in quick-strike raids by one tribe or village against another. The unfortunates captured in such raids lost all rights to existence. The stigma of having once been a slave or having descended from slaves was never expunged. Raiding and slavery were terminated soon after the arrival of European settlers in the late 19th century, but as late as the 1940s informants advised me to avoid speaking to or associating with particular individuals because they were descendants of slaves and therefore unworthy of my attention.

Within the traditional culture, social etiquette and particular practices were rigidly defined for both male and female members. In major part these activities, obligations, responsibilities, and attitudes were rooted in the entrenched class structure of the culture. A gender-exclusive division of labor was a prominent feature of their lives. Men never performed tasks traditionally assigned to women nor did women undertake those activities that were within the domain of men. Thus, women neither carved nor painted;

such activities were male status positions intimately associated with ceremonial, ritual, or even quasi-religious observances.

Among the distinct social castes there was no specialized class of craftsmen. Artists were drawn from the ranks of the aristocratic families and from those near the highest echelon of power within the tribe. Few from the commoner class could aspire to such ranks, primarily because an artist's work dealt with honors and status symbols of the high ranks. A sufficient depth of understanding of the history and symbolism of the subject matter demanded from childhood onwards continual exposure to the stories, rituals, and ceremonies themselves. This lifelong learning was closed to commoners. They were in essence barred from access to the rituals, ritual paraphernalia, and the large body of lore associated with the tribal crests, ancestral history, and power prerogatives.

Moreover, it was a requirement that the artist speak of such matters only with his chiefly patrons. Commoners were forbidden direct communication involving rituals, ceremonies, and their symbolism. A chief could not negotiate with a commoner, only with those of equal or relatively equal social rank. Not only was it beneath the patron's dignity to do so, but he would violate a major tribal taboo by discussing such esoteric matters with ordinary people. Such discourse would result in a loss of face and be seen as a degradation, an indignity. Though artists were entitled to speak with the elite classes with respect to their needs for display and the theater of power, they were to adopt a deferential position in both their mien and language.

There were well-defined ways in which an aspiring young man could enter the circle of carvers and painters. An apprentice relationship with a recognized master was the principal avenue to such a role. The young aspirant probably demonstrated at an early age a precocious preoccupation or predilection for carving or painting. Most commonly, only youths possessing suitable kinship ties found a ready opportunity to apprentice with an established artist. However, a youth's recurrent dreams of being an artist or an apprentice might be interpreted by tribal elders as a sign of supernatural sanction or guidance entitling a youth of higher rank to learn to carve or paint. If such a dreamer showed a compelling desire to enter into the arts, both his parents and lineage leaders would create ways to enable the young man to receive guidance from a respected artist. Whether instigated by predilection, precociousness, kinship ties, or dreams, apprenticeship in the arts required a lengthy service involving hard work, discipline, commitment, and patience.

Under the watchful eyes of his master, a young apprentice learned all the necessary tools of the trade, including how to communicate appropriately with the prospective or actual client. Also, the student was required to learn to satisfactorily fashion the great variety of tools that each medium regards for its execution. But to fashion tools that fit the peculiarities of the boy's particular motor habits and skills was not sufficient. The carving apprentice had to learn all the nuances and subtleties associated with each blade angle and curve. The painting apprentice was further required to learn the drafting skills necessary for the preparation and formalization of the many design elements demanded for a worthy composition. He also learned the secrets of preparing the paints.

The successful apprentice had to become fully familiar with a rich panoply of history and symbolism of the tribes and to know the rules of the structured mode of negotiation and communication required to deal with demanding patrons. The successful apprentice also had to become fully familiar with the methods and techniques of carving and painting. He must know how to utilize the woods best suited to specific tasks or needs, how to conceptualize the design commensurate with the commission at hand, and how to utilize the techniques instilled by the master.

Throughout the apprentice's training he was given little freedom of choice. He imitated the master's techniques; he copied the master's designs, procedures, embellishments. Copying the master was the fundamental learning method followed along the entire Northwest Coast. To duplicate a master's every move, to follow his instructions without question, was the framework upon which every apprentice built his craft. In all things he was expected to follow without question the principles the master established with respect to preparation, analysis, and production of space, as well as color relationships.

When the apprentice had eventually proved himself to the satisfaction of his master, the young man was entitled to accept commissions on his own merit. It was only at this point that the emerging artist began to breathe the fresh air of a new-found freedom that allowed him to accept the challenge of fulfilling chiefly demands. Now he could begin to work toward gaining the recognition and rewards that would accrue if his work found acceptance in the rarefied world of Northwest Coast pageantry. As for the master he would be compensated for training his apprentice in trade goods, food resources and other commodities by the young man or his family.

The Transitional Artists

As noted earlier, the life histories of the artists who prepared house front and screen paintings during the changing 19th century remain elusive. In the early 20th century several men of exceptional talent and experimental minds appeared on the scene. They have proved to be a fragile and uncertain thread linking the rapidly fading traditional past with slowly awakening modern interest.

One of the foremost of these transitional artists was Charley James, also known as Yakuglas, or the Gifted One. Born around 1876, he was the son of a white sawmill operator and a Fort Rupert Kwakiutl woman. Following his mother's premature death, James was sent to live with his maternal grandmother in Victoria. Early on he was drawn to the arts of his mother's native culture, and through whatever means then available he gradually acquired a sense of native carving and painting. He was a prodigiously active artist despite having suffered the loss of his left hand, the result of a shotgun accident (Nuytten 1982:13). Little is known as to his instruction—perhaps he was self taught—but he must have had enormous determination and a profound curiosity in order to persevere in a period in which the native arts were not only being discouraged but more importantly were rapidly disintegrating due to the radically different social and political environment that had emerged.

Charlie James was not only a prolific carver, he also produced a large number of paintings of creatures drawn from Kwakiutl mythology on wooden boards that he sold to white visitors as curios. He employed similar paintings as monumentally sized memorials displaying the crests belonging to deceased members of the tribe; these were erected in village cemeteries (Plates 43, 44, and 45). There is no question that his inquiring imagination and extraordinary productivity had an immense impact on aspiring artists from the various Kwakiutl tribes in the region. He was for a time an instructor in carving at the residential Indian school in Alert Bay where he lived. James painted totem poles, memorial crest figures, masks used in the winter ceremonial dance dramas, in addition to souvenirs for tourists. Not only did these undertakings bring him welcome income, they also helped keep alive the Kwakiutl artistic traditions.

James's most famous student was his stepson, Mungo Martin, who was actually only six or seven years younger. They were as much friends and colleagues as relatives. Mungo Martin, also named Nakapunkim, or Ten Times a Chief, was born in 1880 or 1881 in Fort Rupert. From a tender age he was involved with James in a master–apprentice relationship. This productive alliance proved of immense benefit to the Kwakiutl cultural revival that took place in the years that followed. As a young apprentice Martin was given blocks of wood to carve under James's watchful eye. With these he was expected to recreate the formal characteristics associated with the various mythological beings who inhabited the sea and sky worlds. But following James's practice, Martin was

encouraged to not only carve but to paint on wood. Martin was forever painting on whatever materials might come to hand, including paper dining plates when no other materials were available. All his themes were drawn from the rich mythological heritage of the tribe (H. Hawthorn 1961 and Nuytten 1982).

It was Martin's mother, the daughter of a Scottish employee of the Hudson's Bay Company and a Kwakiutl woman, who first sought a place in the arts for her son. When still an infant she took him to a famous carver and asked that he assure her son's future as an artist. The artist undertook a short ritual: he plucked four of the baby's eye lashes, mingled them with porcupine guard hairs, and made them into a paint brush. He then used that brush to paint signs meant to assure that Martin would one day become a painter. This mystical ritual was efficacious beyond his mother's wildest expectations (British Columbia Indian Arts Society 1982:1).

Unlike James, Martin became a chieftain of his tribe in Fort Rupert circa 1948 when he was in his early sixties. He was the second son of a high-ranking chief who originally came from the Gilford Island people. His older brother Spruce Martin had succeeded their father as chief after being invested with the position and all the prerogatives of the rank through the vehicle of the potlatch. However, Spruce died prematurely some time after 1946 whereupon Mungo, as next in line to the chieftainship, stepped forward to claim the vacated position as traditional practice required. As with Spruce before him, Mungo could not assume this high rank nor validate his claim to so lofty a position until he also potlatched. This sequence of events has remained true for other modern Kwakiutl artists who were born into well-placed families and who eventually succeeded to positions of leadership within their respective tribes.

Martin reached his early twenties before James concluded that he was ready to take work on his own. The student had fulfilled all the requirements stipulated by his master. Martin had proved his mastery of the craft of carving and painting and had absorbed the surviving fragments of traditional lore and symbolism. He shortly thereafter was commissioned to carve a totem pole for a patron residing in Alert Bay (H. Hawthorn 1961:64). It proved his first success. This achievement led quickly to other commissions. One of Martin's most notable projects was a painted house front commissioned by a man named Komogwe, a name derived from that of a mythical being who ruled over all the occupants of the ocean world (Plate 38). It was the most important crest of the leader of this lineage who resided in Gwayasdums village (Nuytten 1982:77).

Despite Martin's growing fame as an artist he was unable to support his family with earned commissions. His primary occupation, like all the other artists before him, was that of a hunter and salmon fisherman. Only those traditional pursuits yielded the means to maintain a lifestyle commensurate with his rank and chiefly position. It was only in his most senior years that he was able to devote his entire effort and energy to painting and carving. Unlike most of the renowned artists of the Northwest Coast, for whom carving and painting were no more than periodic supplements to income, Martin was for 10 years or more at the end of his life able to maintain a reasonable income as an artist. Part of his well-being came out of his association with the University of British Columbia and the Royal British Columbia Museum in Victoria. In his later years he increasingly drew with pencil, crayons, and water colors. His output was prodigious; his hands, nimble and sure, appeared to never rest (Nuytten 1982:77–78).

Martin undertook a ritual parallel to that employed in his case when the mother of his grandson Tony Hunt sought Martin's help in guiding the boy to a life in art. Martin instructed his wife to sew Tony's dried umbilical cord into a piece of cloth from which a crude bracelet was fashioned. Martin wore it while he carved and from time to time he would recite certain chants that he believed to have magical powers. He followed this ritual for four years—the time he believed required for the magic involved to take effect. These rituals were thought to have led to Tony Hunt's ultimate success as an artist.

A contemporary of James and Martin was the Blunden Harbour artist named Willie Seaweed of the Nakwoktak Kwakiutl tribe. Like Martin, Seaweed was born into a family of the highest social status. He was a chief in his own right, both his parents were descended from chiefly lines. Seaweed's entire life was spent in producing carvings and paintings flowing out of Kwakiutl traditions. He was, however, also a daring innovator, having developed a distinctive style in the carving of ceremonial masks, totem poles, painted screens, and house fronts during the early years of the 20th century. Several cloth screens have been attributed to Seaweed's creative and forceful genius (Holm 1983:80–83). Figure 45 is one such example. Others are now located in the collections of various individuals and museums. It is thought that a few examples may also still be among the possessions of some of the leading Kwakiutl families.

Bill Holm wrote a definitive study of Seaweed's emergence as one of the foremost artists of the early 20th century (1983). Unfortunately, Holm was unable to trace Seaweed's formative years. However, by the age of 20 he was an established carver of considerable skill. His precocious achievement somewhat belies evidence of the lengthy apprenticeship with a master usually required to establish oneself. But Seaweed was an exceptional individual; not only did he occupy the most highly ranked position within his tribe but also he was acknowledged as a dancer of great skill, a composer of songs, and a witty and masterful raconteur. In addition he was regarded as unusually generous as befitted his chiefly status.

Seaweed (1873–1967), Charlie James (1876–1948), and Mungo Martin (1880–1962) formed a powerful triumvirate that shaped and directed the revival of Kwakiutl sculpture and painting at a time when these arts had been virtually lost—even forbidden—due to the adoption of Western ways both by personal choice and by the dictates of government and church. These three men collectively set in motion a powerful tide that directed the energies of not only their contemporaries but of aspiring artists of succeeding generations as well. A number of other artists were at work in the various Kwakiutl villages during this period, men like Arthur Shaughnessy (1884–1945) and George Walkus, to name

just two of the second rank. Bennie and Jimmie Dick of remote Kingcome Inlet were also exceptionally talented men. All were in varying degrees productive, forceful, imaginative, and capable artists. All helped to preserve fragments of the Kwakiutl cultural heritage.

It is exceedingly important to note that the traditional meanings, practices, and uses of art amongst the Tlingit had virtually disappeared by the early decades of the 20th century. The few known artists from Tlingit country represent the last dying gasp of the traditional arts among these people at the turn of the century. Neither the mental nor artistic world of the 20th century resembled, save in the most fragmentary way, that of only 50 years earlier. Young artists were not being raised and trained in classic Tlingit tradition. No Haida painters were at work by the late 19th century. The Tsimshian artists had disappeared as well as those from among the Bella Coola tribes in central British Columbia. Northern Kwakiutl artists fared no better. All suffered vast losses in both cultural value and artistic expertise as a part of the severe culture hemorrhaging experienced by all the tribes. This fate was equally shared by the Nuu chaa nulth artists from the west coast of Vancouver Island. The vast bulk of the traditions and practices associated with the painting arts had simply vanished into thin air by the early decades of the 20th century.

But in the remotest recesses of the British Columbia coastal fjords and inlets, far from contact with government agents and white settlers, a small coterie of artists continued the carving and painting traditions of the Southern Kwakiutl tribes. They did so surreptitiously and mostly to serve their own status and ceremonial needs. Here alone along the great stretch of the Northwest Coast was the exception to what was a kind of cultural disappearance. Here alone the practicing and transferring of customs and beliefs of native art continued, mortally wounded, limping badly, but somehow still alive in the minds of the people.

A later artist whose example became a major influence in the development of Kwakiutl art in the middle of the 20th century was Henry Speck (1908–1968), or Ozistalis, of Alert Bay. He moved in the direction of nontraditional media and contemporary forms, most notably a precursor of printmaking. I have known Speck's paintings since the early 1960s. Much of his work portraying supernatural beings on both cardboard and commercial art paper was explicitly produced for the commercial art market. As can be imagined, Speck's work had an enormous impact on Canadian commercial Indian art sales.

Speck's chiefly name, Ozistalis, is derived from the enormous mythical bird, the Great One. The name was first owned by a man who called himself Tzay'komay, Cedar Bark Man. As Speck explained the story to me in 1965, Tzay'komay asked the great bird what his name was. "I am called Ozistalis," the bird answered. "I wish you were a real man," Cedar Bark Man replied. Ozistalis answered by pulling off his bird mask and garment to reveal his human form. The Great One married Tzay'komay's daughter whereupon both the human bird and the name became the special crest of their descendants.

Speck was born into an aristocratic family of the Tlawitsis Kwakiutl tribe living on Turnour Island, which lies to the east of Alert Bay. At an early age he began painting and drawing pictures, claiming his right to do so through his maternal grandfather who had been both a chief and an artist. During the 1960s, only shortly before his death, Speck became something of an artistic celebrity. His paintings were shown in galleries in Vancouver, Ottawa, Toronto, and other Canadian cities as well as Seattle, San Diego, Chicago, and finally in London. An enthusiastic following arose with his growing popularity in Canadian art circles.

I suspect some of the cloth crest screens still extant in Kwakiutl villages were made by Speck during his formative and maturing years. The style and handling of these cloth screens parallel his later illustrations (Plates 46 and 47). Speck was, as were Martin and Seaweed before him, keenly aware of the striking visual impact of the northwest tradition and so sought to employ the same imagery as fully as possible.

Among the northern Northwest Coast tribes, the Tlingit and Tsimshian in particular, both chiefly and artistic functions were filled through a matrilineal system of descent. Thus, the chief's oldest sister's first son was usually elevated to these esteemed positions. Virtually no information is available as to the early training and practice of those who entered an apprenticeship with a master painter. The information about Southern Kwakiutl practices may well have no relevance to Tlingit or Tsimshian practices, because after the 1880s Southern Kwakiutl social systems had largely been replaced by elements of those of the American and

Canadian colonizers. Nor have any in depth studies been undertaken to learn of modern Tlingit or Tsimshian artists and their practices.

The Commissioning of a Painting

In few aboriginal cultures around the world was the artist held in higher esteem by the native society than along the Northwest Coast. In even fewer cases yet was a group of trained artists so central to the aesthetic expressions of native societies. But even in such a relatively unique and apparently desirable setting, the limited opportunities for artists to ply their craft meant that their primary means of making a living required wresting a subsistence from the environment in precisely the same way as their tribal compatriots. Hunting and fishing were the basic pursuits undertaken by all artists regardless of the esteem accorded them or the positions they occupied within their respective tribes. Commissions were, therefore, undertaken only during the less demanding food-gathering seasons. The sole exception to this general practice was the rare occasion when a powerful and rich patron subsidized an artist's needs for a year or more in exchange for immediate attention to a commission. Regardless of the season, a house front or screen painting involved weeks if not months for preparation and execution. A work on such a scale required many resources, often including the assistance of several other people.

Before commissioning a painter the patron chieftain would confer with the artist of his choice as to the general type of house front painting he had in mind and the nature of the upcoming social event for which it was being commissioned. These conferences took place either at the artist's residence or in the long house of the patron. Since the contracts were necessarily verbal, the patron was usually accompanied by either a retinue of assistants or another high-ranking tribal member to act as witness to the negotiations and the nature of the agreement reached (Holm 1983:29). Once a work was commissioned, it was up to the artist to bend himself single-mindedly toward the realization of all the subtleties of the patron's needs and desires and toward completing the work to the chief's approval and satisfaction.

To receive the visiting chief of another village for the purpose of negotiating the painting of a house front or screen conferred great honor upon the artist. It enhanced his standing in the eyes of not only his kinsmen but other tribal leaders contemplating the commissioning of a screen. Receipt of the previously agreed payment only further raised the artist's reputation. It was considered beneath the dignity of a rich leader to quibble about the sum that was to be paid for an artist's services, once the nature of the commission had been agreed upon. The higher the price the greater the prestige for both artist and benefactor. Though no chief worthy of such an elevated social position could honorably haggle over price, the craftsman was in turn expected to refrain from negotiating an outrageous sum. To do so would only be construed as an effort to embarrass and insult a man of honorable station. Furthermore, to do so might even lead to unpleasant consequences.

Payment was necessarily in goods in kind, for the natives lacked a monetary system. Such payments were not limited to foodstuffs and similar basic resources but also included valuable utilitarian objects. With the introduction of a monetary system, Canadian and American currencies tended to replace woolen trade blankets, food supplies, canoes, or metal utensils. Several screens made by Tlingit artists are known to have attracted commissions of several hundreds of dollars. Goods or money was, however, only a part of the payment the artist received. Enhancement of his worth to the tribe, the heightened respect and deference accorded him by other tribal leaders, the augmentation of his fame and recognition, and a personal sense of satisfaction and fulfillment all were further benefits of a successfully completed commission. Widespread recognition of the contribution the artist made to the status and power accorded a particular tribal leader also reflected favorably upon him. Public acknowledgment of the craftsman's role in a work frequently led other chieftains to contemplate a commission. These other rewards were of greater worth in the eyes of the natives than the tangible payment.

Most commonly, the agreement for a painting required the artist to move temporarily to the patron's village to complete the commission, but, on occasion, the project might be executed in the artist's village and then transported to the patron's. The several extant screens in the houses of clans in Yakutat, for example, were painted elsewhere. If the artist was required to move to the patron's village, he was expected to receive the hospitality commensurate with his own elite position in terms of both lineage and his ceremonial function as the creator of the work. He was thus treated with the protocol befitting both his position and the cordiality of a highly visible dignitary.

The Artist at Work

Following the commissioning of a house front painting or interior screen, the artist was compelled to formulate a composition that met the patron's requirements. Models might be constructed to assist in visualizing those symbolic emblems and their relationships as recounted by the patron in the interviews. Not infrequently artists resorted to earlier paintings for examples.

Once the design was in place the practical problems of acquiring the requisite materials had to be resolved. Many plank boards had to be cut, squared, smoothed, adzed, and finally assembled, but not joined, to obtain a surface of the required dimensions. This process was greatly simplified with the introduction of lumber mills into the region. Shrinkage of the wood and its subsequent stabilization in the final production demanded not only careful consideration but much accumulated experience with wood joinery. Holes were usually drilled with special tools at certain points in the planks so they could eventually be united to form an integrated composition without sagging or disjointing. Some house front paintings required as many as 24 individual planks, many in excess of 24 to 30 inches (60.1 to 76.2 cm) wide and 2 inches (5.1 cm) thick. Several interior screens contain 10 or more individual planks of similar dimensions.

All the boards required for a house front or interior painting were assembled on a flat surface. Having previously formulated the composition in his mind's eye or in a model, the artist then began to lay out the larger elements of the composition using charcoal. If the initial drawing was imperfect or in other ways did not meet the artist's satisfaction the offending portions could be rubbed out and redone.

When the general outline was completed on the planks, the black line patterns were then drawn into place. This procedure required considerable time as adjustments in line and design were almost always necessary. The artist had to ask himself, Does the design outline flow smoothly and accurately from one board to the next in a satisfactory manner? Do the design elements require some modification so they work more closely together to form a unified pattern? Might wood shrinkage eventually lead to a distortion of design? If so, would this adversely effect its visual impact on the public?

Preparing the outlines of the crest figure was only the first matter to be resolved. The inner details that shaped and gave character to the figures were as important as the overall pattern in achieving the social effects being sought. They called for as much in ingenuity and creative instinct as the outline. In preparing the intricate surface details within the design the artist typically employed a series of templates or stencils of varying sizes and shapes, which he personally prepared and cut. No two stencils were exactly the same in shape and size. For example, templates representing a simple eye pattern were not interchangeable with those of the more intricate kind. The stencils were cut from the inner bark of red or yellow cedar trees. The preparation of and the uses of stencils was one of the most crucial skills gained through ap-

prenticeship. Stencils were a critical link in the creation of monumentally sized paintings.

Stencils or templates were not only made for the eye patterns. They also were utilized to standardize other elements in the design complex such as limb joints, wings, tails, viscera, dorsal fins, and flukes. The stencils for each painting had to be carefully and properly shaped as they markedly impacted the overall harmony of the painting. Because a multitude of stencils was required for each painting—in some examples 40 or more—it was critical that the artist keep a close mental inventory as to which stencils were to be employed for each particular part of each crest figure's anatomy and features.

It is worthwhile to note the number of templates required to complete a painting such as those illustrated in Figures 22, 24, and 26. As George Emmons recounts, the native artist positioned each stencil at the place to be painted and then traced the outline in charcoal (1990:199–200). Moving from one stencil to the next, the entire design was gradually built. The artists usually started with the face of each figure, followed by the details of and within the body cavity, and then the other features such as appendages (Figures 55, 56, and 57). Following the completion of one side of the outline of a bilateral figure, the templates were then turned over to the opposite side of the figure and the design reproduced in an identical fashion. The typical bilateral symmetry of the traditional crest design gradually took shape in this way.

This job required uninterrupted attention and intense concentration to be certain the correct stencil was being used and that it and its counterparts fit precisely within the anatomical feature depicted. If mistakes were made—and some were inevitable in such a complex effort—the lines of charcoal were washed out and the process restarted from the beginning. To prevent such an unhappy outcome the artist frequently paused to assess the development of the overall effort of the painting. Needless to say, this exacting process was time consuming. It was a task that could not be rushed, nor could it be completed within a stipulated time frame.

Note the details of each painted panel reproduced in this book. Particularly, think of the kind of control implicit in the swelling and flowing of each formline feature. Some swelling and constricting of lines within these various forms were important characteristics of many Northwest Coast paintings. Some lines narrow to almost pencil-line thinness, which required great dexterity as well as virtuosity of control in the use of the brush. Further, it is important to remember that rough wooden surfaces were being painted, not paper. The mastery and control of knife, paint, and brush border on the truly remarkable. Closely examining the painted flat surfaces reveals that the best of the Northwest Coast craftsmen had not only superb command of the medium but an astonishing control of the details. Their work reveals a confidence in their skills that is little short of awesome. Remember that once paint is applied to wood, no amount of erasing will correct mistakes.

Among the artists' most important tools were the many types of traditional brushes. These varied in size from as fine as a pencil point to an inch or more wide. Most projects required as many as 12 to 18 brushes of various widths to obtain the variations in size and nature of the strokes commonly employed. Even the most cursory examination of the illustrations included herein reveals the incredibly diverse kinds of brush strokes used in these paintings.

According to George Emmons the brushes the Tlingit used were largely made from porcupine guard hairs. Stems and handles were mostly made of cedar wood but some were of bone or ivory (1990:196). All brushes were fashioned flat in shape rather than tapered. To assemble the brushes the wooden handles were split and the hairs and bristles were then arranged evenly in the slot to project half an inch (1.3 cm) or more beyond the wood's edge. The handle was then wrapped tightly with split spruce root to secure the bristles in place. I witnessed artists take strands of hair from their heads and in a matter of seconds prepare a brush for immediate use. Hilary Stewart has pointed out that occasionally painters in the southern regions of the Northwest Coast used their fingers to paint rather than brushes (1984:98), but I did not hear of such a technique from the artists I interviewed during the 1940s and 1950s. Exclusively animal hair brushes were used in the north.

The paints were traditionally prepared by pulverizing various mineral elements and mixing them with salmon or trout roe to provide the adhesive. The colors in the illustrations in this book appear to be uniform because they utilize modern methods of reproduction employing sophisticated standardized techniques. The original paintings, by contrast, are characterized by many different shades of red and blue-green, reflecting the diverse sources of pigment as well as the different periods in which the colors were prepared. Even the color black varied in intensity from one area and time period to another.

Artists might proceed with either one of two procedures when applying the paints to the planks. In the first case, the planks were laid flat on the ground, the painting was completed, the planks were joined, and the painting mounted. In the second case, the painting was done on the assembled planks after they had been raised into position on the house itself. Modern Northwest Coast artists, when preparing contemporary museum exhibitions of house front paintings, such as the Tsimshian installation in the Canadian Museum of Civilization, invariably lay the wood planks flat on the floor for the painting (Figures 55, 56, and 57). By contrast, photographs taken during the early decades of the 20th century in a Southern Kwakiutl village portray artists painting from scaffolds; those planks had been raised and secured to the exterior front walls of the long house before painting. Early photographs, however, seldom picture scaffolding. Laying out the planks on a spacious flat surface to work out the design and apply the paint seems to be the earlier or preferred technique.

Some scholars, dissenting from this view, point to the grave mechanical difficulties that would face the craftsmen in raising a fully assembled painting from the ground to its vertical position on the house front. However, it must be recognized that the Northwest Coast Indians were experts in the utilization of the wood resources locked up in the enormous trees among which they lived. They had clearly perfected the technology of raising the enormous beams to build their large long houses. They would have experienced little difficulty in adapting this technology and procedure for raising not only totem poles but also large assembled paintings.

Whether the painting was done before or after mounting the planks on the house front, the problem of securing the planks remained largely the same. The standard means of fastening was to thread thongs of rawhide through many minute holes drilled along the edges of the planks. This lacing held the planks firmly in place for a few years. The lashings were so skillfully executed that they were virtually undetectable. They are hardly visible in the photographs in this book. An alternative technique for stabilizing house front paintings is illustrated in Figure 31. In this case slender poles taller than the height of the assembled planks were placed vertically from the ground up at intervals along both the front and back of the painting. Thongs were then employed to tie the poles together, securing the planks in between. The relative fragility of the lacing holding the planks together was simply not a matter of concern because of the ephemeral use of most paintings. They were soon disassembled, removed, or allowed to decay, or in a few cases were stored for future use.

Further Questions

One might raise the question, Did the artists copy ideas from one another? Copying per se was widely employed as a legitimate means of learning the skills involved in painting and carving, a practice that could also help explain the apparent similarities between particular paintings mounted in widely scattered villages. There is no doubt in my mind that most of the stylistic features common to such paintings were borrowed, incorporated into other work, and embellished by later copyists.

Take, for example, the Tsimshian traits that passed northward into Tlingit country and southward into Northern Kwakiutl villages, gradually infiltrating Southern Kwakiutl and Bella Coola areas as well. Notice the similarity in composition of the Coast Tsimshian artists' work and the paintings later produced for houses in Fort Simpson and Gitlahdamsk and on the Rain Wall Screen in Klukwan (Figures 22, 26, and 10 respectively). Notice the border figures common to them all. To more decisively see evidence of a tradition of copying, compare the miniature border figures in all the above examples with those in Figure 53, a painting made on commercially produced paper. The border figures in all are strikingly similar. The painting reproduced in Figure 53 probably dates back to the late 19th century, and as importantly, it is only 33 by 36 inches (83.8 by 91.4 cm) in size, clearly a work of entirely different scope and intent than its stylistic predecessors. It was acquired by an art dealer in Santa Fe, New Mexico, during the mid-1950s, who then put it up for sale. Notice the sensitive and delicately rendered lines, all of which demonstrate the artist's subtle virtuosity.

These four similar paintings were obviously not the work of the same man for they were done at different times within a period of at least 50 years or more and were used over a very wide geographic area. The connection of elements, or at least the effect of stylistic stimulation, remains convincingly evident, making the case for imitation irrefutable. Most likely a series of borrowings occurred: one artist borrowed and embellished features employed by a predecessor or a competitor, and his work was in turn borrowed by another, and so on through a now unknown chain of artists. All, however, represent the ultimate development of the Northwest Coast painting tradition. None were the work of an artist still seeking to perfect the medium. That end had already been achieved.

It may be useful to note that Tsimshian features illustrated in these various paintings did not always translate well into the work of artists from neighboring tribes. Double and triple eye design characteristics seen in some of the primary figures in Tsimshian paintings, for example in Figures 10, 22, and 26, are not seen in Southern Kwakiutl, Bella Coola, or Nuu chaa nulth paintings. And the use of triple figures for eyes, as in those of the central thunderbird's head in Figure 22, Plate 2, is a style that did not spread throughout the region.

Another question that continues to intrigue and to stimulate contemplation is the matter of the genuine identity of the artists who produced flat paintings. Besides the lack of documentation accompanying the artworks, some cultural practices obfuscated the artists' identities. The more northerly Northwest Coast tribes developed a body of quite specific rules as to which artists could be hired for such commissions. The Tlingit, for example, were barred from hiring an artist who belonged to the same half of the tribe as the patron commissioning the work. If no such person was available or acceptable then the artist had to be found outside of the group, that is, in another tribe. But this rule was not always adhered to for a variety of reasons. Sometimes the appropriate group numbered no artists in its ranks. A more common influence was the wish to keep work within the tribe when possible. Various means were therefore exercised to circumvent the tribal guidelines. An outsider might be publicly designated as the commissioned artist, but the actual work would be done by one from among the patron's own people. The vast array of machinations designed to skirt the observance of tribal rules have been carefully shrouded in secrecy and therefore are not well understood by outsiders.

This question brings to the fore yet another: Did a single artist create a particular painting or were the combined efforts of a coterie of workers necessary? The principal artist may have depended only upon one or more apprentices, or he may have hired trained craftsmen of lesser stature to assist him in such massive projects. Now, reconstructions of house front paintings done in traditional style usually employ more than one artist, several in fact. But this world is vastly different from that of the mid-19th century when Pacific Northwest Coast native culture was at its apogee.

The Remarkable Case of the Rain Wall Screen

Scattered throughout the pages of this volume are repeated references to one distinctive masterpiece, the Rain Wall Screen, once housed in the original Whale House in Klukwan, a village located at the head of the Lynn Canal in southeastern Alaska. Although the fortunes of the Ganaxtedi raven lineage within the Chilkat tribe that owned this screen have fluctuated over time, and the temptation to turn the treasure into cash must have been great, few outsiders have ever been given the opportunity to observe it.

Despite having spent three weeks in this village doing field research in 1949, our team of researchers led by Frederica de Laguna was ultimately unsuccessful in gaining entry to observe this phenomenal painting.

The original Whale House collapsed and vanished shortly after the turn of the 20th century, but the art pieces it contained were transferred to what was initially conceived as a future home built on a concrete foundation. Unfortunately, the house was never fully completed as a residence for the proud lineage. Over the years these incredibly rare and valuable artifacts were increasingly exposed to the elements, to dampness, rot, rain, and wind, as the temporary housing itself declined. Their deterioration and gradual disintegration were evident to those who knew of the pieces, and their growing vulnerability led to considerable consternation toward the raven clan from outsiders who recognized the importance of these possessions.

From the end of the 19th century clan members had truculently rejected all offers by outsiders to buy and properly house the artifacts. Despite increasing and indeed astronomical figures offered, the Klukwan raven clan had consistently refused to sell. The possessions within the Whale House had been valued at several millions of dollars; bona fide offers in this range were made in the early 1980s. Even while the ante rose with each passing year and the fortunes of the clan, the tribe, and the village itself fell on more and more difficult economic circumstances, clan members remained unified in rejecting all offers from outsiders.

The collection consists of numerous ceremonial items such as masks, feast dishes, and dancing batons with carved crest symbols, all emblems of the clan's past greatness and power. But the centerpieces are the four extraordinary 10-foot-tall (3.0-m), sculptured interior house poles and the Rain Wall Screen. The poles were once the supporting pillars of the original Whale House. The Rain Wall Screen, 20 feet (6.1 m) wide by about 10 feet (3.0 m) tall, contains in addition to the painting some low relief surface sculpture, constituting a staggeringly rich array of symbolism. The screen is locked away in the entry compartment meant for the house leader (Figure 10; Plates 14 and 15).

In 1974 the Klukwan tribal council passed a resolution that forbade the sale of possessions of Tlingit artifacts to any purchaser outside the community without the expressed consent of the council. The obvious intent of this ordinance was to thwart the sale of the Whale House treasures. The resolution, however, struck at the heart of the raven clan's right to dispose of its property as its members saw fit. It was only a matter of time before this quarrel resulted in open conflict between the raven clan and the rest of the tribe.

Opposing views began to emerge among the Chilkat tribe as to what should be done with these great historic works of art. The eventual splintering of the former tribal solidarity led to the formation of two factions with respect to these artifacts. Should these great examples of the illustrious Tlingit past be sold to a museum where they would be cared for, preserved, and exhibited for all the peoples of the world to see? Should they be allowed to disintegrate in keeping with the traditional view that their ceremonial purpose had been served and they should not be shared with the outside world? Should they remain in the village as a possible tribal resource, to be used to develop the community as a whole in some ongoing project that might benefit all the members of the tribe rather than one clan group exclusively?

The crisis centered on the question of whether the raven clan could claim the Whale House possessions as exclusively theirs, or whether this princely trove was owned equally by all the members of the Chilkat tribe. The controversy was heightened by the assertion that the raven clan, who claimed exclusive possession under the pretext of the safety of the collection, was only seeking enormous financial gain by offering to place the artifacts in the care of a great and prestigious museum. Certainly the covert incentive, the opportunity to acquire a considerable windfall of cash from the sale, conservatively estimated to be in the neighborhood of between three and five million dollars, was a critical factor. Not only would this sum provide the clan members a handsome windfall but would also boost their status, power, and prestige at the expense of other clans both within as well as outside the tribe.

In a speech given during a council meeting, a member of the Whale House urged, "A Tsimshian made the Rain Wall Screen for us. We bought it for prestige and power. We should sell it for the same reasons" (Carpenter 1975:23).

The controversy over what was to be done with the collection simmered over many years but finally came to a sudden climax in 1984. If ever there was a horror story, that which unfolded in the following 10 years fits the classic mold. On the one hand, the pieces in the Whale House—some say the finest examples in all the Northwest Coast region—and their story epitomized the effect of skyrocketing values placed on unsurpassed examples of Native American art and the fevered quest by well-endowed collectors and institutions. And as importantly the entire collection was in danger of being completely lost in native hands. On the other hand, the matter had degenerated into a bitter quarrel over ownership and over which branches of the tribe were to enjoy the enormous sums of money involved.

As predicted, or expected, the circumstance triggering open confrontation occurred in 1984 when an art dealer offered to purchase the entire collection, including the Rain Wall Screen. The proposed transaction involved in addition to the stipulated purchase price, payoffs to certain clan members who viewed themselves as the rightful heirs according to the Tlingit custom of reckoning descent and inheritance matrilineally. Some of the clan members drove a large vehicle into the village when the rest of the villagers were attending a social function in a nearby community, and proceeded to remove the four house poles and the Rain Wall Screen. The pieces were then moved to another location, packed and crated with great care, and clandestinely moved out of the village under darkness.

The discovery of the loss of the artifacts followed almost immediately thereafter and was reported to the Alaska State Police. In the meantime the treasures were put aboard a ferry bound for Seattle, Washington. The tribal council moved into action. An injunction was issued by the tribal council and the Chilkat tribe against those who had taken possession of the collection. During the ensuing legal battle these priceless pieces of native art languished for nine years in a warehouse somewhere in Seattle. The raven clan members were determined to have the courts decide who were the rightful heirs. But what court was to have jurisdiction in this matter? The State of Alaska? The U.S. federal government? The tribal court?

Legal fees soared. Charges, counter-charges, and recriminations suffused the community. Dissension, disunity, distrust, and accusations of selling out—all these and more flew fast and furiously during the years following the injunction. The agent who represented the purchaser of the collection was portrayed as the devil incarnate and was reviled mercilessly. A continuous tirade of poisonous invective was directed at him, at the buyer of the collection, and at the clan members involved in the "theft." These last became *persona non grata*, their presence in the village made untenable. A consuming hatred spilled over to poison the atmosphere in the village, driven by the shared greed. By 1994 all the litigants were exhausted both emotionally and financially by the ordeal. A U.S. federal court had ruled the matter was to be determined by a tribal court. The tribal judge, an outsider but a Native American, heard testimony from tribal members for months on end. Eventually (1994) he ruled that the art collection was to be turned over to the tribe because it had primary possession. The claim of the tribe took precedence over the claims presented by the clan. (For additional details on this intriguing episode see Herem 1991 and Enge 1993.)

In October of 1994 a celebration was held to mark the return of all the artifacts to Klukwan. Most of the villagers witnessed the physical return of the collection, and the people seemed relieved to have the bitter controversy come to a close. However, much doubt still prevails as to whether the return of the Whale House treasures can heal the social rift that opened in 1984.

The foregoing summary is at best a broad brush-stroke account of the tragic story. The issues involved in the conflict were far more convoluted and complex and have proved difficult to resolve. Some members of the clan have indicated that they might appeal the tribal court's decision. Some have refused to accept the verdict. Others have reluctantly put the matter behind them in the hope of a reconciliation. Meanwhile the legal fees resulting from this decade-long dispute have reached astronomical proportions. My understanding is that the legal bills remain unpaid as both individual and tribal resources have long since been exhausted.

To further complicate the matter, unbeknown to most people in the field, a full scale replica of the Rain Wall Screen was carved and painted during the mid-1960s. It was purchased from a Northwest carver and shipped to New York City. Its present whereabouts are unknown. The tribal values of power, possession, and prestige have come full circle in this unhappy episode.

C·H·A·P·T·E·R VII

A NEW LIFE

"Our spirit moves us to share and to build the pride of we the First Peoples through education, art, and entertainment of our guests and ourselves by reflecting the past, striving in the present, to enhance the future of our native cultures. Our mission shall require great deeds of we the First Peoples—and of our friends."

Welcome sign
at the Khouwutzen (Cowichan)
Heritage Center, Duncan,
British Columbia

FROM THE early 1900s to the mid-20th century, Northwest Coast Indian art and the native culture itself experienced rapid decline and seemed headed for collapse. The population had plummeted, attributable to a variety of tragic causes. The influx of Westerners and the growing presence of the powerful European cultural tradition played a major role in the rapid decline of the native society. Two potent forces, rapid cultural change and dwindling native population, were simultaneously at work turning traditional folkways and practices in complex and unpredictable directions. At the same time, the increasingly dominant Western institutions of state and church sought to convert the natives' world view to Western cultural themes and to recast their practices to Western ways. Both government administrations and missionaries shared the objective of replacing the native traditional lifestyle and all its assorted languages, social beliefs, and spir-

151

itual and aesthetic foundations, dimensions that had over the ages sustained the natives. The prevailing view of those in power at the time was that traditional native activities and pursuits stood in the way of the successful adoption of Western ways of life.

On the other hand, the natives were enormously drawn to the strengths of the newcomers. They were a source of seemingly never-ending wealth, possessors of enormous technological resources, and bearers of a body of knowledge far beyond the advancements of the native culture. Considerable numbers of natives gladly accepted the opportunity to join in this marvelous new dispensation.

The consequence for the native society and its artists was a decline in the social need for the ongoing production of the symbols associated with lineage, clan, and tribal history. The symbols began to disappear. The role of the native artist slowly became irrelevant in the changing circumstances.

But out of the cultural malaise questions began to emerge: Was it necessary to abandon everything associated with the traditional past in order to embrace the desirable aspects of Western culture? Was it wise to pursue policies that would result in the abandonment of everything from the past?

In this period, artists found few commissions. Lacking work that sustained their families or enhanced their status and prestige, creative men drifted into other forms of employment, seeking jobs in logging camps, concentrating on seasonal salmon fishing, working as laborers in the larger Western settlements that were springing up along the British Columbia and southern Alaska coast. Other gifted artists became lethargic, simply drifting along disinterested in the future and what it might hold for them or their talents. The eventual disappearance of the practices and production of the native arts seemed to be a certain outcome.

When I took a position in 1963 as field consultant in the arts for the Indian Arts and Crafts Board in the Pacific Northwest region, an agency within the U.S. Department of the Interior, one of my initial objectives was to undertake an evaluation and assessment of what was actually taking place in the arts of the Northwest. The assessment was darker and bleaker than anything I might have imagined. Scholars, professors, researchers, gallery operators, museum directors—in fact, the entire array of professionals who were connected with the regional native art scene—unanimously proclaimed the hopelessness of a possible resurgence of the native arts in the Pacific Northwest.

However, covertly, with little immediate fanfare, some critical and amazing events were taking place—events that within a short period of ten years turned the entire picture around. Change began in the early 1960s and the tempo was to move with increasing and dramatic intensity. For one thing, the British Columbia Provincial Parliament quietly passed a new Indian Act in which the former prohibition against the native custom of potlatching was dropped. Within more or less one year, potlatching began to reappear as elders came together to pay their respects to deceased ancestors who had died without the appropriate honors being bestowed upon them. Nor was it any longer necessary to potlatch in secret in order to establish a person's rightful claim to a hereditary position within the tribe or to validate the rights of successors to leadership positions.

But these new potlatches lacked an imperative element—the

symbols of hereditary wealth, the crests, masks, and costumes that had always been closely associated with potlatching and other ceremonies. Much of what had survived had long been sold to the museums of the world. A demand for material symbols was renewed among the tribes, and artists and the arts in general were encouraged by this demand.

Unfortunately, many of the most gifted artists had passed away and had not handed on their skills to succeeding generations. It was necessary for the few older men who understood something of the principles and practices involved to assist and encourage the emerging generation. By the late 1960s, a new era in Northwest Coast art was beginning to rise, sustained by a large number of academic, professional, civic, and political leaders, both Indian and white. Many assisted either financially or in the provision of expertise. University professors, entrepreneurs, museum administrators and curators, and government officials—all these began working together to attempt to revive the arts of the Northwest Coast people. Their efforts were to have a remarkable outcome both in political and economic spheres.

In association with this dramatic turn of events, other movements toward traditional practices began to surface. Native people themselves found new interest in rebuilding traditional long houses. Their construction evolved into shared projects geared to the local as well as intertribal communities. Long houses once again became the foundation place for mounting social events and potlatches as well as for serving new needs as modern community centers and museums to house and protect the treasures remaining in tribal possession.

These initiatives continued to bear fruit in the 1970s when the art market for Northwest Coast artifacts began to surge upward like a rocket. In the 1960s the prices for authentic native art from the region doubled in value then doubled again. But in the 1970s it tripled, then tripled once more for the very finest of pieces. Throughout those years I watched in stunned silence and disbelief as such values multiplied. The presumed death of the art of this region, so emphatically forewarned by professionals in the early 1960s, not only did not happen, but the opposite was taking place. A new exuberance and excitement developed that no one had believed possible a few years earlier.

Closely following the increased market value of the artworks, the status of the artist also changed dramatically, soaring beyond traditional tribal boundaries into international prominence. Gallery owners, collectors, museum curators, as well as relative newcomers suddenly aware of the heritage of the region became involved in the growth. Individuals and institutions vied for opportunities to acquire or exhibit the work of the contemporary artists who were emerging on the scene. Artists who had previously worked only within their distinctive cultural milieu of tribal clients had now entered another market that was international in flavor and quality, with quite different aesthetic values. The artists moved forward to experiment with new forms of expression, revitalizing traditional themes in a new context. They also began to work in entirely new media: gold and silver, silk-screen printmaking, fabrics, and more.

Part of the new international quality of the traditional art was to introduce women to the community of native painters and carvers. Earlier tradition had restricted women to basketry and the weaving crafts. But with this new resurgence some took up carving and painting as well as the newly adopted media.

Contemporary native artists sell their products for sums that run into the thousands and sometimes tens of thousands of dollars. Their works are in demand not only from avid, affluent collectors and boosters of the northwest art tradition, but also from those within the newly aware chiefly and aristocratic families whose inventory of required family heirlooms must be replenished. The market has been greatly expanded through the acquisition of works for memorial services for prominent lineage and clan members, for various pan-tribal functions, as well as for architectural accents for new buildings. And museums have increasingly turned toward purchasing works of contemporary native artists. Their acquisitions have been used to mount dramatic shows in Germany, France, and England, as well as truly notable exhibits in Japan.

The Great Surge Forward

This new-found vibrance, this surge of new interest in the native heritage was encouraged and supported by the Canadian and American governments, which provided seed moneys to begin a variety of renewal programs. Much of this money was used to retrain prospective artists to the original standards and in the original techniques of production used by the artists of the past. Government and museum programs not only supported these efforts but played an important role in reviving interest in the Northwest Coast Indian arts generally.

Another dimension to this resurgence that was an equally critical factor was the discovery of Northwest Coast art by Native American artists of tribes of other regions in addition to white artists of the United States and Canada. As general interest in the native arts grew, there was an explosion in the publication of books and magazines; articles devoted to Northwest Coast arts were produced to accompany major shows in some of the leading museums of the United States, Canada, and Germany. Writer after writer extolled the brilliance and virtuosity of the artists and arts from the Northwest Coast past. Whites and Native Americans from outside the Northwest Coast began to duplicate the masterpieces illustrated in this growing volume of publications. They also turned to museum collections and shows to find models to copy. Since few works were available for purchase from Northwest Coast natives, collectors and admirers of the art began purchasing what was being produced by white carvers and painters. Several white men soon gained fame for having acquired by imitation and self-learning the appropriate skills in both carving and painting.

Native artists viewed these white artists with increasing anxiety, concern, and envy. Native artists believed the traditional themes, crests, designs, and patterns belonged to the native tribes of the Northwest Coast; the crest symbols that were being copied had belonged to their ancestors and were their hereditary property. Urged by this outside competition, they came to reclaim the house front and interior screen painting tradition as their private property. Mythical beings that the whites were duplicating were, the natives contended, being torn from their historical roots. Interestingly, these outside artists later became the very teachers employed to train and inspire a coterie of young Northwest Coast Indian artists, because the basic skills for carving and painting had for all practical purposes nearly disappeared among the tribes of the Northwest Coast.

The competitive sense socially ingrained in the native artists motivated them to shake off their lethargy and take up the new challenge of worldwide interest in their art. They were stimulated by a renewed sense of their cultural heritage, and they were spurred to compete for a place in, and a piece of, the fast-developing market for Northwest Coast art. Since outsiders had taken over the art they were challenged to take it back. Though North west Coast Indian artists viewed outside artists as thieves of their lineage and clan symbols, they begrudgingly acknowledged the superior skills the white carvers and painters possessed in the 1960s and 1970s.

The Northwest Coast people had a reputation for shrewdness and toughness earned from their dealings with the 19th-century explorers, fur traders, and travelers in their region. Westerners regularly remarked in their journals on how astutely the natives operated in commerce, demanding what the market would bear for what they had to trade. Analogously, the contemporary Indian artist saw another opportunity in the ballooning market for their traditional artifacts. They would either have to regain now the use of their art tradition or they would surely lose it forever. An increasing number of them turned to learning anew the traditions and principles associated with their ancestors' art and culture.

Though a renewed sense of pride in the past was an important ingredient in motivating the Northwest Coast Indian artist into action, I profoundly believe that as important, if not more important, an ingredient was a determination to take back something of the past that had once belonged to them and that was being utilized for gain by outsiders. Competition and the desire to make money, I believe, were the prime motivations that moved them into reasserting themselves in the 1970s and 1980s. By the 1990s the native art was flowering again and meeting the increasing demand from a growing and enthusiastic clientele.

Resurrecting the House Front Painting

Monumental flat painting began to tentatively appear in a handful of villages in southern Alaska and British Columbia in the 1940s. One Tlingit project had been started under Works Progress Administration auspices in the late 1930s. It proved a failure, but did, however, foreshadow a possible future development. Another forerunner to the resurgence of house front painting was mounted in Victoria, British Columbia, in the early 1940s. The provincial government and the then Museum of Natural History jointly sponsored the building of a large-scale model reconstruction of a Haida-style long house that was to be placed in the center of

Thunderbird Park in the heart of downtown Victoria. It was the first of many such long houses.

After several years of use as a tourist attraction, this long house model was torn down and a new one was constructed on the same site. Designed and created by the museum's chief totem carver, Mungo Martin, it was an authentic scale replica of the house in which Mungo was raised in the village of Fort Rupert. The painting applied to the house front has been referred to as a killer whale crest, but it is actually a mythical or supernatural sea creature known as *tseekis*, something similar to a rock cod or sculpin. It was a family crest of a chief who lived in the nearby village of Kalokwis. Through kinship ties Mungo claimed his right to borrow the design to paint on the house front (Plate 48). This long house and its painted house front became an instant success as a tourist attraction. Huge crowds were drawn to this distinctive building set amid a number of carved totem poles.

In rapid succession other house front paintings appeared in more remote communities to the north. A number of Kwakiutl leaders set aside their many differences and age-old squabbles to begin working together on projects intended to enhance their respective communities. The erection of long houses was the kind of project all could readily support, for few issues of possession, power, or prestige were involved.

The first long house built to serve the social and ceremonial needs of a group of regional tribes was in Courtenay, British Columbia, supported by a Comox tribal chief named Andy Frank. It was a modest affair, completed in 1960. It was, however, to be-

come the model for a more elaborate undertaking a few years later in Alert Bay. The Courtenay house was 40 feet (12.2 m) by 50 feet (15.2 m) in size and boasted a large house front painting depicting a thunderbird or sea eagle carrying a whale, purportedly its source of food (Plate 49). A totem pole commemorating Mungo Martin's only son, David, who was lost in an accident at sea, was raised to the left of the house in May, 1960.

Chief Frank's long house was followed by a major building project sponsored by the Southern Kwakiutl tribes around Alert Bay. The Nimkish tribe and other groups banded together in a joint effort to build a great ceremonial long house in the village. Seventy years earlier several house front paintings had stood in this place but they had long disappeared. The project was started in early 1963 under the direction and guidance of two outstanding men, James Sewid and Henry Speck. The two chieftains were responsible for rallying support for the project not only among the numerous artists in the surrounding areas but among much of the native population as well. It was completed in 1966. The house front design was of a great whale (Figure 54). The tribes' pride in this communal effort was infectious. At a cost of $17,000 Canadian they had succeeded in building a traditional-style long house 70 feet (21.3 m) in length, 50 feet (15.2 m) in width, and almost 20 feet (0.6 m) in height at the roof peak. It rested on a concrete foundation later covered with earth.

The Alert Bay long house soon acquired the name the Marine House. The enormous rafters were individually carved and adzed to resemble kelp from the sea. As Sewid explained to me, this house commemorated one first built by his ancestors in order to memorialize the great mythological flood, which purportedly forced the dispersal of various tribes to the distant regions that they presently occupy. The enormous 4-ton (3.6-metric-ton) beams that formed the framework for the house were donated by major timber companies in the region. The important crests of all the tribes that had participated in this great effort were carved into the upright poles as well as the cross beams.

The Marine House could seat 500 spectators but could accommodate as many as 1000 standing people when the occasion demanded. This long house proved a smashing success for it stimulated further joint tribal activities, social, cultural, and memorial in nature. It was a place where the native peoples could meet—their invited guests among them—to honor deceased ancestors, to validate rights of inheritance, to debate the directions the people would have to take in order to realize future opportunities.

Other villages soon undertook the building of long houses. Several groups of Tsimshian people banded together to raise long houses in their territories. One of the first was in Ksan, near Hazelton, British Columbia. It became a center for cultural renewal including the revitalization of the native arts of carving, painting, and weaving. The first of a series of house front paintings was mounted in 1958 but was a modest example. The house in Ksan became known as the Treasure House and was followed by several additional long houses with more elaborately painted house fronts. These structures served not as dwellings for the people but as classrooms and exhibition spaces for budding artists' work (Plate 50). Ksan has become an important center for developing the arts and crafts in both traditional and contemporary molds (Plate 51). An important building on which a fine house front painting was mounted can be seen in Kitwancool, a conservative community in which many famed artists once resided (Plate 52). The painting was copied from an earlier house screen preserved in the Canadian Museum of Civilization (Figure 25).

The renewed interest in house front painting continued into the 1980s. With increasing and unrelenting vigor, more and more villages sought to emulate the early examples. A large and impressive house front painting adorns a recently completed Bella Coola school called the Learning Place. The exterior walls bear numerous Bella Coola–style designs created by six aspiring artists who reside nearby. At Gitsegyukla, a Skeena River Tsimshian settlement, still another impressive school house has been recently completed whose front space is adorned with symbols representing the natural creatures—and the crests as well—of their environment, the eagle, wolf, frog, killer whale, sun, and more (Plate 53).

These examples are but a few of the house front paintings that have begun to reappear in various Northwest Coast Indian villages. They are, in fact, old practices reworked to meet new circumstances for larger communal benefits rather than for the more narrowly focused lineage or clan ends. With this new community focus, the tribes near Alert Bay, after years of effort and preparation, in November 1980 completed a museum and cultural center to house tribal documents, a library, and numerous cultural artifacts—masks, costumes, coppers—once confiscated from families that had defied the potlatch prohibitions. The new museum was appropriately named U'mista, or Returning Home. The house front painting above the cultural center's main entrance is a duplication of that which once graced the house of the Nimkish chief Tlah go glas (Figure 34; Plate 36).

The Return of the Interior Screen

Just as house front paintings have reappeared, so also have interior screens. I have already alluded to the replica of the Rain Wall Screen that was made in 1967–68 and shipped to New York City. Numerous high quality screens have been painted by an increasingly sophisticated group of artists residing in the Northwest. The Ksan group in Hazelton, British Columbia, has produced some remarkable examples to decorate buildings of a modern architectural style. Notable is the series of massive doors made from red cedar. The doors are positioned at the entry to the Museum of Anthropology at the University of British Columbia in Vancouver. They are among the finest examples coming out of this renaissance. Though the subjects depicted on these screens are steeped in the mythical past—themes that run throughout the work—they reach out to the present as significant masterpieces.

In terms of sheer ingenuity of creation, a series of screen murals was produced by the Ksan artists, carved in low relief as well as painted, representing mythic themes stemming from the Gitksan Tsimshian people. Presented in the traditional colors—black for the formlines, red for the secondary, and blue-green for the tertiary colors—this mural painted on red cedar wood adorns the mezzanine of the Royal Bank of Canada's main office in Vancouver, British Columbia. It is a colossal example, 120 feet (36.6 m) long and 8 feet (2.4 m) high, by far the largest example of any screen in existence. It is composed of three massive central designs flanked on each side by three subsidiary panels.

Interior screen paintings have proliferated in other settings and other regions as well, adorning numerous public buildings, health dispensaries, community centers, tribal offices, and private industrial facades or interiors. A community center in Seattle, the Daybreak Star Center, features a large painted screen with killer whale crests prominently displayed. The Puyallup Health Center near Tacoma, Washington, features an enormous thunderbird that dominates the entire interior wall of the main building.

Artists are no longer required to derive their right to practice from an elite lineage, from the chiefly and aristocratic families of the past. Contemporary northwest artists are a product of the recent tendency for the democratization of all aspects of life. Young men and women not blessed as the scions of aristocratic families are nevertheless now encouraged to work in the traditional media and to expand their creative talents in the perpetuation of traditional forms.

The above examples together with many others too numerous to mention unequivocally demonstrate that house front and interior screen painting, which once seemed in eclipse and about to disappear forever, have almost miraculously reappeared to elicit the profound appreciation of audiences so numerous and widespread that they would confound those ancestors who originated the forms. These expressions in form and design, in color and in flat dimension, will almost surely continue to evolve as distinctive forms, to meet the changing social and aesthetic requirements for those people touched by them.

These riches from the past—these forgotten riches—have come back rediscovered, to appear in a totally different age and in circumstances very foreign to their origins. The fruit springing from this ancient time is thriving as the ancestors never would have believed, all to awaken future dreams and greater visions of the past.

DRAWINGS

Figure 1.1. The left panel of the interior screen of the Killer Whale House in Klukwan, Alaska. Tlingit.

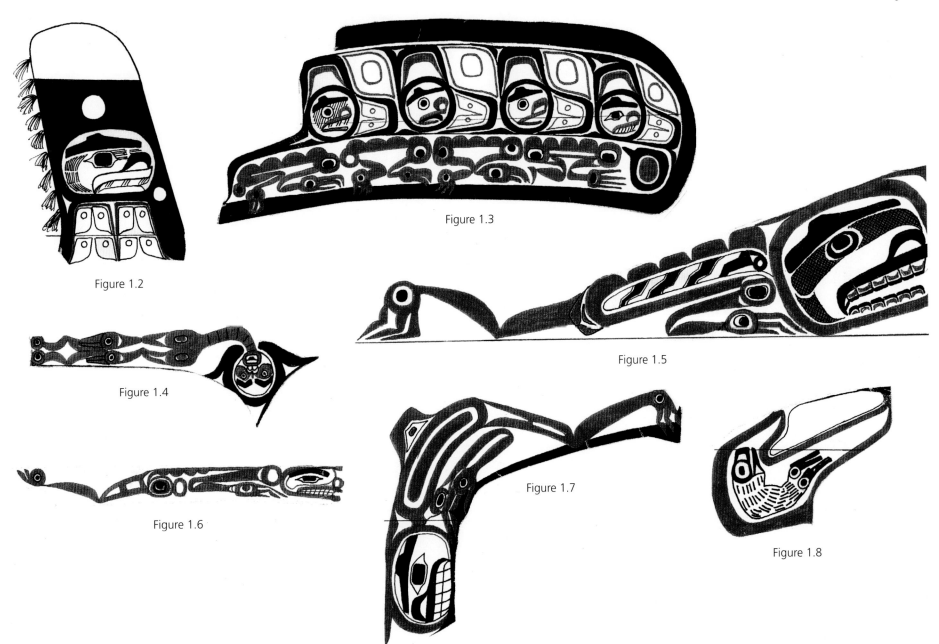

Figure 1.2

Figure 1.3

Figure 1.4

Figure 1.5

Figure 1.6

Figure 1.7

Figure 1.8

Figures 1.2 to 1.8. Detail of Killer Whale Screen in Killer Whale House in Klukwan.

Figure 2. Raven Screen from the Beaver House in Angoon, Alaska. Tlingit.

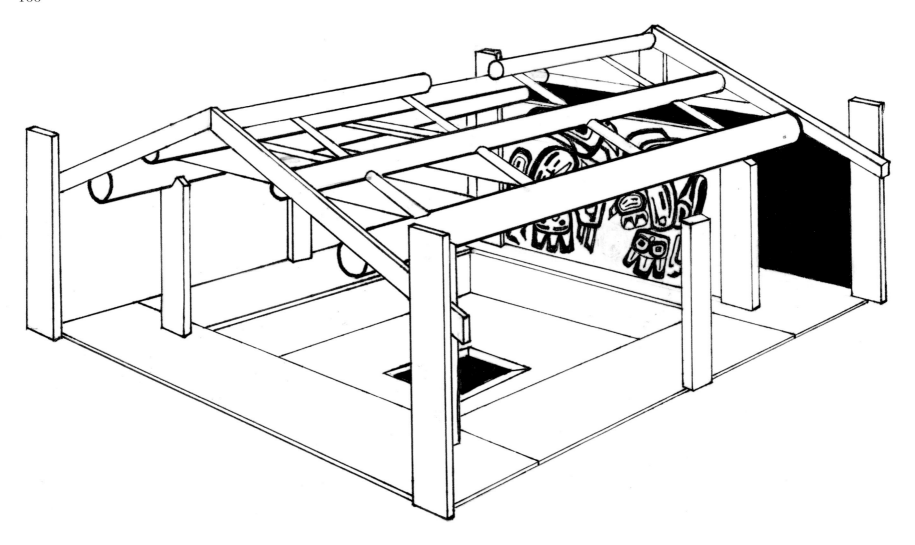

Figure 3. Framework of a traditional Tlingit house from southeastern Alaska.

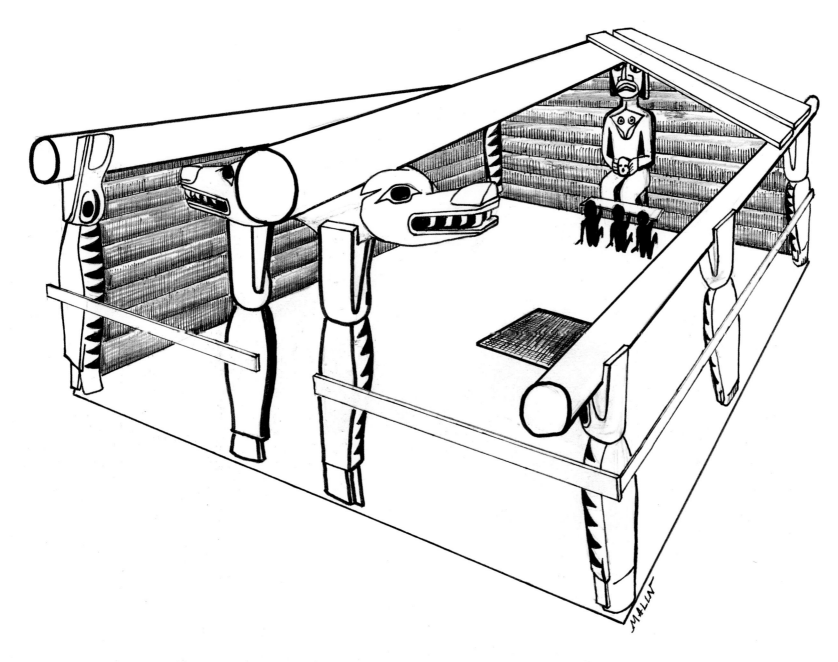

Figure 4. Framework of the Sea Lion House in Hwa'tis, British Columbia. Koskimo tribe, 1950.

168

Figure 5.1. Left side of the Coast Tsimshian house front painting on the Sea Monster House at Lak Kwalaams, Fort Simpson, British Columbia.

Figure 5.2. Blow hole detail of the whale on the left side of the Sea Monster House painting at Fort Simpson.

Figure 5.4. One of several rib designs in the whale on the left side of the Sea Monster House painting at Fort Simpson.

Figure 5.3. Blow hole detail of the whale on the right side of the Sea Monster House painting at Fort Simpson.

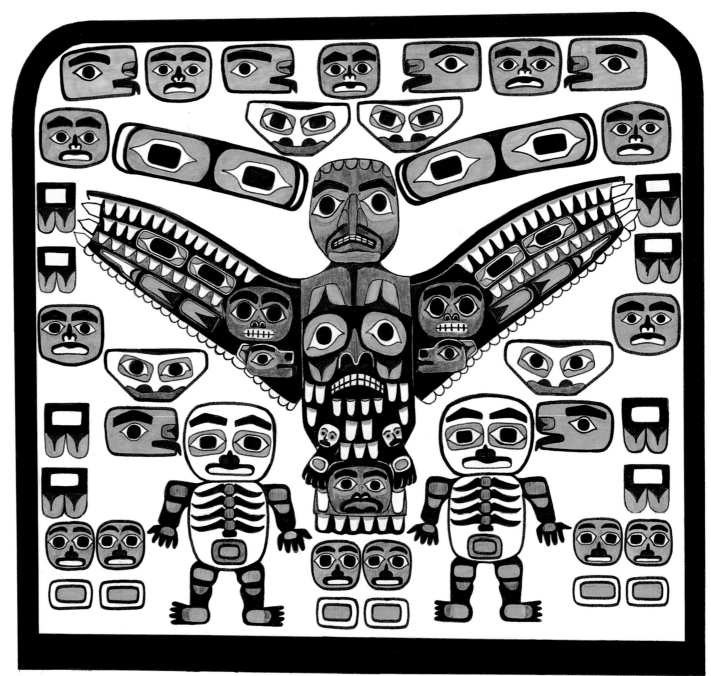

Figure 6. The Thunderbird Screen from the Drum House in Yakutat, Alaska. Tlingit, 1950.

Figure 7. The Beaver Screen in the Wolf Bath House in Yakutat, Alaska. Tlingit, 1950.

Figures 8.1 and 8.2. The Thunderbird and Whale Screen from the Hopachisat tribe of the Nuu chaa nulth.

174

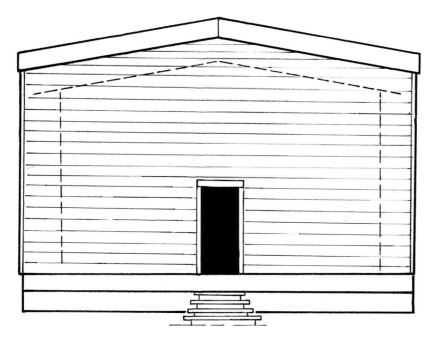

Figure 9.1. Facade construction in the Southern Kwakiutl style.

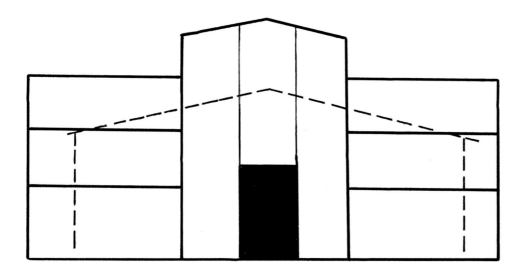

Figure 9.2. Facade construction in the Bella Coola style.

Figure 10. The Rain Wall Screen in the Whale House in Klukwan, Alaska. Tlingit.

MALIN

Figure 11. The Brown Bear Screen in the Killer Whale House in Klukwan, Alaska. Tlingit.

Figure 12. Raven Screen in the Frog House in Klukwan, Alaska. Tlingit.

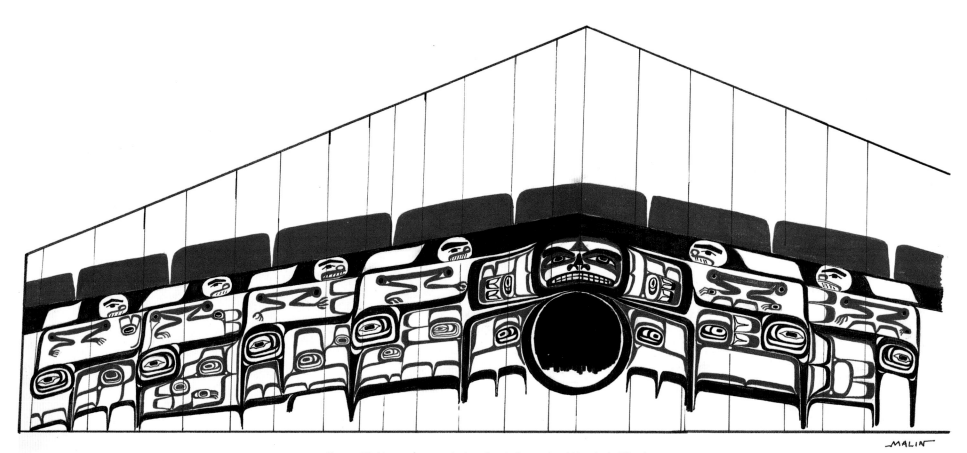

Figure 13. House front painting that belonged to Taku Jack. Tlingit.

Figure 15. One of the four raven figures in the Raven Screen possibly from Hoonah, Alaska. Tlingit.

Figure 14. Brown Bear Screen
from the house of the Tlingit
Chief Shakes in Wrangell, Alaska.

Figure 16.1. Primary formlines of the frontal view of a raven.

Figure 16.2. Secondary and primary formlines combined.

Figure 16.3. Tertiary and primary formlines combined.

Figure 16.4. All three elements combined in final piece, a detail of Figure 2, Raven Screen from the Beaver House in Angoon, Alaska.

Figure 17. House front emblem painting for the Tlingit Chief Anahootz of Sitka, Alaska.

Figure 18. Interior screen from the Eagle's Nest House in Sitka, Alaska. Tlingit.

Figure 19. Central figures of the Raven and Coho Salmon Screen
from the Moon House in Sitka, Alaska.

Figure 20. Tlingit Grizzly Bear Screen.

Figure 21. House front painting of a halibut from Tuxikan village, Alaska. Tlingit.

Figure 22. Painting on the front of the Thunderbird House of the Coast Tsimshian Chief Sqagwet of Lak Kwalaams near Fort Simpson, British Columbia.

MALIN

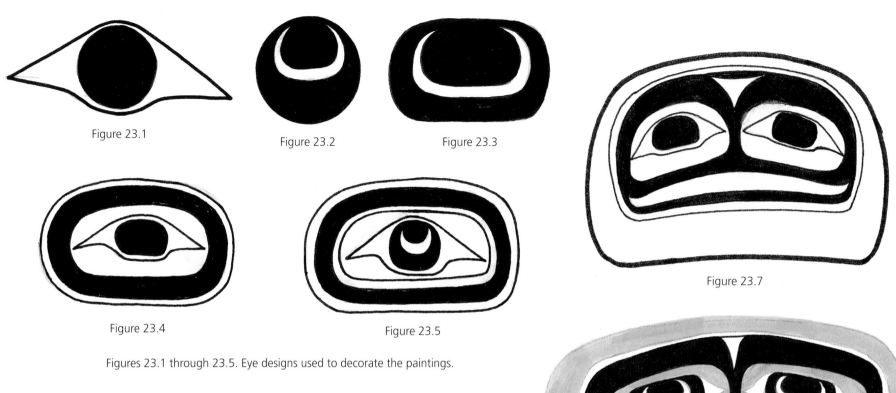

Figure 23.1

Figure 23.2

Figure 23.3

Figure 23.7

Figure 23.4

Figure 23.5

Figures 23.1 through 23.5. Eye designs used to decorate the paintings.

Figure 23.8

Figures 23.7 through 23.9. Double eye designs.

Figure 23.6. The salmon-trout eye design.

Figure 23.9

Figure 23.12

Figure 23.10

Figure 23.13

Figure 23.11

Figures 23.10 and 23.11. Frontal face designs.

Figures 23.12 through 23.15. Profile face designs.

Figure 23.14

Figure 23.15

Figure 23.16. Tlingit raven crest design in profile.

Figure 23.17. Tlingit eagle crest design in profile.

Figure 23.18. Tlingit eagle crest design in frontal view.

Figure 24. Coast Tsimshian house front painting of grizzly bears from Fort Simpson, British Columbia.

Figure 25. Interior screen painting of a raven from the Gitksan Tsimshian.

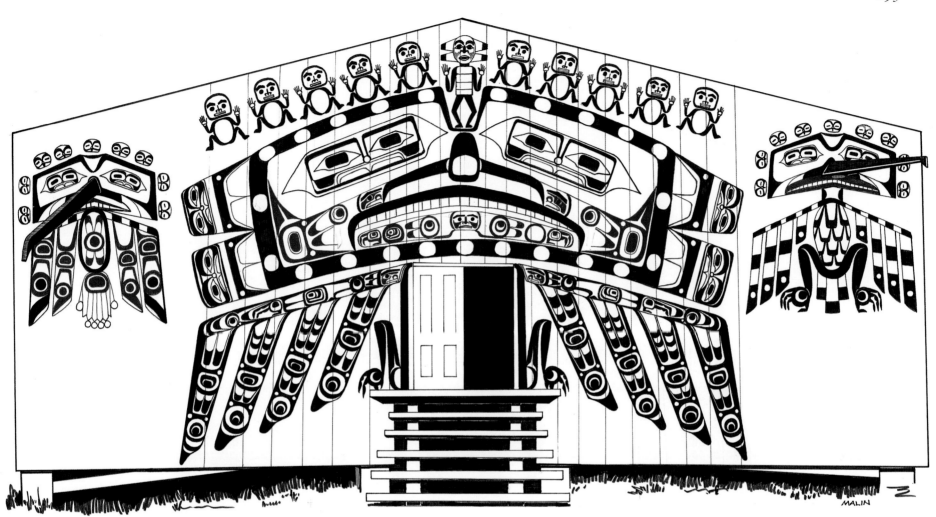

Figure 26. House front painting belonging to Chief Minesqu of the Nishka Tsimshian from Gitlahdamsk, British Columbia.

Figure 27. House front painting of a two-headed killer whale from the Nishka Tsimshian.

Figure 28.
Interior screen in
the Eagle House
from Howkan,
Alaska. Haida.

MALIN

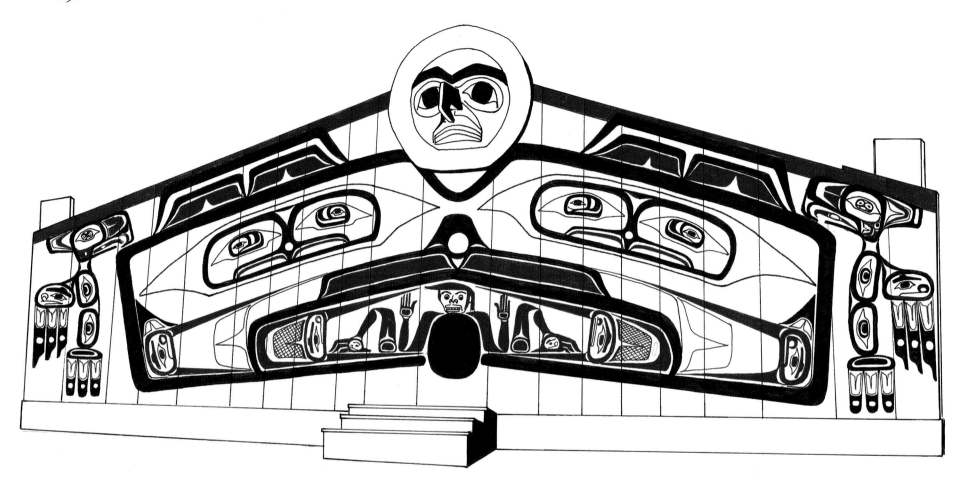

Figure 29. House front painting of the Moon House, Chief Gold's residence near Skidegate on the Queen Charlotte Islands.

Figure 30. Ravens in a facade painting from the Northern Kwakiutl village of Klemtu, British Columbia.

Figure 31. Thunderbirds in a Bella Coola house front painting from Komkotes village.

Figure 32. A house front design from Humdaspi, a Southern Kwakiutl village.

Figure 33. A house front from Humdaspi showing a whale's face.

Figure 34. The Southern Kwakiutl Thunderbird and Whale House of Chief Tlah go glas from Alert Bay, British Columbia.

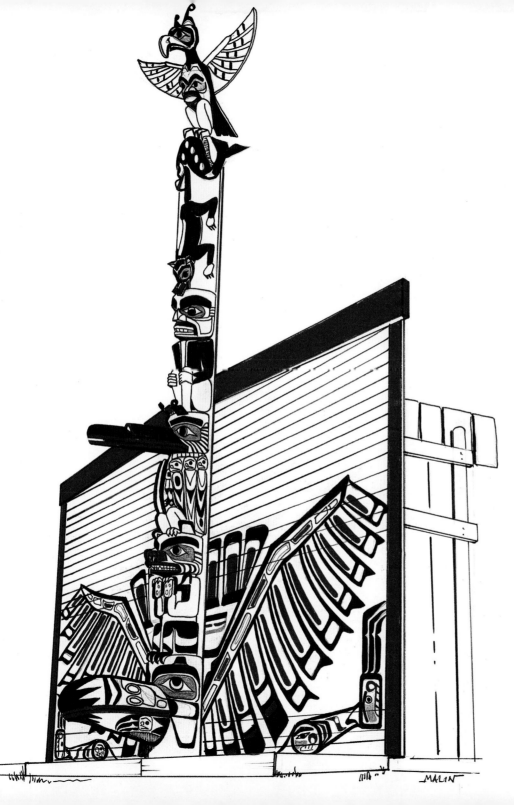

Figure 35. Totem pole and house front painting belonging to Chief Wakias, a Southern Kwakiutl from Alert Bay, British Columbia.

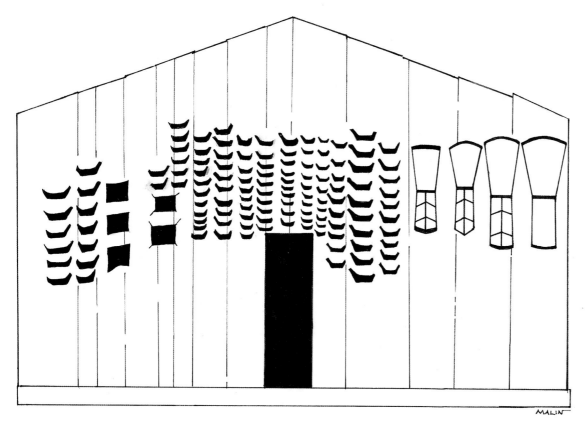

Figure 36. Atypical house front painting representing wealth given away during the owner's potlatches. Alert Bay, British Columbia.

Figure 37. House front painting of a thunderbird and a whale belonging to Quatsino Sam, a Koskimo Indian from Hwa'tis, British Columbia.

Figure 38. Southern Kwakiutl house front painting belonging to Chief Johnny Scow of Gwayasdums, British Columbia.

Figure 39. Southern Kwakiutl house front from Gwayasdums, British Columbia.

Figure 40. Whale House belonging to
Johnny Moon, a Southern Kwakiutl of
H'kusan village, British Columbia.

MALIN

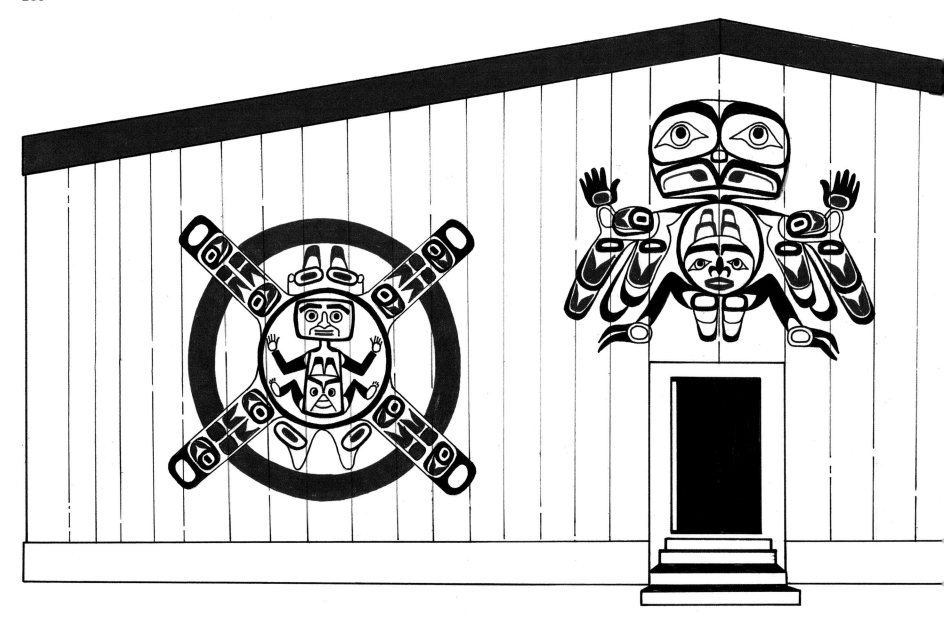

Figure 41. Southern Kwakiutl house front showing a thunderbird and two sun crests. Humdaspi, British Columbia.

Figure 42. Interior screen from the Sea Lion House of Chief Tza'kyus, a Koskimo Indian from Hwa'tis, British Columbia.

Figure 43. Painted cloth screen from the Southern Kwakiutl of Knight Inlet, British Columbia.

Figure 44. Painted cloth screen from the Southern Kwakiutl of Alert Bay, British Columbia.

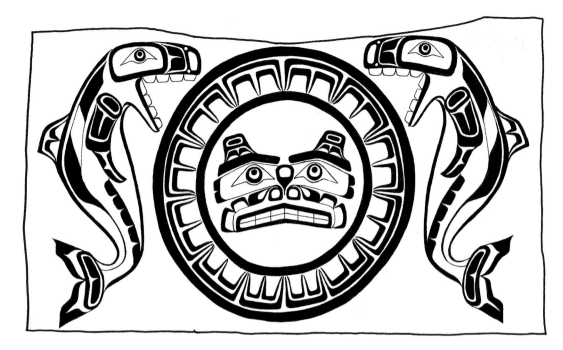

Figure 45. Painted cloth screen from the Southern Kwakiutl of Blunden Harbour, British Columbia.

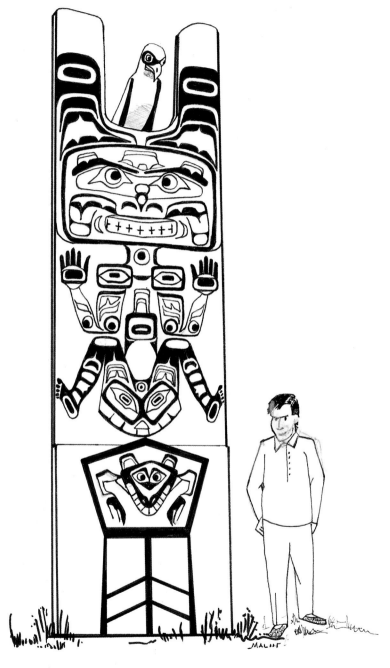

Figure 46. A temporary totem board from the Southern Kwakiutl of Alert Bay, British Columbia.

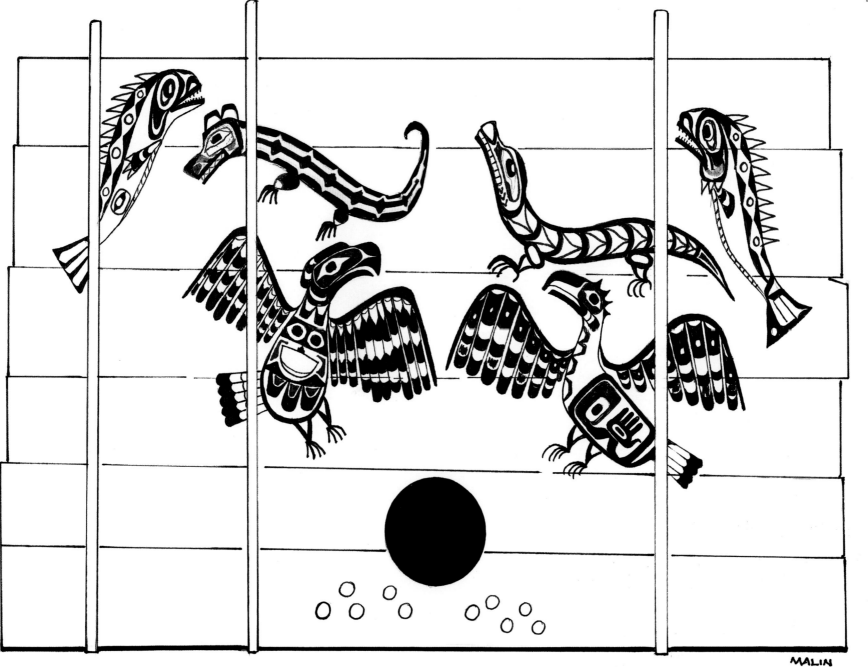

Figure 47. A reconstructed Nuu chaa nulth house front painting from Port Alberni, British Columbia.

Figure 48. A Nuu chaa nulth interior screen from unknown location.

Figure 49. A Nuu chaa nulth cloth screen from unknown location.

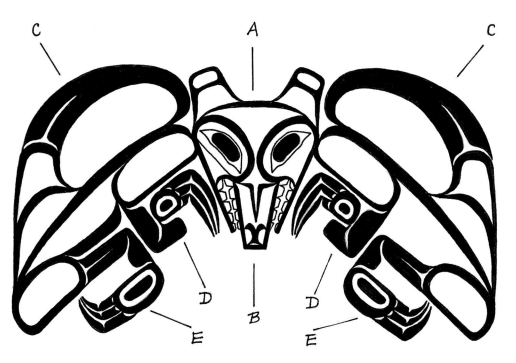

Figure 50. At Ksan, a wolf crest in bilateral symmetry on an interior screen from the Tsimshian of Gitksan, British Columbia. The label A denotes the wolf's head, B its nose, C its body, D the forelimbs, and E the hind limbs.

Figure 51. Tlingit house front painting from Angoon, Alaska.

Figure 52. A miniature interior screen reproducing the larger house front from Angoon, Alaska.

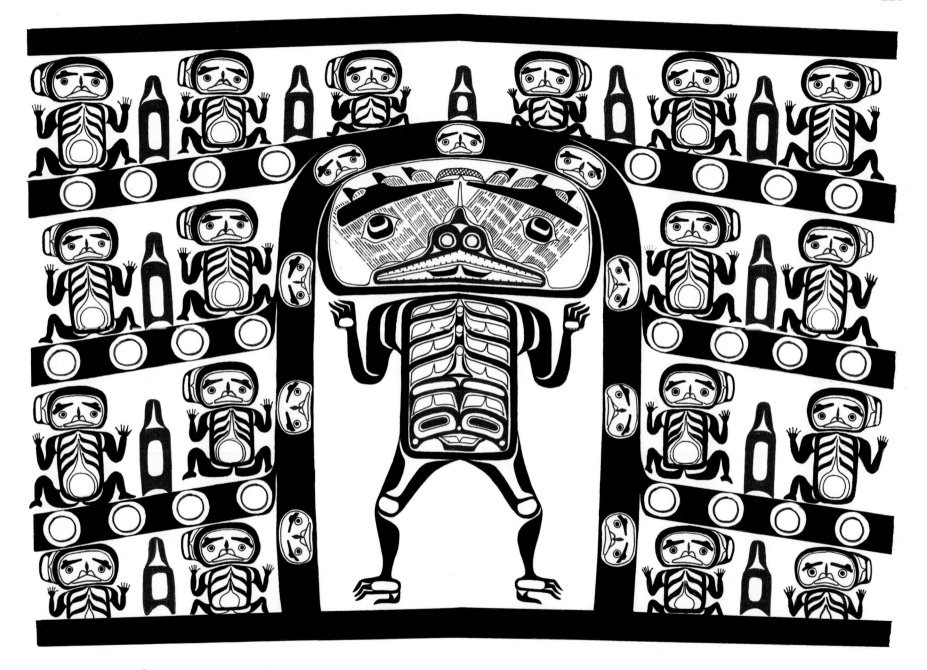

Figure 53. A design painted on commercial paper probably in the late 19th century. The artist is unknown, but the style suggests Coast Tsimshian origin.

Figure 54. Modern house front painting on Southern Kwakiutl community house in Alert Bay, British Columbia, 1965.
The long house and painting were destroyed by fire in 1996.

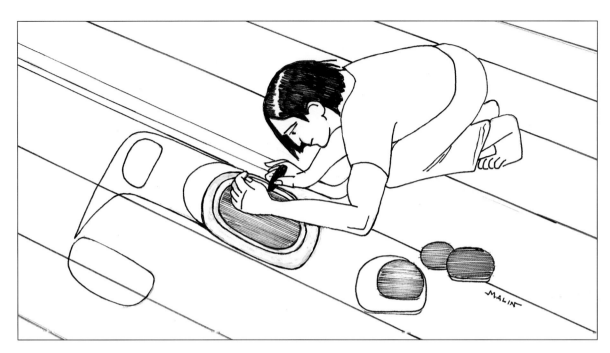

Figure 55. Artist applying template forms to a large-scale plank painting.

Figure 56. Artist applying paints to formline patterns.

Figure 57. Artist applying paints to formline patterns.

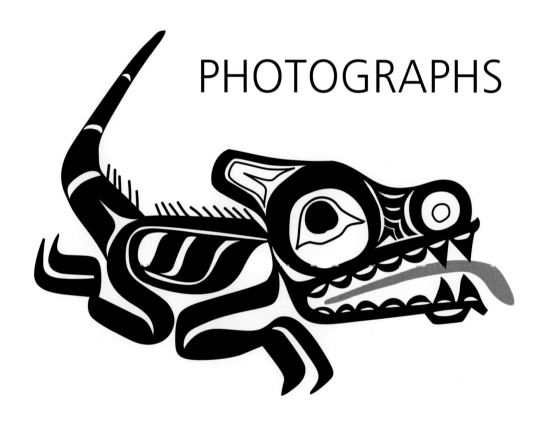

PHOTOGRAPHS

R. C. Bureau of Mines

Plate 1. Interior view of Chief Kudenaha's Killer Whale House belonging to the raven clan in Klukwan, Alaska. This photograph dates to the 1890s and shows only one of the two existing screens. When I observed both screens during an expedition to Alaska in the summer of 1949, the central painted and carved boards representing a grizzly bear were nowhere in sight. Photograph courtesy British Columbia Archives and Records Service, HP 76733.

Plate 2. The mighty house of Chief Sqagwet of the eagle clan in the Gitando tribe of Tsimshian at Fort Simpson, British Columbia, circa 1879. This magnificent house front painting represents three thunderbirds and is the high point among numerous examples that probably once graced the village in the mid-19th century. Photograph courtesy British Columbia Archives and Records Service, HP 88656.

Plate 3. A superb example of an interior screen from the Tlingit village of Angoon, Alaska. It had been removed from the traditional house interior and placed in a modern cottage at the turn of the 20th century. Photograph courtesy Alaska State Library, Vincent Soboleff Collection, PCA 1-410.

Plate 4. A scene identified as the Koskimo village called Hwa'tis in Quatsino Inlet, northern Vancouver Island, photographed by James Dawson in the 1870s. I spent 10 weeks researching this region in 1950. Photograph courtesy National Archives of Canada, PA 37941.

Plate 5. The collapsing remnant of a Northern Kwakiutl house front painting from the village of Klemtu, British Columbia, photographed by George Emmons in the 1890s. Photograph courtesy Royal British Columbia Museum, PN 1160.

Plate 6. Disintegrating remnants of a traditional long house at Gwayasdums village on Gilford Island off the northeast coast of Vancouver Island. The 20-foot (6.1-m) carved figure portrays the mythical being who brings wealth and is represented here as a welcoming figure for visitors. It stood in front of Copper Johnson's house. The dwelling on the left belonged to James King. Photograph courtesy British Columbia Provincial Museum, circa 1927.

Plate 7. The frame construction of a mighty house located in Memkomlis village near Vancouver Island's northeast coast. The monumental beams of cedar each weighed several tons. Photograph by Edward Curtis, 1914, courtesy Archives of British Columbia, 74551-D-8357.

Plate 8. This view of Gwayasdums village, Gilford Island, was taken by F. J. Barrow in 1933 or 1934. Note the large painted house front on the left that represents a raven crest. The remains of two large frame houses can be seen at the center and right. Photograph courtesy British Columbia Provincial Museum, PN 2440.

Plate 9. This photograph captures an event that apparently has never been duplicated. Five house front paintings simultaneously adorn houses in the Bella Coola village at Komkotes. Richard Maynard photograph, 1873, courtesy British Columbia Provincial Museum, PN 7195b.

Plate 10. A house front painting of superb quality and exceptional complexity, the likes of which has seldom been duplicated, represents the mythical sea creature Nagunaks. It is possible that it was never used as there is little evidence of weathering, but some have suggested that small parts were touched up or repainted. The artists are unknown. From Fort Simpson, British Columbia, circa 1870, photograph courtesy Smithsonian Institution, 2241.

Plate 11A. Two Nuu chaa nulth house screens from the Port Alberni region of Vancouver Island, dating to the last part of the 19th century. An important event or potlatch is in progress. The photograph captures the decorative placement of such screens within the interior of the lineage house. Photograph courtesy Vancouver Public Library, 9287.

Plate 11B. A close-up photograph revealing the details of Plate 11a, circa 1930. The youngster standing between the screens is William Tatoosh, Sr. Courtesy Vancouver Public Library, 9284.

Plate 12. Ee'lis, the Nimkish village located at Alert Bay, British Columbia, circa 1909. Note the arrangement of the houses, in a row paralleling the beach front. All have facade constructions. The five totem poles standing in front of some houses appear to date from the 1890s and thereafter. Photograph courtesy British Columbia Provincial Museum, PN 2684.

Plate 13. An elaborately carved and painted house front of four large poles and a crossbeam connecting to each of the four topmost crest figures. It was raised in a Kwakiutl settlement at New Vancouver, or Tsatsichnukwomi. All the symbols portrayed represent great spiritual power and wealth, and it is certain the owner was a person of considerable means. Photograph courtesy British Columbia Archives and Records Service, HP 62435.

Plate 14. The interior screen in the original Whale House at Klukwan, Alaska, before 1890. This is the famed Rain Wall Screen, considered a rare masterpiece. The original house collapsed over a century ago, and the screen has never since found a secure permanent home. Ownership has been a source of contention within the tribe. Photograph courtesy Alaska State Library, Winter and Pond Collection, PCA 87-13.

Plate 15. An unidentified elder sitting before the great Rain Wall Screen. The close-up shows the details of the surface low relief carving and painting. Photograph courtesy Alaska State Library, Dale Butler Collection, PCA 306-440.

Plate 16. A painted interior screen assembled out-of-doors for photographing is an exceptional work and reveals great subtlety of line and composition. This is the only known photograph of this screen, and one can assume it was eventually destroyed. From the Taku Tlingit near Auk Bay, Alaska, probably before the 1890s. Photograph by D. H. Nelles, courtesy Public Archives of Canada, PA 37695.

Plate 17. Converted into a house front, the interior partition screen from the house of Chief Shakes of Wrangell, Alaska. It once graced the property of the Nan yan-yi clan in the *shinkukedi* or wolf half of the Stikine Tlingit tribe. It is a rare and exceptional masterpiece, representing a grizzly bear. It probably dates from the early to mid-19th century.

Plates 18A and 18B. The Raven Screen—this painting possibly depicts episodes in the mythology of Raven, the Tlingit culture hero. The panels may originally have been a possession of the Hoonah Tlingit but were collected in Sitka, Alaska. The Denver Art Museum acquired these magnificent paintings in 1938. Photograph courtesy Denver Art Museum, PTL-3, 1939.140.1 and 2.

Plate 19. This photograph was taken between 1900 and 1928 and reveals the Raven Screen positioned outdoors for photographic purposes. Tlingit people sitting in front of both panels provide an approximation of the screen's size.

Plate 20. Crest paintings applied to an early 20th-century cottage front in Angoon, Alaska, the Killer Whale Dorsal Fin House. The Daqlawedi clan of the wolf half of the tribe owned it. Informants disclose that the designs were painted in 1896 by Yehlh Nawu, or Dead Raven, a Tlingit artist. Note the modest-size totem pole positioned to the left of the house. Photograph courtesy Alaska State Library, Vincent Soboleff Collection, PCA 1-61.

Plate 21. Clan house members stand in front of the Killer Whale House in Angoon. The crest of the clan is prominently displayed and dates back to the turn of the century. By 1949 only the barest outline of the painting was visible. Photograph courtesy Alaska State Library, Vincent Soboleff Collection, PCA 1-62.

Plate 22. The interior painting, the Raven and Coho Salmon Screen, may date back to the 1890s. At one time it graced the Moon House interior in Yakutat for the Humpback Salmon People, but it is now housed in the Sheldon Jackson Museum in Sitka. Photograph courtesy Alaska State Library.

Plate 23. The Golden Eagle Screen, possibly from the Drum House in Yakutat, Alaska, is dated from around the turn of the century. The artist is Yehlh Nawu, or Dead Raven. Photograph courtesy American Museum of Natural History, Department of Library Services, 328732.

Plate 24. A Tlingit house front painting on the Dog Salmon House in Tuxikan village in southern Alaska. The painting dates back to the latter decades of the 19th century. Photograph courtesy Tongass Historical Society, Ketchikan, Alaska, THS 76.8.7.2.

Plate 25. A house front painting from the Cape Fox Tlingit village called Gash in southeastern Alaska. The crest represents the grizzly bear. The entire dwelling was purchased from the Tlingit in the last decade of the 19th century and was rebuilt and displayed for a time in Bronx Park, New York. Photograph courtesy University of Washington Libraries, Special Collections Division, Harriman Expedition, UW 2306.

Plate 26. An interior house screen reconstructed from a single surviving board, now in the Portland Art Museum. There is no certainty as to its symbolism. It possibly originated from the Coho House of the Tlingit at Sitka, Alaska.

Plate 27. This photograph is especially valuable because it provides an overview of Fort Simpson, British Columbia, from the mid-1870s. The row of Tsimshian long houses and totem poles stretching along the water's edge are clearly revealed with the aid of a magnifying glass. Photograph courtesy Vancouver Public Library, 8551.

Plate 28. An enormous painting is depicted on Chief Minesqu's house at Gitlahdamsk village on the Nass River in northern British Columbia. The prominent crest represents an episode in the illustrious history of the chief's family. Photographed in 1903, courtesy British Columbia Provincial Museum, PN 4110.

256

Plate 29. This photograph reveals with poignant finality the fate of many Northwest Coast masterpieces in sculpture and painting. Once belonging to Harry Edenshaw's family in Klinkwan in southern Alaska, the painting has collapsed and fallen into ruin. Photographed in 1901 by C. F. Newcombe. Photograph courtesy British Columbia Provincial Museum, PN 40.

Plate 30. A house front at Kimsquit, a Bella Coola village, in 1881. Notice the vertical pole supports at both sides of the house combined with vertical and horizontal supports at the center. Photograph courtesy British Columbia Provincial Museum, PN 9517.

Plate 31. A Bella Coola house front painting from the 1880s is combined with a vertical carved pole that provides an entry into the house. The human figure depicted in the pole is dressed in Western-style clothing. Note the support poles which provide greater stability for the painting, but these at best are but a short-term arrangement. Photograph courtesy American Museum of Natural History.

Plate 32. The last interior screen painting known to be surviving *in situ* in the 1920s, when it was photographed. It probably was destroyed shortly thereafter. It represents a fierce grizzly and was located in the home of an important Bella Coola chief. Photograph courtesy National Museum of Canada, 56924.

Plate 33. A view of the Southern Kwakiutl village at Humdaspi on Hope Island, northern Vancouver Island, taken in the 1880s. The three houses at the right of the photograph have painted fronts. The house at the extreme right has excellent clarity, but the third from the right is mostly obliterated by weathering. By 1912 this view had been completely transformed; no trace of the paintings could be found. Photograph courtesy Archives of British Columbia, 33584.

Plate 34. Photographed in the 1880s, this house front painting, representing a raven on the sun with grizzly bears at either end, is in Fort Rupert. It suggests a design with close affinities to more northern neighbors, perhaps the Heiltsuq or Bella Bella Kwakiutl. Fort Rupert people played a pivotal role in traditional Kwakiutl politics and potlatching during the latter half of the 19th century. Photograph courtesy British Columbia Provincial Museum, PN 7303.

Plate 35. This 1862 photograph reveals a newly established village located at Alert Bay on Cormorant Island off the northeast coast of Vancouver Island. A three-masted schooner lay offshore beyond the right side of this print. There are no standing totem poles or house front paintings to be seen at this particular time. Photograph a gift to the author from James Sewid, 1965, but the photographer is unknown.

Plate 36. Chief Tlah go glas's house at Alert Bay in the 1870s. The painting represents a thunderbird. Notice the prominent wooden beak appendage projecting from the bird's head. The house has a facade, which appears typical of Kwakiutl architecture during that time period. Photograph courtesy Vancouver Museum, 231.

Plate 37. A scene along the waterfront in Alert Bay village during 1910–12 shows this part of the pathway constructed with wood planks. In addition to six standing totem poles, there are possibly three house front paintings along this section of the village. Photograph courtesy Vancouver Museum, 1132.

Plate 38. Gwayasdums village on Gilford Island photographed during the first decade of the 20th century. The painted facade house front at the right decorated the Sea Monster House and belonged to the Scow family. The painting depicts the face of a powerful sea being, a crest of the Scow family. Photograph courtesy Royal British Columbia Museum, PN 235.

Plate 39. Copper Johnson's house front painting photographed in 1912, about a dozen years earlier than in Plate 6. Notice the figure of a copper that shapes the entryway to the house. Photograph courtesy British Columbia Provincial Museum, PN 10726.

Plate 40. Two house front paintings from the Kwakiutl village of Tsatsichnukwomi, or New Vancouver, probably dating from the early 1880s. By the turn of the century the village had been abandoned and the former inhabitants settled in other villages. Several houses along the shoreline were constructed with facades. Photograph courtesy Royal British Columbia Museum, PN 242.

Plate 41. A life-size diorama representing a dramatic moment in the winter dances of the Southern Kwakiutl tribes on Vancouver Island during the late 19th century. The backdrop is a painted cedar wood screen employed to symbolize the two separate worlds of the Kwakiutl, the ethereal supernatural realm behind the partition and the profane world as viewed from the audience. Photograph courtesy Chicago Natural History Museum, 16242.

Plate 42. An intensely dramatic moment in a Kwakiutl potlatch in Alert Bay, British Columbia, during the first decade of the 20th century. The man holding the copper that symbolizes wealth and power may be explaining its name and history to those present, or he could be issuing a challenge to rival chieftains. The painted construction in the background is a temporary totem. Photograph courtesy British Columbia Archives and Records Service, HP 99790.

Plate 43. A crumbling mortuary painting representing a bullhead crest, standing in the graveyard at Fort Rupert, British Columbia. It is dated around the 1930s and was believed to be painted by the Kwakiutl artist named Dick Price. Photograph 1947.

Plate 44. A Christian-influenced graveyard in Alert Bay during 1912–15. Mortuary paintings representing killer whale, thunderbird, eagle, and wolf crests can be identified in this photograph as well as coppers symbolizing wealth. The wolf crest at the right is reported to mark the grave of the Nimkish chief Tlah go glas. Photograph courtesy City of Vancouver Archives, IND.P.111, N.59.

Plate 45. Copper symbols proliferate in this photograph taken within the Alert Bay graveyard in the first decades of the 20th century. The height of these paintings can be judged by the adults standing in the lower left corner. Photograph courtesy British Columbia Archives and Records Service, HP 59314.

Plate 46. An example of Henry Speck's paintings from the mid-1950s and later. This painting in Alert Bay is about 6 feet (1.8 m) in width. It represents a thunderbird holding a double-headed serpent, both important crests of the people. Photograph circa 1965.

Plate 47. Another Henry Speck painting, this is on wood and represents a thunderbird carrying a whale in its talons. The work is also from the mid-1950s. Photograph circa 1965.

Plate 48. The Great House, called Wawaditla, displays a painting created by the famed Fort Rupert artist, Mungo Martin. Standing in Victoria's Thunderbird Park, the painting represents a sea creature known as a *tseekis,* a sculpin or rock cod. Photograph 1970.

Plate 49. Chief Andy Frank's long house located in Courtenay, B.C. It was constructed in 1960 to house pan-tribal meetings and ceremonial events. The painting represents a *kwikwis*, or sea eagle, carrying a whale. Photograph circa 1965.

Plate 50. Totem poles and house front paintings emerge once again side by side in several buildings at the Ksan cultural center near Hazelton, B.C. The project was implemented in the 1950s to reignite interest in Tsimshian culture. It became a vital cultural and artistic center by the 1970s. Photograph 1978.

Plate 51. A second house front painting located at Ksan cultural center. These buildings are not dwellings but rather storage and classroom spaces for students and participants of Tsimshian arts and history studies. Photograph 1978.

Plate 52. The community cultural center in the remote Tsimshian village of Kitwancool in the upper Skeena River territory. The house front design was inspired by a traditional screen painting illustrated in Figure 25. Photograph 1979.

Plate 53. The house front painting at the elementary school located in Gitsegyukla, a Tsimshian village in the upper Skeena River region in northern British Columbia. In an excellent example of the blending of the old with the new, the figures represent creatures in Tsimshian mythology. Photograph courtesy Charles Rhyne.

BIBLIOGRAPHY

Barbeau, Marius. 1950. Totem Poles. 2 vols. National Museum of
Canada Bulletin, no. 119. Ottawa, Ontario.

Blackman, Margaret. 1984. *Visual Ethnography of the Kasaan Haida in
the Tsimshian and Their Neighbors of the North Pacific Coast*. Eds. Jay
Miller and Carol Eastman. Seattle: University of Washington Press.

Boas, Franz. 1897. *The Social Organization and Secret Societies of the
Kwakiutl Indians*. Report of the U.S. National Museum for 1895.
Washington, D.C.

Boas, Franz, ed. 1916. *Tsimshian Mythology* by Henry Tate. Annual
Report of the Bureau of American Ethnology for 1909–1910.
Washington, D.C.

Boas, Franz. 1955. *Primitive Art*. New York: Dover Publications.

British Columbia Indian Arts Society. 1982. Mungo Martin. Sidney,
British Columbia: Gray's Publishing Ltd.

Carpenter, Edmund. 1975. Introduction to *Form and Freedom: A Dialogue on Northwest Coast Art* by Bill Holm and Bill Reid. Houston:
Rice University Institute of the Arts.

Cole, Douglas. 1985. *Captured Heritage: The Scramble for Northwest Coast
Artifacts*. Seattle: University of Washington Press.

Cook, James. 1784. *A Voyage to the Pacific Ocean*. 3 vols. London: W. and
A. Straham for G. Nicol and T. Cadell.

Curtis, Edward. [1915] 1970. *The Kwakiutl*. Vol. 10, *The North American
Indian*. New York: Johnson Reprint Corp.

de Laguna, Frederica. 1972. *Under Mt. St. Elias: The History and Culture
of the Yakutat Tlingit*. Vol. 7, *Smithsonian Contributions to Anthropology
Series*. Washington, D.C.: Smithsonian Institution.

Drucker, Philip. 1940. *Kwakiutl Dancing Societies*. Berkeley: University
of California Press.

Drucker, Philip. 1950. *Culture Elements Distributions: The Northwest
Coast*. Berkeley: University of California Press.

Drucker, Philip. 1951. *The Northern and Central Nootkan Tribes*. Bureau
of American Ethnology Bulletin 144. Washington, D.C.

Duff, Wilson. 1964. *The Indian History of British Columbia: The Impact of
the White Man*, vol. 1. Victoria, British Columbia: Provincial Museum of Natural History.

Easton, Bob. n.d. Plank House Architecture of the Northwest Coast. Pamphlet of the Arco Center for the Visual Arts. University of British Columbia Museum of Anthropology.

Emmons, G. T. 1916. The Whale House of the Chilkat. Anthropological papers of the American Museum of Natural History. New York.

Emmons, G. T. 1930. The Art of the Northwest Coast. *Natural History Magazine*. May–June, pp 282–292.

Emmons, G. T. 1990. *The Tlingit Indians*. Ed. Frederica de Laguna. Seattle: University of Washington Press.

Enge, Marilee. 1993. Treasures of the Tlingit. *Anchorage Daily News*. 4–8 April.

Feder, Norman, and Edward Malin. 1962. Indian Art of the Northwest Coast. *Denver Art Museum Quarterly*. Winter.

Forrest, Robert. 1982. Rediscovering a Masterpiece. *Heritage/West*. Fall, pp 15–20.

Garfield, Viola. 1939. *Tsimshian Clan and Society*. Seattle: University of Washington Press.

Garfield, Viola. 1948. *The Wolf and the Raven*. Seattle: University of Washington Press.

Garfield, Viola. 1966. *The Tsimshian Indians and Their Arts*. Seattle: University of Washington Press.

Hawthorn, Audrey. 1967. *The Art of the Kwakiutl Indians and Other Northwest Coast Tribes*. Seattle: University of Washington Press.

Hawthorn, Harry. 1961. The Northwest Coast. In *The Artist in Tribal Society*. ed. Marion Smith. Glencoe, Illinois: The Free Press.

Herem, Barry. 1991. The Curse of the Tlingit Treasures. *Connoisseur Magazine*. March, pp 85–90.

Holm, Bill. 1965. *Northwest Coast Indian Art: An Analysis of Form*. Seattle: University of Washington Press.

Holm, Bill. 1983. *Smoky Top: The Art and Times of Willie Seaweed*. Seattle: University of Washington Press.

Holm, Bill. 1990. Northwest Coast Indian Art. In *Handbook of North America*, vol. 7. Washington D.C.: Smithsonian Institution.

Holm, Bill, and Bill Reid. 1975. *Form and Freedom: A Dialogue on Northwest Coast Art*. Houston: Rice Institute of the Arts.

Howard, O. O. 1898. Famous Indian Chiefs. *St. Nicholas*, vol. 35, no. 7. May, pp 622–623.

Jonaitis, Aldona. 1986. *Art of the Northern Tlingit*. Seattle: University of Washington Press.

Kan, Serge. 1989. *Symbolic Immortality: The Tlingit Potlatch of the 19th Century*. Washington, D.C.: Smithsonian Institution.

Keithahn, Edward. 1962 . Heraldic Screens of the Tlingits. *Alaska Sportsman Magazine*. February, pp 16–19.

Keithahn, Edward. 1963. *Monuments in Cedar*. Seattle: Superior Publishing Company.

MacDonald, George. 1983. *Haida Monumental Art*. Vancouver, British Columbia: University of British Columbia Press.

MacDonald, George. 1984. Painted Houses and Woven Blankets. In *The Tsimshian and Their Neighbors of the North Pacific Coast*. Eds. Jay Miller and Carol Eastman. Seattle: University of Washington Press.

McIlwraith, T. F. 1948.   *The Bella Coola Indians*, 2 vols. Toronto: University of Toronto Press.

Malin, Edward. 1986. *Totem Poles of the Pacific Northwest Coast*. Portland, Oregon: Timber Press.

Miller, Judy, Elizabeth Moffatt, and Jane Sirois. 1990. Final report of the Native Materials Project. Canadian Conservation Institution.

Miller, Polly. 1967. *Lost Heritage of Alaska*. Cleveland: World Publishing Company.

Munro, Margaret. 1988. Indian Art Comes to Light. *Canadian Geographic Magazine*. August–September, pp 66–70.

Nabakov, Peter, and Robert Easton. 1989. *Native American Architecture*. New York: Oxford University Press.

Newman, Peter. 1987. *Caesars of the Wilderness*. New York: Viking.

Nuytten, Phil. 1982. *The Totem Carvers*. Vancouver, British Columbia: Panorama Publications.

Oberg, Kaverlo. 1973. *The Social Economy of the Tlingit Indians*. Seattle: University of Washington Press.

Olson, Ronald. 1940. *The Social Organization of the Haisla of British Columbia*. Berkeley: University of California Press.

Olson, Ronald. 1954. *The Social Life of the Owikeno Kwakiutl*. Berkeley: University of California Press.

Olson, Ronald. 1955. *Notes on the Bella Bella Kwakiutl*. Berkeley: University of California Press.

Olson, Ronald. 1967. *Social Structure and Social Life of the Tlingit of Alaska*. Berkeley: University of California Press.

Reid, Bill, and Bill Holm. 1975. *Form and Freedom: A Dialogue on Northwest Coast Art*. Houston: Rice Institute of the Arts.

Sismey, Eric. 1961. H'kusan, a Kwakiutl Village. *Beaver Magazine*. Winter.

Stewart, Hilary. 1984. *Cedar: Tree of Life to the Northwest Coast Indians*. Seattle: University of Washington Press.

Suttles, Wayne. 1976. Productivity and Its Constraints. (Mimeo.) Portland, Oregon: Portland State University.

Tepper, Leslie, ed. 1991. The Bella Coola Valley: Harlan Smith's Fieldwork, 1920–1924. Canadian Museum of Civilization Bulletin, no. 123. Hull, Quebec.

Vastokas, Joan. 1973. The Shamanic Tree of Life. *Arts Canada*. Dec. 1973–Jan. 1974, pp 125–149, 184–187.

Walens, Stanley. 1981. *Feasting with Cannibals*. Princeton: Princeton University Press.

INDEX

Italicized numbers denote pages of illustrations.